EUROPE: A PHILOSOPHICAL HISTORY

PART 1

Europe is inseparable from its history. That history has been extensively studied in terms of its political history, its economic history, its religious history, its literary and cultural history, and so on. Could there be a distinctively philosophical history of Europe? Not a history of philosophy in Europe, but a history of Europe that focuses on what, in its history and identity, ties it to philosophy.

In the two volumes of *Europe: A Philosophical History* – *The Promise of Modernity* and *Beyond Modernity* – Simon Glendinning takes up this question, telling the story of Europe's history as a philosophical history.

In Part 1, *The Promise of Modernity*, Glendinning examines the conception of Europe that links it to ideas of rational Enlightenment and modernity. Tracking this self-understanding as it unfolds in the writings of Kant, Hegel and Marx, Glendinning explores the transition in Europe from a conception of its modernity that was philosophical and religious to one which was philosophical and scientific. While this transition profoundly altered Europe's own history, Glendinning shows how its self-confident core remained intact in this development. But not for long. This volume ends with an examination of the abrupt shattering of this confidence brought on by the first world-wide war of European origin – and the imminence of a second. The promise of modernity was in ruins. Nothing, for Europe, would ever be the same again.

Simon Glendinning is Professor of European Philosophy and Head of the European Institute at the London School of Economics and Political Science.

'In these timely volumes, the idea of Europe – the site of so much contemporary political strife – receives a philosophical interrogation commensurate with its nature. Glendinning's rigorous and compelling delineation of modern Europe's conception of itself, as at once philosophy's historical cradle and its cultural offspring, deftly draws upon the very self-understanding he analyses to confirm its current exhaustion, and to affirm its capacity for radical self-renewal.'

Stephen Mulhall, University of Oxford, UK

'In this remarkable two-volume book, Simon Glendinning inhabits and works through a "philosophical history of the philosophical history" of Europe. This is exemplary work, its readings developed with erudition, patience, and rigor. By the end of the second volume we come to see how the traditional concept of Europe is "exhausted", but not thereby left entirely hopeless or without promise. This is a sustained, often brilliant, exercise of reading the unfolding deconstruction of the dominant European understanding of Europe, one that can indeed stand as perhaps its own best example of what the old name "Europe" can still call forth in philosophy today. A magnificent achievement.'

Geoffrey Bennington, Emory University, USA

EUROPE: A PHILOSOPHICAL HISTORY, PART 1

The Promise of Modernity

Simon Glendinning

LONDON AND NEW YORK

First published 2021
by Routledge
2 Park Square, Milton Park, Abingdon, Oxon OX14 4RN

and by Routledge
605 Third Avenue, New York, NY 10158

Routledge is an imprint of the Taylor & Francis Group, an informa business

© 2021 Simon Glendinning

The right of Simon Glendinning to be identified as author of this work has been asserted by them in accordance with sections 77 and 78 of the Copyright, Designs and Patents Act 1988.

All rights reserved. No part of this book may be reprinted or reproduced or utilised in any form or by any electronic, mechanical, or other means, now known or hereafter invented, including photocopying and recording, or in any information storage or retrieval system, without permission in writing from the publishers.

Trademark notice: Product or corporate names may be trademarks or registered trademarks, and are used only for identification and explanation without intent to infringe.

British Library Cataloguing-in-Publication Data
A catalogue record for this book is available from the British Library

Library of Congress Cataloging-in-Publication Data
A catalog record has been requested for this book

ISBN: 978-1-138-58032-9 (hbk)
ISBN: 978-1-032-01580-4 (pbk)
ISBN: 978-0-429-50743-4 (ebk)

Typeset in Bembo
by KnowledgeWorks Global Ltd.

To the memory of Maurice Fraser

CONTENTS

List of abbreviations   ix
Acknowledgements   xii
Preface   xiv

Introduction: Our selective memories of Europe   1

PART I
European cultural identity   **15**

1 Ideas of culture   17

2 Greek, Christian and beyond   30

PART II
Europe's modernity   **49**

3 From barbarism to civilisation   51

4 The European idea of man   61

5 The cosmopolitical animal   75

PART III
The history of the world 89

6 Perpetual peace 91

7 Attained freedom 104

8 Real happiness 120

9 Complete democracy 135

PART IV
A sense of an ending 155

10 Europe in crisis 157

11 Dispiriting Europe 173

12 The grand tour: looking back and looking forward 192

Bibliography *196*
Index *202*

LIST OF ABBREVIATIONS

This list is specific to the works cited in this book, which is the first of two parts. The bibliography provides a complete list of works referred to across both Part One and Part Two, many of which were germane to both.

AR	Jacques Derrida, *Acts of Religion*
AT	Emmanuel Levinas, *Alterity and Transcendence*
BB	Ludwig Wittgenstein, *Blue and Brown Books*
BFM	Jacques Derrida, "Back from Moscow, in the USSR"
BGE	Friedrich Nietzsche, *Beyond Good and Evil*
Bentham	Jeremy Bentham, *An Introduction to the Principles of Morals and Legislation*
Bloom	Allan Bloom, *The Closing of the American Mind*
BT	Martin Heidegger, *Being and Time*
CD	Sigmund Freud, *Civilization and its Discontents*
CES	Edmund Husserl, *The Crisis of European Sciences and Transcendental Phenomenology*
CF	Jacques Derrida, *On Cosmopolitanism and Forgiveness*
CHPR	Karl Marx, *Critique of Hegel's Philosophy of Right*
CHU	Stanley Cavell, *Conditions Handsome and Unhandsome*
CM	Karl Marx, *The Communist Manifesto*
CPR	Immanuel Kant, *Critique of Pure Reason*
CR	Stanley Cavell, *The Claim of Reason*
Davies	Norman Davies, *Europe: A History*
DG	Deland Anderson, "The Death of God and Hegel's System of Philosophy"
DP	Andrew Buchwalter, *Dialectics, Politics, and the Contemporary Value of Hegel's Practical Philosophy*

EH	Francis Fukuyama, *The End of History and the Last Man*
EIT	Rodolphe Gasché, *Europe, or the Infinite Task*
EO	Jacques Derrida, *The Ear of the Other*
EP	Dermot Moran, "'Even the Papuan is a Man and not a Beast': Husserl on Universalism and the Relativity of Cultures"
HIE	Pim den Boer, *The History of the Idea of Europe*
History	Aristotle, *History of Animals*
HFK	G.W.F. Hegel, *Faith and Knowledge*
HLW	Rebecca Comay, "Hegel's Last Words"
HP	Paul Valéry, *History and Politics*
HPR	G.W.F. Hegel, *Philosophy of Right*
HSR	Robert Perkins, "Hegel and the Secularisation of Religion"
IBWD	Bernard Williams, *In the Beginning was the Deed*
IM	Martin Heidegger, *Introduction to Metaphysics*
Kant	Immanuel Kant, *Kant's Political Writings*
Keiser	Wolfram Keiser, *Christian Democracy and the Origins of European Union*
LH	Martin Heidegger, "Letter on Humanism"
LLF	Jacques Derrida, *Learning to Live Finally*
MK	Adolf Hitler, *Mein Kampf*
OH	Jacques Derrida, *The Other Heading*
OfH	Jacques Derrida, *Of Hospitality*
OG	Jacques Derrida, *Of Grammatology*
OL	J.S. Mill, *On Liberty*
OS	Jacques Derrida, *Of Spirit*
OSE	Karl Popper, *The Open Society and its Enemies*
PE	Paul Valéry, "La Politque de L'Esprit"
PF	Jacques Derrida, *Politics of Friendship*
PG	Jacques Derrida, *The Problem of Genesis in Husserl's Philosophy*
PH	G.W.F. Hegel, *Philosophy of History*
PI	Ludwig Wittgenstein, *Philosophical Investigations*
Politics	Aristotle, *Politics*
PT	Carl Schmitt, *Political Theology*
RB	Emmanuel Levinas, *Is it Righteous to Be?*
RC	Mitchell Cohen, "Rooted Cosmopolitanism"
RFGB	Ludwig Wittgenstein, *Remarks on Frazer's Golden Bough*
RG	J.S. Mill, "On Nationality and Representative Government", in *Three Essays*
RHJ	P.G. Wodehouse, *Right Ho, Jeeves*
RS	I. Bernard Cohen, *Revolution in Science*
S1	Geoffrey Bennington, *Scatter 1*
SE	Pierre Rosanvallon, *Society of Equals*
SHE	Simon Jenkins, *A Short History of Europe*

SM	Jacques Derrida, *Specters of Marx*
SR	V.I. Lenin, *State and Revolution*
TDC	T.S. Eliot, *Notes Towards the Definition of Culture*
TIML	David Wiggins, "Truth, Invention, and The Meaning of Life"
UE	Judith Butler, "Uncritical Exuberance?" (unpaginated online text)
UNESCO	Jacques Derrida, "Of the Humanities and the Philosophical Discipline"
UWC	Jacques Derrida, "The University Without Condition"
VM	Jacques Derrida, "Violence and Metaphysics"
WH	Stephen Houlgate, "World History as the Progress of Consciousness"
WL	Simon Critchley, "What's Left After Obama?" (unpaginated online text)

ACKNOWLEDGEMENTS

I would like to thank the following people for their support, encouragement, inspiration, and suggestions large or small: Catherine Audard, Sonja Avilijaš, Matthew Bell, Robert Bernasconi, Chiara Bottici, Richard Bronk, Kevin Cahill, Amit Chaudhuri, Rebecca Comay, Robert Eaglestone, Kevin Featherstone, Katrin Flickschuh, Cristóbal Garibay-Petersen, Rodolphe Gasché, Victoria Glendinning, Denis Guénoun, Robert Hancké, Bjarke Morkore Stigel Hansen, Stephen Houlgate, Christine Irizarry, Peggy Kamuf, Anna Ksiazczakova, Oisín Keohane, Mareike Kleine, Ingrid Kylstad, Elissa Marder, Michael Morgan, Alan Montefiore, Michael Naas, Kalypso Nicolaides, Paula Zoido Oses, Alois Pichler, Tahir Rashid, Alison Stone, and Jonathan White.

This volume is dedicated to my friend and colleague Maurice Fraser, with whom I taught a course called "The Idea of Europe" for over a decade at the LSE. Very sadly, Maurice died while I was completing the first draft of this text, and I am very sorry that I won't get to hear his warm and generous praise for getting it published, and his robust and unstinting criticism of what I have written.

Material from this book has been presented at academic conferences, seminars and lectures at universities in Amsterdam, L'Aquila, Baltimore, Cambridge, Edinburgh, Groningen, Haifa, Little Rock, London, Luxembourg, Memphis, Moscow, New York, Nottingham, Oxford, Rochester, St Petersburg, Utrecht, Warwick, and Wolverhampton; at public events in Edinburgh, Hay-on-Wye, and London; and at various schools, primary and secondary, in England. I would like to thank the participants at all of these occasions for their thoughtful comments and contributions.

Most of the thinking that belongs to the development of this book was first presented in lectures and seminars with students in the European Institute at the London School of Economics and Political Science. I would like to thank them for their patience, enthusiasm, and ideas.

Acknowledgements xiii

The first draft of this book was completed while I was Visiting Professor at the University of Bergen, Norway, in 2015–16. I am extremely grateful to Alois Pichler for facilitating that. My sincere thanks go to Geoffrey Bennington and Stephen Mulhall who read through the penultimate draft of both volumes, and offered generous and helpful suggestions for improvement. I would also like to express my thanks to Tony Bruce for taking on this project, reviewing a complete draft, and, with Adam Johnson, overseeing its development. The second draft of this volume was read by my wife, Anjali Joseph. She then read it again along with the second volume in its penultimate draft. Her comments and objections were challenging, and my gratitude is endless. It is unquestionably a better book as a result. Its failings are all mine.

Oxford, 2021

PREFACE

What does it mean to be European?

We later civilisations...we too now know that we are mortal

– Paul Valéry

I

What does it mean to be European? This question is an old one. Today it belongs to discourses on culture and cultural identity. But it is not so long ago, less than a hundred years in fact, that this question was treated in terms of spirit and spiritual identity. Nevertheless, whether the subject is a culture or a spirit, the relating of its developmental history would likely be thought the (proper) business of history as a discipline. This book, across two volumes, attempts to make a contribution to understanding Europe's developmental history from the perspective of philosophy.

Making historical sense of Europe makes good sense to us: what happens in history, we are inclined to think, only "acquires meaning" if we see "effect following cause over time" (SHE, p. 4). I too want the account I am giving to make meaningful an historical development. My aim is to provide a way of reading the emergence of a distinctively European understanding of the world and the significance of our lives; to provide a kind of surveyable portrait of this becoming-European world. But I do not proceed through an exploration of the European archive in search of a narrative linking first causes to contemporary effects. It is not a casual explanation of an historical development, but the interpretive excavation of the major scansions or mutations of an historical self-understanding.

Modern social science has its way of surveying cultural self-understandings too: through surveys (questionnaires, interviews, focus groups, and so on). The investigation attempts to find out what people think on some subject by asking them what they think about it. Eurobarometer surveys, for example, monitor the evolution of public opinion in all EU Member States, providing rich data sets for both quantitative and qualitative research not only on what matters to people politically and socially, but also on their perceptions of belonging and identity. I will look at some of its survey data later too. But what might it mean to undertake an investigation of a distinctively European self-understanding philosophically? What testimony or testimonial could provide its material for thinking? It might be supposed that the only inquiry left open to us here would belong to the history of ideas: seeking out representative articulations of a developing idea of Europe. However, one would not have to reach too far back historically to find that such articulations of an "idea of Europe" have consistently folded back onto the "idea of philosophy" and its history, the two almost invariably entangled with each other: tied together, especially, in the virtually ubiquitous identification of ancient Greece as the true starting point of a history of Europe.

It is perhaps tempting to think that the entanglement of Europe with philosophy stems from this historical starting point: Europe is the place, European culture is the culture, that has most continuously nurtured and cultivated philosophy, at least in its Greek name. But there is a more radical interpretation. As the young Jacques Derrida put it in his 1953/54 *Diplôme* dissertation, summarising Edmund Husserl's investigation of "spiritual Europe" in the 1930s, the idea is not simply that "Europe is the cradle of philosophy" but that "Europe is itself born from the idea of philosophy" (PG, p. 155). That would be an extraordinary tangle.

One thing that belongs to the idea of writing a book called "Europe: A Philosophical History" is to register this more radical interpretation as internal to the history of Europe as that is conventionally understood. Europe's history is radically, that is to say, originally or in its roots (*radix*), tied to the philosophical. In this book, I will not take this idea to express a merely historical fact but as an interpretive key. I will press forward with the guiding idea that Europe is itself a philosophical phenomenon in this sense: it has forged and formed itself historically by giving itself a Greek, and especially Greek philosophical origin. Europe's understanding of its own history unfolds in the wake of and in the light of that Greek origin. Europe's history is already something of a philosophical history.

That Greek commencement does not, of course, fall from the sky: it has its history too. As Husserl acknowledged, for example, "the Greeks themselves tell of the wise Egyptians, Babylonians, etc., and did in fact learn much from them" (CES, p. 279). I will come back to this historical regress, which, as Husserl stressed, cannot stop at the Egyptians or Babylonians or anyone else. However, in more and less troubling ways, it remains the case that what the Greeks called *philosophia* has been a fundamental and ineluctable reference point for understanding Europe's history and identity. The *particular* culture that has called itself "European" has marked itself out as the heritage of a fundamentally philosophical, that is to say, *universal* outlook. The Europeans, in their understanding of the world and the significance of their lives, have conceived themselves as the ones who "*specialize* in the sense of the *universal*" as the French poet and essayist Paul Valéry once said…of the French (HP, p. 436).

In this book, I will highlight the fundamental role in the formation of this outlook of a distinctive understanding of what it means to be the living thing that we human beings all are: a distinctive anthropology. This anthropology, too, comes down from the Greeks, from the Greek philosophical conception of the human as the *zōon logon echon*, the living thing with the capacity for the "*logos*", a word meaning, roughly, "word", although what this "*logos*" word has been understood to mean is a central part of the unfolding European story too.

From the perspective of this anthropology, the history of European humanity would, in one respect, simply belong to the history of that living thing. However, within Europe's history, where Hellenic culture is carried first into the Imperial Roman and subsequently into the Medieval Christian power domains, Europe's own history comes to have, in addition, an altogether different sense. With the fateful translation of *zōon logon echon* as *animal rationale* that took place in that history, *empirical* history opens to the idea of a *universal* history: the developmental history of what Europeans, in their different languages, have called "Man".

At issue is the movement of an empirical history, Europe's history, that would belong to – and has identified itself as belonging centrally to – a history of the self-realization of Man *as* Man; an historical movement, then, towards the proper end or *telos* of Man.

Attesting to and thereby raising the stakes in the movement towards that *telos*, Europe, and especially Europe in its self-consciously "modern" (enlightened, rational, scientific) condition, conceives itself as setting the heading towards a state of peace, freedom and well-being for all humanity. On the basis of its understanding of Man and his teleology, Europe forges its cultural identity in universally exemplarist and missionary terms. This is Europe's modern promise, the promise of Europe's modernity.

The idea that Europe has a universal significance by virtue of its originary relation to philosophy is strikingly expressed in Immanuel Kant's prediction in 1785 of "a great political body of the future" arising on "our continent" – a Federation of European Nations or a European Union – that will likely provide a guiding example "for all other continents" to follow (Kant, pp. 51–2); Europe in this way participating in and producing a movement of world history towards a condition of universal peace, freedom and well-being for all. The particular history of "our continent" is thus grasped in relation to the universal destiny of Mankind; in terms of the teleological movement towards a maximally rational life for all humanity. However, the global "cosmopolitan existence" posited by Kant as the final end of a world-historical teleology of Man's self-development is not just a philosopher's idea of humanity's collective destiny: the very idea of such a human universality, of humanity finally living in peace, in a universally fitting condition, is essentially philosophical. That idea belongs, as we shall see, to the idea of providing a distinctively philosophical history, the history of Man.

In this book, I will argue that this conception of the history of Man, this conception of Man and his teleology, has been the fundamental framework of all European thinking about Europe. Within that framework, Europe's involvements in what today are conceived as processes of "globalisation" are not to be understood merely as the upshot of the hegemonic political and economic ambitions of colonialist or imperialist Europeans – as an historical *geopolitical* development broadly conceived. Rather, those involvements should be understood in terms of the development of a culture that has conceived itself as destined to spread out worldwide according to principles finally inseparable from reason itself as an inherent capacity of Man. The idea of Europe's modernity – its break from its own former regionally-traditional ways of being human – is thus conceived as a new historical stage for humanity at large, opening what might be called a *geophilosophical* development, with a European world enlarging from a cultural beachhead first established, above all, by philosophy.

In Kant's great texts on this theme, the work of a distinctively philosophical or universal history is to relate the rise of a cosmopolitan hope spreading out from Europe on a world-wide scale. I believe a cosmopolitan hope is still a hope. However, one would have to be naïve in the extreme not to recognise that this hope, as much as the European Union whose very existence it inspired, is in our time, fragile, faltering, and threatened. Moreover, its historical unfolding seems far from hopeful or promising: when one compares how classic texts of philosophical history represent Europe's modern character – as rational, scientific, enlightened, free – with the way Europe's modern history has come to appear to us today – in its imperialism, colonialism, world wars, Stalinism and National Socialism, the Holocaust, and so on – the difference can seem absurdly great. The idea of Europe's promise seems more than ever a fundamentally problematic Eurocentric fantasy, and a very dangerous fantasy at that, a horror story. Europe henceforth defined, in an anti-Eurocentric recoil, only by its crimes.

Supposing, as it is undeniably necessary to suppose, that the Eurocentrism internal to the old philosophical discourse of Europe's modernity is simply no longer acceptable, what, if anything, can we say about Europe, its history and its promise, today? Europe forged itself by *calling itself to appear*, and to appear always, as an exemplary *avant garde* for global humanity on the way to its proper end. This self-understanding has, today, itself become a problem. So where should we go from here? Could Europe set a new heading for itself, beyond its old modern self-understanding? Over two volumes this book aims to track the historical development of the modern European self-understanding, and takes a stand on its future. There remains, I will argue, something still unexhausted in the old spirit of Europe.

II

This volume begins, however, with the anti-Eurocentric recoil against the European heritage that most marks our time: a recoil, for example, against the old canons, the texts of the Dead White European Males, a recoil that sees in Europe's history only a sequence of disasters, prejudices, and exclusions, a history of violence and exploitation; anything but an unexhausted promise. In some parts of academia, this anti-Eurocentric recoil against the Eurocentric norm has become a new norm, and not without justice, as we shall see. Indeed, given the anthropocentrism, ethnocentrism, and androcentrism that has been so powerfully installed in all Eurocentric thinking about Europe, one might wonder if there is anything more to say: Europe today is worn-out, moribund, exhausted, over.

In a recent effort to explore Europe as "a philosophical concept", Rodolphe Gasché boldly plays with fire when he asserts that thinking there is no more to say, thinking we now know what to think when we think about Europe today, is a kind of structural failure on the part of one of the most influential forms of contemporary Europe-related thinking:

> Undoubtedly, there are many who confidently pretend to know exactly what Europe has stood for, and continues to stand for – namely a hegemonic phantasm and moribund worldview. By depicting Europe and the West as a homogeneous power of domination over the rest of the world, postcolonial criticism of European imperialism, and its construction of non-European cultures, knows perfectly what Europe is. Indeed it knows it so well that it indulges in the same lack of differentiation of which it accuses the West in its relation to its others. It thus turns Europe into the blind spot of its own discourse. (EIT, p. 16)

The charge of presenting as homogenous something rather differentiated and complex might be turned against Gasché here. Moreover, he does not stop to consider that it is precisely in a time when Europe appears least promising – a Europe increasingly dominated either by technocratic governance or crude and vulgar democrats and populists – that its past can appear clearly only in terms of its disasters and crimes.

Nevertheless, I share Gasché's dismay at the "lack of differentiation" in the anti-Eurocentric recoil. Indeed, as we shall see, what is most striking is its failure to see that its own recoil has a long and profoundly European pedigree. Without wanting at all to obscure or underplay the dominant Eurocentrism of the modern European self-understanding, this book attempts the kind of differentiated vision of Europe that Gasché rightly demands.

No doubt there are endless ways one might go about it. In this book, I make a case for taking seriously the thought that gives Gasché's book its subtitle: to think of an investigation of Europe as "a Study of a Philosophical Concept". I believe that an effort to come to terms with the situation facing Europe today – the challenge to its centrality and the fragility of its still-modern institutions, including its Union – cannot be made without an engagement with the idea of philosophical history, and an appreciation of its vicissitudes. This book will be, in the main, a philosophical history of philosophical history, and will track the conception of Europe and European identity that unfolds there.

When I get to philosophical history in some detail in Part Three of this volume, I will not merely be reviewing what philosophers have had to say about Europe. The intention, right from the start of this book, is to undertake an investigation of the dominant modern European self-understanding. I will start with considerations concerning Europe's history and culture which are, mostly, familiar. But this familiar surface will reveal a more subterranean ground: as presupposing a particular conception of Man as an historical being. It is here that we make decisive contact with philosophy, and especially with philosophical history. As we shall see, philosophical history, the history of Man and his teleology, provides the very language of our language of Europe, its history, its modernity, and its cultural identity.

III

Following the course of Europe's history by following the major and dominant scansions in the history of philosophical history is not something I could have done alone, and I have benefited from many scholarly contributions. However, long stretches of the journey taken in this book are guided above all by pointers from the philosophical interest in Europe and its heritage that I have found in the work of Jacques Derrida. I am sure there are turns in my thinking which do not follow Derrida's. Nevertheless, I simply could not have got going without his assistance. From his earliest writings (including, as we have already seen, his *Diplôme*) to his final interview only months before his death, Europe was a regularly recurring theme in his work, and he dedicated a whole book to the topic in *The Other Heading: Reflections on Today's Europe* (1992). But it is not just a quantitative point. Derrida's work taught me that a satisfactory attempt to attain a reflective appreciation of Europe's contemporary cultural condition simply cannot duck reading the great texts of the European philosophical tradition on Europe. Moreover, there is a key claim that he makes in this context which I not only follow but try to defend: that Europe first becomes a theme for philosophy in the course of attempts to develop what is called philosophical history or universal history, a form of history that was, throughout its modern formation, a teleological history of the self-realization and de-alienation of Man. Reflecting on Kant's discussions of the movement of human history as part of a general teleology of nature, Derrida states the claim as follows:

> In this teleological ruse of nature, Greco-Roman Europe, philosophy and Western history, are the driving force, both capital and exemplary, as if nature, in its rational ruse, had assigned Europe this special mission: not

> only of founding history as such, and science, but also the mission of founding a rational philosophical (non-novel-like) history and that of "legislating someday" for all other continents.... The teleological axis of this discourse has become the tradition of European modernity. One encounters it again and again, intact and invariable throughout variations as serious as those that distinguish Hegel, Husserl, Heidegger and Valéry. One also encounters it in its practical form, sometimes through denial, in a number of politico-institutional discourses, whether on the European or world scale. (UNESCO, p. 6)

Europe first appears as a theme for philosophy when philosophy attempts to give a teleological account of world history, a rational philosophical universal history of Man. The classic philosophical discourse of world history is, that is to say, inseparably a discourse of Europe's exemplary modernity, and its centrality to the movement of world history. I take as my principal task in this book to conduct the detailed work of following this discourse through the major texts of philosophical history, and "in its practical form" in the formation of the European Union.

Derrida has his illustrative list of thinkers belonging in their differences to this traditional discourse of European modernity: Kant, Hegel, Husserl, Heidegger and Valéry. Derrida's list guides the progress I make through philosophical history, although I will add Marx and Freud to the list covered in this volume. However, while I will regularly have Heidegger in view in this book, I will not be going very far into his Europe thinking; not least because, finally, his thought is not even Eurocentric. As Derrida himself noted in *Of Spirit* "it is not Eurocentric in virtue of this first raising of the stakes: it is a Central-Europa-centrism" – a Germanocentrism (OS, p. 70). Germany will figure rather centrally in most German philosophical history, but in Heidegger, it really is all about the unique distinction of the Germanic world and its language, and I do not want to get sidetracked by that.

After a general discussion of familiar approaches to European identity in the first two parts, this volume will follow the history of European philosophical history from the Enlightenment up to the outbreak of the Second World War, from Kant to Husserl. In doing so we will see how, for reasons that are internal to the way Europe's history has in fact unfolded, the discourse of Europe's modernity undergoes a widespread weakening during the first half of the twentieth century, and philosophical attempts to come to terms with Europe emerge at that time as a discourse of modern Europe's crisis, a spiritual crisis, a crisis of spirit.

Philosophical history does not grind to a halt in the challenge to the centrality of Europe and its culture which becomes increasingly impossible to avoid in the second half of the twentieth century. However, with the fascinating exception of the work of Francis Fukuyama in the early 1990s, philosophical history begins to take on the task of thinking and rethinking its own history, and to "think Europe" beyond its modern self-understanding and its crisis. This is the development explored in the second volume of this book, *Beyond Modernity*. Beginning in that sequel with a sidestep (back) to Friedrich Nietzsche as the prophet of Europe's so-called "postmodernity", the second volume will bring us up to our own time, and its considerable instabilities and uncertainties, drawing into the discussion contributions from Isaiah Berlin, Francis Fukuyama, and finally from a number of more recent thinkers, including Jean-François Lyotard, David Wiggins, Stanley Cavell, Bernard Williams, and Judith Shklar, as well as from Derrida. By the book's close, I hope to have shown how the loss of faith in a teleological sense of world history that marks our time implies not merely a crisis of Europe's modernity but its exhaustion. That is to say, the crisis is not merely an event within the history of Man and his teleology, but a crisis (if that is still the best word here) for that history. What we will witness and attest to is the inner dissolution of Europe's old "modern" understanding of the world and the significance of our lives. We live in the time of the unravelling of the discourse of Europe's modernity and its promise. Where the first volume runs historically from Kant to the outbreak of the Second World War, the second runs from the Cold War to Brexit and the Covid-19 crisis.

Trying to make sense of a Europe and a European identity worth identifying with beyond its exhausted Eurocentrism and its anti-Eurocentric recoil is not something one can achieve without more ado – especially if one is to avoid unwittingly repeating it all. These are discouraging times. But I hope to show that even a worn-out Europe today retains something of its modern promise; beyond its Eurocentrism and anti-Eurocentrism, Europe's possibilities, especially regarding its democratic heritage, remain, I believe, still unexhausted.

IV

In 1926, casting his eye over a Europe that seemed to him without aspirations of its own beyond being "governed by an American committee", Paul Valéry invited his reader to imagine being given "unlimited power", and in possession of "the firm intention of doing your best" (PH, p. 228). Go on: imagine it.

"Well, what are you going to do? What are you going to do TODAY?" (PH, p. 228, capitals in original).

Sixty-four years later, but in a dialogue across the (to)days with Valéry, Derrida takes up this question, if not apparently the fantasy it was attached to, and speaking for himself did more than speak for himself:

> Is there then a completely new "today" of Europe beyond all the exhausted programs of *Eurocentrism* and *anti-Eurocentrism*, these exhausting yet unforgettable programs? (We cannot and must not forget them since they do not forget us.) Am I taking advantage of the "we" when I begin saying that, in knowing them now by heart, and to the point of exhaustion – since these

unforgettable programs are exhausting and exhausted – we *today* no longer want either Eurocentrism or anti-Eurocentrism? (OH, pp. 12–3, emphasis in original)

Derrida wonders if he is taking advantage of the "we", unsure whether in speaking this way of what he wants for Europe, he is overreaching himself, and is really only speaking for himself. He must have believed or felt that he wasn't. How far that "we" might reach must have remained, however, very unclear, very uncertain, perhaps very limited; but the honest faith of the belief would be that its reach might grow, that its growing power might, one day, unlimit itself, opening a completely new "today" for Europe, that it might even "one day take over without any resistance at all" (OH, p. 140).

I am more than happy to be included in the embrace of Derrida's "we today". Indeed, I could wish nothing more for this book, these two flawed pebbles on the beach, than its having belonged to the history of that new "today" for Europe. For that reason, if, now, I were to attempt to narrate this European story as if from outside, everywhere free of the first person-plural, this book would not only present a stupid pretence at academic objectivity but, for me, would simply lose its voice. I am (among other things) a European myself, culturally European: my position is anything but that of a detached scientific observer. And in a more or less continuous way, I will risk taking advantage of the "we", a signatory of the preface to what remains to come for Europe.

In more conventional prefatory form, let me anticipate something of the complications this appeal to the "we" introduces into the writing of this book. Sometimes when I write about "us" or "we", and about what is "ours", that gesture makes a traditionally philosophical appeal to human universality or, at least, anonymity; it makes a claim on your attention, staking itself on making a claim to anyone's. There are no guarantees when one claims to speak for all others. As the American philosopher Stanley Cavell puts it, "I have nothing more to go on than my conviction, my sense that I make sense. It may prove to be the case that I am wrong, that my conviction isolates me, from all others, from myself" (CR, p. 20). In the face of this threat to one's sense of making sense Cavell himself then moves very quickly to affirming that "the wish or search for community" involved in his appeal to what "we" say is, at once, "the wish or search for reason" (CR, p. 20). Where one's making sense is in question, that transition is perhaps understandable, but it is not an altogether neutral sense of one's words making sense: "reason" is not a neutral word for what might gather me with all others and myself. Indeed, far from risking isolating him from all others or himself, it immediately reinscribes his search within a quite specific heritage of understanding what the search for human community means, a heritage that is, I want to say, already specifically European. Even if it is not a speech only to Europeans, it is certainly an address that emanates from something European, a culturally European place, even if that place is the enigmatic variation called "America", a variation that Cavell explored as deeply as anyone.

Cavell says that the appeal to what "we" say is "a claim to community". When such a claim is made in a philosophical voice, it seeks "the basis upon which [community] can or has been established"; it cannot presuppose it (CR, p. 20). Hence, Cavell conceives his claim to community as necessarily risking his own isolation and erring, even from himself. This is strictly unavoidable. However, a philosophical investigation of Europe multiplies the difficulties when it is itself also composed in a European voice. Sometimes when I write in this book about "us" or "we", and about what is "ours", that gesture is a claim to a specifically European community. That this gesture cannot claim to embrace all others does not altogether change the situation Cavell imagines himself in, and in certain ways intensifies its risks.

Speaking in the name of "we, the Europeans" is a claim to community every bit as much as a philosophical or universal claim to community is. However, even if, today, one can seek a more inclusive reach for that European claim than once one could, it still, undeniably, leaves others out. That is a potentially distressing situation, adding to the distressing isolation Cavell bears witness to: not simply the risk of its isolating me (which it does risk), but the certainty of its isolating others, the ones the search throws out of Europe, as the non-European. If I am speaking in the name of "we, the Europeans", I am making a claim to community, and counting myself in. However, while my conviction, my sense that I make sense, may prove wrong, while my conviction may isolate me, I simply cannot wish my claim to community might speak for all others, and it would be altogether mad to suppose, today, that it might be a claim of reason.

One of the most distinctive things about us is that we sometimes speak in ways that elide and paper over implicit distinctions, selections and exclusions. We know, we cannot forget, that in Europe's past, for example, a text that addressed itself to "we, the Europeans" would likely have been an address to "my fellow Europeans", a speech to "fellows", to *males first*, even if it concerned itself with European women. When Valéry invited his reader to imagine that "you were given unlimited power", he not only gives no indication whatsoever that this "you" is a European, though I can only render his words as making sense if he did suppose that, but he explicitly presumes that you are a man: "Suppose you were given unlimited power. You are an honest man…" (HP, p. 228).

That is not all that will likely have been presumed in such an address to Europeans. I'm not sure whether, in Europe's past, any of those honest Europeans, even if they were women, were ever conceived as being people of colour. That an address to Europeans can, today, make a claim (hesitantly and unevenly) to address a more inclusive collectivity is part of the story I will relate, part of the long and ongoing democratic movement in Europe. But it remains "exclusionary". However widely spread across the globe it is today, the modern European understanding of the world is not everyone's, not everyone is culturally European.

And yet, precisely because of this world-wide-isation, this globalisation, of the European world, the European story does not only belong to those who might search or wish for a European community, or to those who might risk speaking in the first-person plural in its name. Among the "all others" that there are, if you yourself are marked historically as non-European, or call yourself non-European, you too can take an interest in and contribute to this European story. After all, it will certainly have taken an interest in you, albeit an interest which has most often been distressing and humiliating. For example, as I have already indicated, those who have called themselves European have liked to think that the culture of "our continent" promises to embrace a distinctively cosmopolitan point of view; a culture that cultivates an ideal of hospitality that demands that we welcome others to our places when they visit legitimately, and behave peaceably in the places of others when we do the same, since, say, "we are all rational beings" or "we are all sons of God". Without presuming this sense of its basis, I want to cleave to that cosmopolitan promise too. But we also know, and have long known, that "our continent" has and remains, in fact, very rarely so promising: "If we compare with this ultimate [cosmopolitan] end the *inhospitable* conduct of the civilised states of our continent, especially the commercial states, the injustice which they display in *visiting* foreign countries and peoples (which in their case is the same as *conquering* them) seems appallingly great". Who said this? These are the words, once again, of the anthropocentric, androcentric, and Eurocentric thinker Immanuel Kant, writing in 1795 (Kant, p. 106).

I hope that the investigation of Europe and European cultural identity that follows will avoid the too-rapid simplifications that so often accompany the story of Europe, and, more broadly, will help to shed light on what it means to be European today, and what it might mean tomorrow. I will not overlook that my search itself emanates from something European, a culturally European place – even if that place is the enigmatic variation called "England". When Europe has been in question in European philosophy, "England" has never been far from the centre of discussions. But its historical place in Europe has always also been somewhat semi-detached; the continent isolated by the fog in its Channel. Moreover, the very name of this European place is not so straightforward. The English philosopher John Stuart Mill tumbled into the hellish circumlocution "England (or rather Scotland)" when speaking of the provenance of David Hume as the greatest "negative thinker" that "England" has to its name (UOL, p. 55). Complications are added further by the fact that this place sometimes goes by the State name the "United Kingdom", a name which, as Derrida once observed, shares in that form something of the distinction of the USSR in that it is not even the name of the place of a people, literally not the name of a "pueblo" (BFM, p. 49). This is a distinction that (I think) it, now, no longer shares with anywhere in the world, and which may not long remain. Nevertheless, peopled and placed as I already am, and with nothing more to go on than the conviction that I've attained a nose for the thing, when I speak in the name of "we, the Europeans" it may prove to be the case that I am wrong, that my conviction isolates me, from other Europeans, from myself, and indeed from what makes sense to any others. But the search is on: not as a detached observer, but in the midst if not the middle of it all, I seek the basis upon which European cultural identity has been established, and how it can, once more, be re-established.

INTRODUCTION

Our selective memories of Europe

> *A higher situation for mankind is possible, in which the Europe of nations will be obscured and forgotten, but in which Europe will live on in thirty very ancient but never antiquated books.*
>
> – Friedrich Nietzsche

I

Before it all becomes too obscure, and already forgotten, I want to tell a story about "the Europe of nations"; a story about the Europe that made its way from the optimism of Enlightenment cosmopolitanism to the still faltering steps of today's European Union. It will be related across two volumes, and follows the elaboration and falling apart of a European culture that called itself (to be) "enlightened" and "modern"; a culture that called on itself to break from a past dominated by myth, magic, superstition, illusion, delusion, and dogmatic authorities, and to set itself on a new heading towards a rational, scientific, and free way to be for Man.

This will not be, however, a straightforward work of European history. It does not chart the events and episodes that have taken Europe from then to now. It tracks, rather, the movements and mutations of an historical self-understanding.

It is, then, a story that concerns the stories "we, the Europeans" have told about ourselves when we tell ourselves who we are. It is not at all irrelevant whether this self-understanding is faithful or unfaithful to the reality of Europe's history. In many ways, it has, over time, simply been overwhelmed by that reality. But I am not relating it in order either to criticise it or to affirm it from an historical or political point of view. Taking an interest in those points of view, especially an interest in contesting views of "what actually happened" in Europe's history, is a definite characteristic of the "subject" whose self-understanding I am trying reflectively to relate, and I will certainly be getting involved with it myself as we go along. Nevertheless, my primary interest and point of departure is more existential than historical or political: if you are yourself a European, or have been significantly informed by the modern European understanding of the world, then the subjectivity that is interrogated here is yours, and I will be relating the story of the development of the understanding of the world that you have inherited, and whose inheritance you are.

That subject undoubtedly has "roots" in a tradition. Indeed, it finds itself already in a world, already provided with a historical memory. But, as Martin Heidegger stressed, tradition can transmit the past in ways that make it only more "*inaccessible*" and "*concealed*" (BT, p. 43, emphasis in original): the most basic sources of our understanding of the world and the significance of our lives can become obscured and be forgotten. While I do not set out a political-historical critique of that understanding, in another sense this investigation does conduct its critique. I am attempting to come to terms with the terms through which this subject has understood itself. The fundamental term here is, I believe, "Man" or "Mankind", and it is, therefore, the distinctive anthropology of European humanity that I will want to home in on and to excavate from within the more familiar expressions of European cultural identity. This can also be called "critique" because at issue is something like its own conditions of possibility; the most basic, originating and abiding sources, the *archē*, of European cultural identity. This will draw us into Europe's history, but it is not a merely historical task: the "sources" in question are not behind us, but still with us – though in our time they are, I believe, nearing exhaustion. We are in this event, we the Europeans. I call the discipline which takes an interest in the fate of the fundamental *archē* of European subjectivity the philosophy of Europe.

Philosophy is not only the *how* of this investigation, its standpoint, but will relate radically to its *what* as well. The texts that I will explore in this book are not only philosophical texts; each also draws the history of Europe into an essential relation with philosophy. In these texts, Europe's cultural identity is invariably conceived as rooted in an originally Greek ideal of philosophical inquiry. The important thought here, and one I will defend in this book, is that this conception is itself Europe-producing. Europe is not to be identified as an independently specifiable (geographical) place where philosophy was first elaborated and developed. On the contrary, Europe's history and identity are inseparable from the cultivation of originally philosophical ideas concerning the individual and social forms of life thought proper to "Man".

As I explained in the Preface, this volume will explore the development of the dominant discourse of Europe's modernity as found (primarily) in the work of those thinkers most centrally concerned with history as philosophical history or a history of Man: Kant, Hegel, Marx, Freud, Valéry, and Husserl. It concludes (historically speaking) with the outbreak of the Second World War. The second volume starts with a step back in time: to the distinctive contribution to understanding Europe's story that we get from Nietzsche. It will then track the movement of this European story in texts that took it up most directly after the Second

World War, (primarily) taking in work by Isaiah Berlin, Francis Fukuyama, Jean-François Lyotard, David Wiggins, Stanley Cavell, Bernard Williams, Judith Shklar, and Jacques Derrida.

Kant, Hegel, Marx, Freud, Valéry, Husserl (Volume 1) – Nietzsche, Berlin, Fukuyama, Lyotard, Cavell, Williams, Shklar, and Derrida (Volume 2). That's mostly a lot of men, and mostly a lot of Dead White European Men. It says a great deal about the unravelling of the classic discourse of Europe's modernity, its massive loss of credibility, that this kind of focus and interest is not only increasingly rare, but feels fundamentally at odds with the contemporary intellectual climate, positively antediluvian. For example, it was as long ago as 1989 that Stanford University, one of the world's most prestigious universities, abandoned its previously compulsory first-year course in "Western Culture" and replaced it with a course called "Culture, Ideas and Values" which had a far more diverse selection of texts (in terms of gender and ethnicity) for students to study. The times they are a-changin' – and not only in America.

On the other hand, this desire for change has a lineage of its own. Indeed, I think it belongs to and is a particularly powerful expression of the coming to the end of the line of Europe's dominant old modern self-understanding; it is symptomatic of that ending. In order to introduce the kind of work in the philosophy of Europe that I will pursue in this book, I want further to explore this trend of abandoning what were often called "Western Civ" courses in America, and the culture wars still rumbling on (everywhere) over the place (if any) of Europe's heritage and history in universities, and in our world.

II

Writing in the mid-1990s with a cautious even-handedness about the change to Stanford's undergraduate program, and the growing trend at American universities to make similar changes, the British historian Norman Davies noted that the "Western Civ" courses were being abandoned "for their alleged Eurocentrism" (Davies, p. 29).

While the qualification "alleged" shows something of Davies's anxieties about the complaint against the old courses, and I'll come back to that, he is not at all uncritical of the "limited vision of Europe" they tended to offer (Davies, p. 29). He has two main objections to them, the second of which clearly acknowledges the merits of the accusation that these courses were indeed Eurocentric. The first, which reflects Davies's passion for and knowledge of what was still typically framed as "East" Europe, is the tendency of historians to focus almost exclusively on a supposedly more significant "West" Europe. This is a tendency we will see more or less constantly in this book, because the philosophers covered here have also exhibited it, and it is the dominant and dominating conception of Europe found in philosophy that I want to explore. But Davies is right, and today scholars are at least learning to say "Central", where once, especially during the Cold War and in its wake, they said "East". His second complaint is more directly related to the trend of abandoning (allegedly) Eurocentric courses. While he wants historians of Europe to overcome their "West"/"East" obsession, his most trenchant criticism is reserved for their pervasive tendency to present "idealized" representations of Europe's "past reality" more generally:

> The *really vicious* quality shared by almost all accounts of "Western Civilization" lies in the fact that they present idealized, and hence essentially false, pictures of past reality. They extract everything that might be judged genial and impressive; and they filter out anything that might appear mundane or repulsive. It is bad enough that they attribute all the positive things to the "West", and denigrate the "East". But they do not even give an honest account of the "West"... Such hagiography is no longer credible. (Davies, pp. 28–29, emphasis mine)

It is significant that the prejudices and exclusions running through the old "Western Civ" courses were once thought credible. And we will come back to that too. But given Davies's clear-eyed appreciation of a subject in denial, one might be even more puzzled why he regards the charge of Eurocentrism as only "alleged". Is there really room for thinking that, actually, this whole subject was not guilty of that? Perhaps. One reason might be that a number of the authors studied in the old courses were writing well before ideas of "Europe" as a place began to dominate the cultural life of the inhabitants of the "little promontory on the continent of Asia" (HP, p. 31). Although the name is ancient, Davies notes that the "community of nations" that had previously conceived their cultural identity in Christian terms began to think of themselves more "neutrally" as European "in a complex historical process lasting from the fourteenth to the eighteenth centuries", with "the decisive period…reached in the decades either side of 1700 after generations of religious conflict"; a period in which the earlier concept of "Christendom" had become "an embarrassment" (Davies, p. 7). So writers from an earlier period could hardly be accused of (in Davies's helpfully brief definition of Eurocentrism) "regarding European civilisation as superior and self-contained" (Davies, p. 16). Davies might want also to add that if the courses really are on the development of that civilisation and not some other one, then sticking to the authors who have been most continuously influential in the formation of *its* culture is not Eurocentric anyway: it is nothing more than "keeping to the subject" (Davies, p. 16).

"Keeping to the subject". It's a nicely ambiguous phrase, and one which, without prejudice to Davies's point, I will want to exploit here. For, rather unambiguously, if there is one "subject" that such courses, in fact, keep to, it is, precisely, a White European Male subject. It is his little promontory. And keeping only to that, with the prejudices it sustains and the exclusions it practices, is, for those looking to change the curriculum, central to the problem.

Eurocentrism as Davies defines it may not be everywhere – or even anywhere – affirmed in the selected texts studied. But the anti-Eurocentric recoil is against the selection, the canon, and against the very idea of keeping to just this subject, and of wanting us to regard it (him) as *the* subject worth keeping to, to the exclusion of every other subject identity. And this is why the challenge is so tremblingly painful and fraught. Those texts never were just selected as representative samples of Western or European culture. No, they were selected as ones whose reading was thought most deeply appropriate to the formation of the kind of refined subjectivity that should be striven for through a higher education. These are not mere samples but examples: exemplary contributions to the development of (and even to the idea of) the very institution in which they were being preserved, and to the wider culture to which this kind of institution belongs. Universities have wanted to teach courses covering the likes of (and this is Stanford's old list) "Virgil, Cicero, Tacitus, Dante, Luther, Aquinas, More, Galileo, Locke, and Mill" because the culture of this culture is the one that has been regarded (by those who want to keep to the subject) as normative *for us*: it ought to be handed down as ours, and to become yours. Keeping to this subject, for those who have wanted to keep to it, its "devotees", is not only what we would have to do if, as Davies rather weakly affirms, we want to "illustrate the roots" of our own culture and values (Davies, p. 29), it is the subject we should keep to if we want that culture and those values to have a future.

As Jean-Paul Sartre put it "to choose between this or that is at the same time to affirm the value of that which is chosen; for we are unable ever to choose the worse. What we choose is always the better; and nothing can be better for us unless it is better for all" (EH, p. 29). For anyone who finds themselves in keeping to this subject, there is a terrible loss in its abandoning.

Davies is keenly aware of the "really vicious quality" of the denial internal to so many "Western Civ" courses: such subjects keep only to what is thought impressive and filter out everything that might be felt repellent. However, Davies is not unequivocally supportive of the anti-Eurocentric recoil either, and has some sympathy for defenders of the old subject. According to Davies, the "great paradox" of the recoil is that the European values so relentlessly celebrated by "the devotees" of the old subject – "tolerance, freedom of thought, cultural pluralism" – are now "under attack" from those who have, he declares, "benefitted most" from them (Davies, p. 31).

Later in this introduction, I will outline why I think we should be alert to denial on both sides of this scene. But I don't think Davies's "great paradox" really captures what is at stake here. For a start, is there really anything so very paradoxical to this situation? Isn't it understandable if people who have been drawn into a culture where tolerance, freedom of thought, and cultural pluralism have been celebrated, might want, in the name of those virtues, to overcome its still existing prejudices and exclusions? Indeed, if, despite its prejudices, those who have benefited from its virtues find a way to open the old space to people who are not White, not European and not Male, and who have typically not so benefited, then, good.

I have referred to "prejudices and exclusions" that are fostered by courses that are, in their normative selection if not always in their actual content, Eurocentric. These are not academically abstract matters, and the prejudices match the exclusions. At the time of the challenge to them, there really were no texts by people of colour, no texts by non-Europeans, and no texts by women on the Stanford course. And those who mounted the challenge were saying: this is not good enough, this is not who we want to be, neither inside nor outside the university, keeping to this subject is the wrong choice, the worse choice. The subject of these courses could no longer be affirmed as the subject to which we want to keep. What Davies calls a "great paradox" might be better (and I think more fairly) expressed as some kind of progress.

The subject one keeps to if one keeps only to the hegemonic canon is a certain White European Male. The real irony here is that the committed desire to keep to that subject has itself opened the space to its opposite, to an anti-Eurocentric recoil that is run through by an equally committed desire: the desire to overcome discrimination on the basis of anyone's skin colour (not-White), ethnicity (not-European), or sexual characteristics (not-Male) – and, beyond that eponymous trio, other cases of discrimination too – on the basis of sexuality, class, religion, and species, for example – and hence a desire to make a radical break with that old subject. Today, we can no longer make sense of the culture that would privilege the writings of the DWEMs as normatively ours: we want to challenge the prejudices and exclusions that are preserved, and preserved so transparently, when we keep to the old subject of "Western Civ". And so at Stanford out went "Virgil, Cicero, Tacitus, Dante, Luther, Aquinas, More, Galileo, Locke, and Mill" and in came "Rigoberta Manchu, Frantz Fanon, Joan Rulfo, Sandra Cisneros, and Zora Neale Hurston" (Davies, p. 29).

We may want to speak of "keeping to the subject" in the new courses too, but that is misleading insofar as the new course is characterised precisely by its project of diversification. It is not devotion to another singular subject identity but to a diversity of subject identities (each of which has, no doubt, its own security gates and guards).

In this respect, the scene is not symmetrical. But we should remember that the charge of Eurocentrism is more strongly and coherently aimed at "the devotees" of the old subject than it is to the DWEMs whose work was selected and kept to. And at this level, there is not only symmetry but an uncanny likeness between the devotees on each side. It's not a singular subject over against a subjectal diversity but: two lovers of responsible diversity. The one feels his or her love for tolerance, freedom of thought, and cultural pluralism under attack, the other feels his or her love for the same thing finally expressed.

These devotees, are they finally even two? There are certainly two programmes in view, but one is the anti-Eurocentric "mirror" of the other; and as such, they belong together as two basic expressions of the same "subject": the one more self-congratulatory and backslapping, the other more self-hating and self-accusing.

The idea that there is an internal relationship between these two programmes comes from the work of Jacques Derrida. Although he is often positioned firmly on one side of this debate (the anti-Eurocentric side), his work seems to me to be crucial to understanding its general logic. Derrida is well and widely known for identifying an "ethnocentrism" within the tradition of Western metaphysics. Indeed, in the opening lines of one of his earliest books, *Of Grammatology*, he is explicit about this, stating as a main aim to focus on the "powerful ethnocentrism" that is "in the process of imposing itself on the world" (OG, p. 3). Much less well known or well recognised, however, is his identification within *"the history of (the only) metaphysics"* of an "anti-ethnocentricism" too. Discussing the anthropology of Claude Lévi-Strauss, for example, Derrida states that:

> one already suspects…that the critique of ethnocentrism, a theme so dear to [Lévi-Strauss], has most often the sole function of constituting the other as a model of original and natural goodness, of accusing and humiliating oneself, of exhibiting its being-unacceptable in an anti-ethnocentric mirror. Rousseau would have taught the modern anthropologist this humility of one who knows he is "unacceptable", this remorse that produces anthropology. (OG, p. 114)

In later writings, Derrida would more often speak of Eurocentrism and anti-Eurocentrism, but it is the same basic idea. Eurocentrism and its anti-Eurocentric recoil constitute, in their opposition, what he calls one of the "fundamental schemas" of the metaphysical heritage that he sought in his work of deconstruction to go "beyond" (UNESCO, p. 8), going beyond the "exhausted and exhausting… programs of Eurocentrism and anti-Eurocentrism" (OH, p. 13).

As will very often be the case in this book, I will be following Derrida's initiative in reading what might be called "the philosophy *of* Europe" (in its double sense: both "from" and "about"). In the case of the American culture war over "Western Civ", Derrida's approach invites us to see the two programmes as two sides of the same "spirit", the same modern European spiritual production of spirit. And it is a modern European spirit that is, on both sides, in denial: on the one (historically dominant) side, a spirit-in-denial that defines Europe only by its achievements; and an (until recently far less forceful but always present) "opposing denial" (UNESCO, p. 13) which defines Europe only by "its crimes" (LLF, p. 45). The laborious work of reading this near-exhausted modern European spirit/subject that I will be exploring in this book does not, as we shall see, set out to destroy, reject, or abandon it. On the contrary, it wants to uncover another European spirit, at once more realistic and more promising, at work within the work of that modern European spirit-in-denial. Within it and going beyond it. This other spirit is, as Derrida emphasised, indissociable from a certain "motif" of democracy and democratic perfectionism that we will see coming increasingly to the fore in our journey through the history of philosophical history (UNESCO, p. 11).

III

One might argue that the premise of this way of seeing things immediately overlooks that it took the intervention of something at least partly non-European – the non-DWEM writers that figured in Stanford's new course, for example – to make the case against the old subject. But insofar as that is true, that case still had to be received, entertained, and at least to some extent welcomed, from the inside. And I think the old subject was, in a fundamental and distinctive way, already hospitable to that. What I have in mind here is a central characteristic of the modern European spirit that Derrida highlighted in his engagement with the spirit(s) of Marx and Marxism in his book *Specters of Marx*. Speaking of a *certain* "spirit" (we might say "subject") of Marxism that he says he still wants to "keep" to (despite the "totalitarian monstrosity" marking its "whole history"), Derrida emphasises that spirit's essential readiness for *self-critique*:

> To [continue to] take inspiration from a certain spirit of Marxism would be to keep faith with what has always made of Marxism in principle and first of all a *radical* critique, namely a procedure ready to undertake its *self-critique*. This critique *wants itself* to be in principle and explicitly open to its own transformation, re-evaluation, self-reinterpretation. Such a critical "wanting itself" is necessarily *rooted*, it is engaged in a soil that is not yet critical, even if it is not, not yet, pre-critical. This spirit is more than a style, even though it is also a style. It is the heir to a spirit of the Enlightenment which it cannot renounce. (SM, p. 88, translation modified)

Derrida is especially concerned with roots in this passage. The word "radical" relating to the roots of something, just as much as it refers to a thought which breaks with something. The anti-Eurocentric recoil might well be called and call itself "radical" in relation to the old subject. But the radical spirit that Derrida says he is inspired [*s'inspirer*, enspirited] by is not the one that wants to break with something else and to go beyond that, but which "wants itself" to be able to *break with itself*, beyond itself – and to remain faithful to itself in so doing, indeed to keep more and more faithful to itself in so doing. This radical critique is rooted in a tradition which that critique's own historical sense can (must) never renounce even as it breaks from it. Remaining faithful to itself by calling for "self-critique" is to keep to a spirit (or "subject") of critique which preceded it, in the soil of which it is rooted, and which it wants to radicalise, that is to say realise, for the first time explicitly as it were, as properly what it is: as critique. "To critique, to call for interminable self-critique", *that's* critique (SM, p. 89) and that's what had "not yet" been attained by a spirit of critique – "a spirit of the Enlightenment" – hitherto, though the Enlightenment had in a certain way already promised that, and was not simply opposed to it.

I will argue that this "wanting itself" to be open to a break with itself beyond itself – and thereby keeping faithful to itself – a culture that can put itself in question (philosophically, politically, aesthetically, etc.) is a distinctively modern European spiritual engine, and has belonged – or does "not yet" not belong (this engine can become, as J.S. Mill anticipated, "stationary") – to the modern European "subject" well before Marx came on the scene, and is that in which a Marxist spirit of radical critique as interminable self-critique is rooted. And I think that it is this modern subject's own "spirit" that the devotees of anti-Eurocentrism put into play with such righteous zeal against the conservative devotees' desire to keep to it – the former thereby forgetting, or wanting to forget, the roots of its own "radicalism" in a European world. In short, this kind of opposition to Eurocentrism is, as Derrida says, an anti-Eurocentric mirror of the idealising Eurocentrism that is as inaccurate about Europe as the one it mirrors; both sides contenting themselves with what is, undeniably, a very selective "memory" of Europe's origins and of Western history (UNESCO, p. 8).

IV

Davies's "great paradox" may not be so great or so paradoxical, but I think he is right to see something paradoxical in the American culture war over "Western civ". In my view, however, it is a much deeper paradox than the one about "contemporary American intellectual life" that he wants to identify (Davies, p. 30): something paradoxical about the modern European "subject" itself. Ventriloquising this European "subject" or "ego" in the context of an analysis of its paradigmatically "national" self-affirmation, Derrida voices the "the logical schema" of this paradox as follows:

> "I am (we are) all the more national for being European, all the more European for being trans-European and international; no one is more cosmopolitan and authentically universal than the one, than this 'we,' who is speaking to you." Nationalism and cosmopolitanism have always gotten along well together, as paradoxical as this may seem. (OH, p. 48)

I think one can fill out this paradoxical schema of the modern European subject all the way down: no one has been more viciously nationalist, racist, Eurocentric and sexist than this subject; no one more internationalist, cosmopolitan, universalist, and egalitarian. With Europeans understanding themselves as both nationally rooted and cosmopolitan in outlook ("men of universality" as Paul Valéry put it, specifically about the French), this paradoxical European cosmo-nationalism will be a recurrent theme throughout this book, a constant wrinkle in the formation of the European subject.

Within the basic text of this modern European subject, there is a key word for distributively sorting out the cohabiting of vices and virtues that an effort to unpick this paradox might hope to achieve, a word I have already had recourse to – progress. Indeed, the contrast between what Mill called a "stationary" civilisation and a "progressive" one has been fundamental to the modern European self-understanding. The idea is that Europe's culture (its spirit) has a distinctive heading: it is moving away from a cultural condition of mere repetition of local customs by constructing for itself a cultural condition that welcomes and is striving for its own development, improvement, transformation, perfection. Progressive thought is, that is to say, internal to the heritage of the Dead White European Males. And wanting to make room for something other than the DWEMs – wanting to make a political and intellectual space that can peacefully accommodate linguistic, religious and other human differences – comes down to us through their thought. As we have already seen in the Preface, it is, in fact, *right there* in the skull of Immanuel Kant – in the skull of that old Prussian racist, Eurocentrist, sexist, and yet radically cosmopolitan thinker. The political "progressive" today belongs to the progressive heritage of the DWEMs too, in wanting to overcome still prevailing moral faults.

This is perhaps a good place to introduce a first complication. What if this classical interest in progress is itself in some way paradoxically problematic? What if it too belongs to the Eurocentric/anti-Eurocentric programme? What if, to use an expression from Derrida, what we have called progress hitherto is not progress "worthy of the name"? Can there be progress in thinking about progress? Can we, in the name of progress, distributively sort out the vices and virtues of the classical interest in progress, and construct something better, something worthy of the name? What if the idea of distributively sorting out virtues and vices, good and evil, is itself something we need to overcome or get beyond? This does not mean we have to lose interest in the classical interest in progress or emancipation. Indeed, I believe Derrida would not be alone in feeling that "nothing seems to me less outdated" than this classical interest (AR, p. 258). Why, after all, did Nietzsche write a book called "Beyond Good and Evil", and want to affirm nevertheless, in a chapter called, precisely, "Our Virtues", that, regarding his learning to "*despise*" the "solemn words and the formulas of virtue", the "moral preaching" of "modern" progressives: "this too is progress" (BGE, p. 129)? We may be, as I will suggest, more resistant to the classical understanding of that classical interest in progress than Europeans of yesteryear knew how to be. But this means: if we have, notwithstanding that resistance, not lost interest in it, we will have to re-learn what retaining and cultivating that interest can mean in our time.

In this book, over two volumes, I will do what I can to keep to a certain spirit of the subject of this classic interest, and to tell the story of the Dead White European Male in deconstruction: of the rise of his little promontory – and of his crisis, decline, and, in our time, his near exhaustion. I do not do so to resurrect him – nor to bury him. But want rather to make a contribution to the progress of "a long historical labour" that is already underway: a "long and slow" development that promises to take him beyond himself, "beyond the old, tiresome, worn-out and wearisome opposition between Eurocentrism and anti-Eurocentrism" (UNESCO, p. 8) – and beyond the anthropocentrism, ethnocentrism, and androcentrism which marks that heritage so stubbornly, sometimes through denial. This, for me, remains Europe's promise: the cultivation of the spirit of critique as self-critique. As this book makes its progress we will see how deeply this is tied to a European concept of democracy.

Derrida's work sets a direction for thinking on this topic that I have found increasingly powerful and thought-provoking. While it is not limited to an academic context at all, his work does belong there, and makes its way from there. It is not surprising, therefore, that he was very critical of conservative conceptions of "the Humanities and their ancient canons" (UWC, p. 208). Indeed, when it came to the academic subject that he kept to most closely and continuously, philosophy, he called for its transformation. In relation to the ambitions for diversification in contemporary anti-Eurocentric challenges, it is notable that, with respect to that transformation, he was particularly insistent (and I will come back to this more fully in Chapter 11) that "what we are more and more aiming for are modes of appropriation and transformation of the philosophical in *non-European* languages and cultures" (UNESCO, p. 8). On the other hand, he was equally insistent that this should not be understood as a motivation for an anti-Eurocentric recoil which would affirm only "something that would no longer have any relation to what one believes one recognizes under the name philosophy" (UNESCO, p. 8). For Derrida, there was no question either of simply abandoning the "ancient canons", or of altogether replacing them with those who, as Davies put it, do not "suffer the stigma of being Dead White European Males" (Davies, p. 29). On the contrary, Derrida affirmed, as clearly and frankly as he could, that these are "canons which I believe ought to be protected at any price" (UWC, p. 208).

It will strike some readers as strange to see Derrida associate himself so personally ("I believe") with the protection of the classical European intellectual heritage "at any price". Perhaps for good reason. The foregrounding of the Eurocentrism of Western metaphysics was, as I have indicated, visibly central to his work from the start. As he put it in his final interview, given to *Le Monde* in August 2004:

> Since the very beginning of my work – and this would be "deconstruction" itself – I have remained extremely critical with regard to European-ism or Eurocentrism, especially in certain modern formulations of it, for example, in Valéry, Husserl, or Heidegger. I have written a great deal on this subject and in this direction (especially in *The Other Heading*). Deconstruction in general is an undertaking that many have considered, and rightly so, to be a gesture of suspicion with regard to all Eurocentrism. (LLF, p. 40).

And yet his robust defence of the ancient canons made this defiance compatible with something else too: with wanting the European heritage to have a future, to speak in the name of "we, the Europeans" in a future-producing way, in relation to "a Europe to come", and in the hope that the deconstruction of the Eurocentric heritage might forge an opening for "an other Europe but with the same memory" (LLF, p. 41). Commitment to this other Europe – including in that a "geopolitical" Europe which could and should "unite", he said, against both "the politics of American global dominance" and "Arab-Muslim theocratism" – this commitment was, he confessed, "my faith, my belief" (LLF, p. 41).

"With the same memory", but unfiltered: recalling everything that has happened in Europe – "because of the Enlightenment, because of the shrinking of this little continent and the enormous guilt that pervades its culture (totalitarianism, Nazism, fascism, genocides, Shoah, colonization and decolonization, etc.)" (LLF, p. 40). This "other Europe" is thought, as Derrida put it, in terms of Europe's openness to "perpetual self-critique" (LLF, p. 45). With this capacity for faithful self-development beyond itself, there is, Derrida suggests "a chance for a future" – for a Europe that would be other to the one that is content either with "reaffirming a certain history, a certain memory of origins", and, equally other to the one that, as in a mirror, "contents itself with being opposed to, or opposing denial to, this memory"(UNESCO, p. 8); other to the one that gives itself over to the viciously idealised self-congratulatory backslapping of traditional Eurocentrism – and other too to the self-righteous, self-accusing, root-forgetting radicalism of contemporary anti-Eurocentrism.

Derrida's faith or belief holds fast to a Europe that is both to come, but which, in virtue of its own "perfectible heritage" (LLF, p. 45), is in a certain way already with us, has always been with us – from the very starting point that "we, the Europeans" assign to ourselves as our Greek-philosophical commanding commencement. As we shall see in the final chapter of this volume it is with philosophy above all, "under its Greek name and in its European memory", that there is a "chance", Derrida says, a chance "which more than ever remains a chance", for this "other way" for Europe beyond Eurocentrism and anti-Eurocentrism (UNESCO, p. 8). Why is philosophy this "other way"? In this book, I will work towards conceiving the project of philosophy as inseparable from the will to make a contribution to the universal community. From the beginning, philosophy was never simply Greek and its European history, which is inseparable from Europe's history, has never been simply European either. Not merely because it is, in reality, informed and indebted to non-Greeks and non-Europeans, which it certainly is and we should never forget it. Indeed, the culture of the "Greek origin" already was, in fact, "bastard, hybrid, grafted, multilinear and polyglot" (UNESCO, p. 8)). Nor because it is or could ever be "spontaneously or abstractly cosmopolitical or universal" (UNESCO, p. 8). But because, forever tied to some milieu (there is always some localised idiomaticity), it is, in its project, never tied to any definite milieu: not Greek, not European, not anywhere. And for this reason, "Europe" too, which has always wanted to root itself in this radically philosophical "soil" (a soil which is itself always a matrix of roots), is always more than and other than merely one region or regional culture among others on the surface of the global totality: its geopolitical significance and identity is, as I suggested in the Preface, irreducibly caught up with a geophilosophical, cosmopolitan, universal trajectory.

In principle, Dead White European Male philosophy exceeds the Dead White European Male philosophical heritage that it has also cultivated and defended. It surpasses that subject even as its devotees have (on both sides) jealously kept to it. And now, today, we should (must) say too: that surpassing should be practised and, indeed, should be available to be practised by people of colour, by the non-European, by women – by all.

V

I mentioned a moment ago that it might come as a surprise to find Derrida so keen to defend and protect the ancient canons ("at any price"). His sense of deconstruction as entailing a "gesture of suspicion with regard to all Eurocentrism" perhaps explains that. But he also (and perhaps for that reason) got hopelessly caught up in the culture war between those who wanted to defend and those who wanted to reject the Western tradition. For example, in America, his work seemed to mark the final disastrous chapter in "the closing of the American mind". "Deconstructionism" (as it somehow always got called when it was denounced) was denounced as "the last, predictable, stage in the suppression of reason and the denial of the possibility of truth" (Bloom, p. 379). In response to this kind of reception, Derrida began to insist more expressly that deconstruction did not reject the heritage:

> I love very much everything that I deconstruct in my own manner; the texts I want to read from the deconstructive point of view are texts I love, with that impulse of identification which is indispensable for reading. They are texts whose future, I think, will not be exhausted for a long time… Plato's signature is not yet finished… – nor is Nietzsche's, nor is St Augustine's. (EO, p. 87)

It was a slow burn, but over the years readers have begun to learn that Derrida did not write in a critical fury against the European philosophical heritage, but for the sake of that heritage in its endless perfectibility, out of love for it, concerned above all to forge a future for it, and a future for it of just the sort he thought most faithful to it, most (in) keeping with it: a future beyond its own anticipated future. For this is the thing about the texts of the Dead White European Male philosophers – these texts *also* promise a future that is not White through and through, not European though and through, and not Male through and through. And more: these Dead White European Male philosophers – they're not even dead through and through; their signatures are "not yet finished". They are not simply exhausted but remain to be read – they too belong to the Europe to come, they too belong to and sustain Europe's promise.

Derrida's signatories in the last quotation happen not to be listed in chronological order, but together they – Plato, St Augustine, Nietzsche – form a perfect line-up collectively to designate what he once called "those places towards which we are still timorously advancing" (PF, p. 103). As we shall see, there is a (not unjustified) temptation to affirm only Greek and Christian discourses as the epitome of the places that should be called (culturally, spiritually) "European". But Derrida wants to add something more, and so do I. "One should, more prudently, say", says Derrida, "'Greek, Christian and beyond'" to designate those European places (PF, p. 103). This would be a Europe that can and should comfortably take into itself, "at the very least", the profound Judaic and Islamic contributions belonging to its historical formation. However, "and in Nietzsche's wake", this "beyond" signifies something else too, something not just empirical or sociological, but philosophical: "the entire passage beyond" that we have begun to catch sight of in the spirit of self-critique that belongs to the European spirit: "that is to say, everywhere, in every place, where a tradition thus tends of itself to break with itself, not being able to do so, by definition, in anything but an irregular and a trembling fashion" (PF, p. 103).

Greek, Christian and beyond: the places cultivated by this tradition of more than one tradition, these are European places, the places of Europe's still trembling promise. Let's get closer to such places, and work our way towards their abiding sources – the *archē* of the modern European world. As a preliminary to and motivation for the turn to the philosophical history of philosophical history, the first part of this volume will conduct a brief guided (if somewhat wandering) tour of the most familiar places and faces of European subjectivity and identity, beginning with questions concerning cultural identity itself.

PART I
European cultural identity

1
IDEAS OF CULTURE

> *I wonder then at those who have parted off and divided the world into Libya, Asia, and Europe... Let it suffice; we will use the names by custom established*
>
> – Herodotus

I

Where shall we begin?

> We must begin *somewhere where we are* and the thought of the trace...has already taught us that it was impossible to justify a point of departure absolutely. *Somewhere where we are:* in a text already where we believe ourselves to be. (OG, p. 162. trans. mod.)

Derrida affirms a fairly radical sense of what Heidegger called our "thrownness" into an historical world here, which would mean that it is always already too late to hope to enter the "text" that periods and places us in "the right way" in any absolute sense. We must begin "somewhere where we are", already in a world, in a text already, already fitted out with an understanding of the world and the significance of our lives.

Time and space are the fundamental forms of our sensibility, but they are not pure forms: they are always and already localised in periods and places. Our inquiries into Europe begin then not only with a thought about some period and place but already from that. The Modern philosopher said "I think therefore I am", but this "I am" is always an Abrahamic identification: "*hineini*", "Here I am".

Asking about the becoming-European of a world I am already in, a world, inhabiting what Derrida here calls "a text", with all its traces and ghostly hauntings of other periods and places: on the inside not the outside of the very "thing"

I want to interrogate or describe. I can only circle back on myself, making my way inside the inheritance that I am, that I already inhabit as the locale or localisation of my subjectivity, in which my being, including my being European, has its being. Not just its "outer" environmental whereabouts but right inside the inside, haunted by the vestiges of a history which I do not just "have" but which period and place me from the start. Can we home-in on the homeland of this European subject that I am? Can we track down its sources, the *archē* of its formation?

In the passage from *Of Grammatology* I have just quoted, I omitted Derrida affirming, regarding "the thought of the trace", that it is a thought "*qui ne peut pas ne pas tenir compte du flair*" (OG, p. 233) – a thought which cannot not take "flair" into account (originally translated as "which cannot not take the scent into account"). It is not only not a question of tracking an independent object, but finding a way to come to terms with the whereabouts of this "somewhere where I am" cannot just be an application of a programmatic "know how" or "method" either. Familiar and yet not known or conceptually fixed, getting on the scent of it, hunting it down, sniffing it out, knowing your way about in this text, will require a certain ear or nose for what might matter, and an awareness that inherited orientations can also block our access or stand in the way or send us off track.

Cautiously, then, and for starters, let us accept that the "somewhere" of this European world where we, the Europeans, are is not "everywhere". Europe is, Herodotus records (without knowing how it came to be so), parted off and divided from elsewhere – from Libya and Asia, he says. So even if no one is a European through and through, not every subject, not every man and woman, is counted in some way as a European. By the act of "those who have parted off and divided the world" (supposing there was such an act or – *concesso non dato* – that this act is over), some find that they are, and others find that they are not, definitively not, European. Some are from elsewhere and outside, foreign to Europe, even if not, today, always or in all ways entirely foreign to everything European. Elsewhere Europeans are the foreigners, even if not, today, always or in all ways entirely foreign to what is non-European there.

How should we understand the differences that this parting and division among humanity invites us to acknowledge, or at least demands that we think? How deep do they go? What logic or science, if any, does this kind of identity or identification follow? In Europe "race" has been a powerful watchword in these matters, and race theorists (racists) have chased a hope for finding a natural basis for their beliefs and commitments. But even if there is none, and they certainly have none, this does not mean that the idea of racial differences is irrelevant to the parting and division. Indeed, it would highlight and foreground the importance of something like the culture in which these ideas emerge and take hold. It is always within and out of an understanding of the world that is cultivated in a cultural "way of life" – a *way* that is, as Derrida puts it, always "nature's *way out* of itself in itself" (OH, p. 27) – that any ideas of or impulses, racist or not, towards parting and dividing the world become active or actual.

What does it mean to belong to some culture or other, or some culture rather than another? As a prelude to asking about Europe's specific "cultural identity" (supposing it has one), this chapter will be concerned with the following question: if there are any human cultures that at least look different from one another in their ways, or that do or would avow themselves as different from each other in their ways, or have been regarded as different from each other in their ways, in short, if there appears to be more than one human culture, how should we conceptualise human cultures as such?

There seem to me to be only four general conceptual possibilities. Someone might want to affirm that what is proper to a culture, what makes it properly a culture, is that it is [select one of the following]:

1. identical to itself
2. different to the other
3. identical to the other
4. different to itself

The first is a radically non-relational conception. A culture is conceived here as fundamentally self-contained, self-enclosed, and self-producing (associated with ideas of autochthony, autopoiesis, endemism, and nativeness), and it simply has the cultural identity it has made for itself. For any culture, its difference to some other culture (parting and dividing them) will be thought of primarily in contingently differential *historical* terms: in terms of the different ways different human groups happen to have made themselves over time.

The second is a radically relational conception, where it is only through the movement of setting-oneself-over-against-another (parting and dividing them) that a culture comes to be and to be had at all. For any culture, its rivalrous and antagonistic difference to some other culture will be thought of as a *constitutive* relation.

The third supposes that there is, in the end, only one culture, that of human culture in general, and hence that the commonalities between putatively different cultures are fundamental. For any culture, its apparent difference from some other culture (parting and dividing them) will be thought of as real enough in its active effects but ultimately *superficial* in their reach.

And the fourth? The fourth, and the one I want to endorse, is, once more, a formulation of Derrida's, and is central to his discussion of culture in his Europe book, *The Other Heading*. It is doubtless the most "strange and slightly violent" formulation of the four, at least syntactically, a feature that Derrida admits (OH, p. 10). So what does it mean? Without excluding the possibility of all sorts of comparisons between cultures that identify themselves in some way as parted and divided from others (for example, by linguistic or religious differences), and without excluding the lived reality of identity-forming antagonisms and hostilities between cultures, the fourth affirms that what we call "a culture" is *itself* and *within itself* always and already open to all of the differential assessments highlighted in the other three conceptions of differences between cultures (differential histories, differentiating antagonisms, differential appearances): the reality of *a* culture – what, following Heidegger, I will call its *Dasein* (its "being-there") rather than its objective presence – has its own (gathered, home) life only in and through and even in view of this kind of "difference *with itself*" (OH, p. 9). On this view, a culture that *really* is one really is not *one* (with itself).

This claim about cultures – Derrida calls it an "axiom" for his discussion of cultural identity (OH, p. 9) – is, first of all, conceptual (a "dry necessity", Derrida says), a conceptual claim about their non-objective or non-object-like, character. But this necessity is not without empirical implications or consequences. It belongs to this conception, for example, that radical homogeneity, and hence any assertion of the strict purity of a people or assignment of a single origin, is strictly incompatible with the *Dasein* of a culture. What Derrida said about the culture of the "Greek origin" that we cited in the Introduction applies everywhere there is the "being-there" of a culture: it will have "always been bastard, hybrid, grafted, multilinear and polyglot" (UNESCO, p. 8).

The idea of vital internal differences within any culture is not original to Derrida. T.S. Eliot, who admits (not out of false modesty but genuine thoughtfulness) that his effort to think about the "relation" between culture and religion "is so difficult that I am not sure I grasp it myself except in flashes" (TDC, p. 30), is nevertheless confident that, in the European example (the case he is describing as his own, but he will not stop there), "we *must not* think of our culture as completely unified" (TDC, p. 31, my emphasis). He continues:

> The actual religion of *no* European people has *ever* been purely Christian, or purely anything else. There are *always* bits and traces of more primitive faiths, more or less absorbed; there is *always* the tendency towards parasitic beliefs; there are *always* perversions… And it is only too easy for a people to maintain contradictory beliefs and to propitiate mutually antagonistic powers. (TDC, pp. 32–3, my emphasis)

Calling a variation either a parasite or a perversion is not a neutral gesture. And I might say to a defensive Eliot, just as I will later say to a protective Marxist, that these perversions are possibilities that belong (as possibilities) to the structural difference to itself of the "original" formation. (As if anything Christian could be purely Christian.) Nevertheless, I think Eliot is right to affirm that there is always the "trace" of the other within the gathered European culture, and that this is true of any culture. This is not a merely (happy or unhappy) empirical accident. On the contrary, while "difference to itself" can sunder the being-gathered-with-itself that is minimally required for any culture, it is also its condition of possibility: it is the life-giving life of a cultural way of life. As Eliot also affirmed, a "uniform" and "self-contained" culture is at best "lower grade" (TDC, p. 58), and at worst "would be no culture at all" (TDC, p. 62). A certain "friction" within itself is "vital" if a culture is not to "decay": an "indefinite number of conflicts" are thus "favourable" to the *Dasein* of a culture. "Indeed", he says: "the more the better" (TDC, p. 59). Of course, where "divisions have gone too far" that's an end to it too, and it becomes "a danger to itself". Nevertheless, this existential threat to the *Dasein* of a culture is also its vital chance, and so, Eliot concludes, internal "friction" is "necessary" (TDC, p. 59), and hence that "a people should be neither too united nor too divided, if its culture is to flourish" (TDC, p. 50).

Derrida's discussion of this idea is more circumscribed than Eliot's (and yet I'm sure there are aspects of his "axiom" that I am not going to fill out in what follows (see *S1*, Chapter 6)). Nevertheless, I think we can broadly summarise the fourth conception under two heads, two variations of what Derrida calls the "law" of "difference to itself" of any cultural *Dasein* (OH, p. 11). The first concerns the necessary "friction" within the today of every culture that will have any chance of a tomorrow. The second concerns a culture's history, its yesterday. Under the latter head, the emphasis is on an irreducible dimension of allochthony and allopoesis within any structure of cultural autochthony and autopoesis. There is an abiding and politically potent tendency to identify a culture as fundamentally self-enclosed and self-sufficient: of producing itself out of itself without any essential communication with others or external systems, without any essential dependence on or descent from migrants or colonists from elsewhere. It will tend then to affirm endemism as the proper condition of a culture: its belonging to a definite milieu, an original place that is its indigenous and native soil. It is the thought of the culture of a distinctive and unique "people and a land" ("blood and soil") and their "rootedness in a homeland". Against this tendency Derrida's axiom affirms that the development of its gathered "being itself" of any cultural *Dasein* invariably includes the traces of another such culture ("another such culture"; please note, the point goes all the way down): either (a) from the past that is already something of "a foreign country" or (b) from cultural graftings from somewhere altogether elsewhere. Regarding (a), we need to recall, as Eliot insists, that people putatively from "our own" culture in earlier times will always "be different from ourselves" (TDC, p. 18), and (taking in (b)) those people will have always also included migrants or foreigners, just as in our own time. Ultimately, it will have all begun with nomadic or itinerant migrants or colonists anyway: "all stability in a place" is, as Derrida puts it, "a stabilization or sedentarization" (SM, p. 82). No archeo-anthropology can long deny that the ancestors of those we call "the Europeans" all arrived from elsewhere. Wanting to come from (only) here, wanting to have a single origin for your own culture, a unique and unprecedented point of departure for a people in a place, and a monogenealogy without any traces of the culture of the other, is not only an idealisation or falsification of the empirical history of a culture and its identity, but will always be its "mystification" (OH, p. 11). Indeed, when being-in-place wants to have or have had original roots there, we can be sure, as Derrida suggests, that this is "rooted first of all in the memory or the anxiety of a displaced – or displaceable – population" (SM, p. 83). There is, in short, no pure origin of a pure culture in a native land,

and its contemporary (gathered, home) life will (if it is not all over for it) always be a place of "frictions".

Derrida's axiom of cultural identity is not a flat denial of the *Dasein* of a culture, its having an identity and genealogy: it is "not to not have an identity" (OH, p. 9). Rather it is to have an identity that can be formed and forged only in the crucible of this "difference to itself" as the formal "law" of all cultural formation, internal to the creation of a culture, internal to culture as an artifice of nature or the creation *of* a creature.

II

And how will Europe bear on this law? For the moment let us take this as a question regarding Europe's future, its "tomorrow", and hence about our responsibility in this, we Europeans of today. Will Europe confine itself to the being-gathered-to-itself that self-difference makes possible? Will it destroy itself in a counter-to-gathering-dispersion? Or, as Derrida affirms, will Europe strive to be "an exemplary possibility of this law" (OH, p. 11), cultivating it, refining it, taking responsibility for it?

It is fascinating to see that, in relation to this question of Europe's future with this law, Derrida (who is himself picking up on a related theme in the writings of Paul Valéry) and Eliot both turn away from directly political concerns – questions of European political integration and disintegration most obviously – and towards what Valéry will call a "quasi-political" interest in the work of a scattered and varied group of people in European society who have been, in Eliot's words, among the most "highly valued" contributors to its culture, and hence have the greatest bearing on the future of Europe in relation to the cultural crucible of self-difference (TDC, p. 42). This group does not comprise creative artists themselves but those who spend time devoted to their work. Derrida cites Valéry making a similar distinction: taking an interest not only those who create "the material of culture" (artists, writers, poets, composers, and so on) but "as valuable as those who created it", those who respond in a particular way to that material. Both Valéry and Eliot struggle to find a good name for this more than merely supporting cast. Eliot resists calling them "men of culture" since "no one can be accomplished" in all domains of cultural activity, and he simply lists examples: "the scholar", "the intellectual", and "the amateur or dilettante" (TDC, p. 23). Valéry too lists "connoisseurs" and "matchless amateurs", and recalls that they were once spoken of ("with a touch of irony") as "men of taste", but he doesn't save that name either (HP, p. 202). Derrida will describe them as "men capable of repetition and memory" (OH, p. 70), because they are those who dedicate themselves to the reading and re-reading (or seeing and seeing again, or hearing and hearing again) of the material of culture in such a way as to (as Valéry puts it) "fix the authority of a work and a name" (HP, p. 202) – which they do without attaining a hallowed name for themselves. Nevertheless, they are the ones whose work of dedicated appraisal and appreciation maximises the value of the otherwise barely differentiated "arsenal of documents and instruments accumulated over the centuries" (HP, p. 201, cited OH, p. 70), by selectively turning the value of some of it into a "solid value", forming, through their work of repeated attention and memorialisation, what Valéry calls (solid) "ideal capital" from the (scattered) "material" of culture (HP, p. 200–2).

Supposing this anonymous and heterogeneous group has been fundamental to the formation of and development of Europe's culture hitherto, then its future looks bleak. Valéry claims to see "the gradual dying out" of such men in Europe (HP, p. 202). Eliot too emphasises the growing rarity of this wider "body" of people (TDC, p. 24), who together form an "upper group level" of our culture. It is "deterioration on the higher levels" that is of greatest concern, says Eliot, and this is a concern, he insists, "not only to the group which is visibly affected, but to the whole people" (TDC, p. 26) since the contribution "of more highly cultured groups does not leave the rest of society unaffected: it is itself part of a process in which the whole society changes" (TDC, p. 25). Indeed, for Eliot, this is because it is this higher-level group that contributes most to making "life worth living" for everyone (TDC, 27). Members of this group are not to be thought of as a culture's "creators" in any clear sense (TDC, p. 37), but up to now their work has been, nevertheless, the main agent of development and change in European cultural history: they have been the most effective future makers for the culture, the most significant contributors to making the *Dasein* of any culture "*worth while*" (TDC, p. 27, emphasis in original).

Eliot was convinced that this "upper group level" of Europe's culture was withering in his time. But even its survival is no cause for hope if this group becomes so separated from the rest of society that the two are present together only as "in effect distinct cultures" (TDC, p. 26). Both Valéry and Eliot believe that this is happening, and that Europe is becoming as a result increasingly "lost to books" (HP, p. 203). This does not mean we no longer read. On the contrary, "we read too many new books…and periodicals", says Eliot (TDC, p. 86). Valéry too stresses the way publishing houses and the media totally swamp us with reading material (HP, p. 203). For Eliot, however, giving oneself over to this reading gluttony is really to "sacrifice the reasons" for "serious reading", which are the very opposite of "feverishly" reading everything (TDC, p. 86). In a similar vein, Valéry suggests "that there is an element of suicide in the feverish and superficial life of the civilised world" (HP, p. 201).

For a culture so consumed with endless consumption of immediately consumable "news" and the readily digestible "new" and "novel", the very existence of an upper group level is increasingly felt irrelevant. Not only is it isolated from the rest of society but the (supposedly) more egalitarian culture of consumption, championing what is immediately entertaining and "available for all", can come to see it as positively anti-democratic, and as a result "a culture which is only accessible to the few is now deprecated" (TDC, p. 33). At the end of the day (and perhaps at the end of Europe's day), both Eliot and Valéry are at one in thinking we are witnessing the perilous progress of the "disintegration" of European culture (HP, p. 201, TDC, p. 26). "Our own period is one of decline", says Eliot (TDC, p. 19). "Our cultural capital is in peril", says Valéry (HP, p. 201).

There are differences between Valéry's and Eliot's rhetoric and emphasis. But really that matters not one bit since their work on this subject is an example of the very thing they discuss: their work is precisely the work of the nameless type "for whom, *or against whom*" one might want to think and work (HP, p. 202, my emphasis). And this is because of what they have read and what they judged for themselves – with no judge above them – worth the time to read and read again. (*Mea culpa*.) Derrida, summarising, citing, but also (in a slightly qualified way as we shall see in a moment) affirming and approving Valéry's diagnosis, describes these "men capable of repetition and memory" as those who are:

> prepared to respond, to respond *before*, to be responsible *for* and to respond *to* what they had heard, seen, read, and known for the first time. Through this responsible memory, what was constituted as "solid value" (Valéry emphasizes these two words) produced at the same time an absolute surplus value, namely the increase of a universal capital: "...whatever they wished to read, hear, or see again was, by recapitulation, turned into a *solid value*. And the world's wealth was thus increased" (HP, p. 202). (OH, p. 70)

As a result of its capitalisation by these men capable of repetition and memory, the material of European culture becomes more than of merely European wealth or worth, but a claimed contribution to the world's wealth, to human culture in general, for everyone or anyone anywhere. In the case of Valéry and Eliot, we have an interestingly "meta" example of this type: they are readers whose own work of recapitulation and responsible memory gives "solid value" not to particular materials of culture but to the culture of such ideal capital formation. A distinctive form of ideal capital thus appears in their work: "the ideal of 'European culture'" itself (TDC, p. 62). This is not just the maximisation of this or that material of culture but the maximisation of the very space of such maximisation, the site of the most intensive cultivation of cultural capital: this maximisation is "Europe, or the image of Europe", says Valéry (HP, p. 323).

But now, as an ideality or ideal image, this Europe or image of Europe also "exceeds the borders" of any regional particularity (OH, p. 68). European culture has its regional history, but its "worth" cannot be limited to that region, it too has "an absolute surplus value": it has, says Eliot, "an area but no definite frontiers...We are pressed therefore to maintain the ideal of a *world* culture" (TDC, p. 62). Here, Europe would not just be a sample of culture but the exemplary possibility of something prototypically universal. As Eliot puts it:

> The notion of a self-contained European culture would be as fatal as the notion of a self-contained national culture: in the end as absurd as the notion of preserving a local uncontaminated culture in a single county or a single village of England. We are therefore pressed to maintain the

ideal of a world culture, while admitting that it is something we cannot imagine. We can only conceive it, as the logical term of relations between cultures. Just as we recognise that the parts of Britain must have in one sense, a common culture, though this common culture is *only actual* in diverse local manifestations, so we must aspire to a common world culture, *which will not yet diminish the particularity of the constituent parts*. (TDC, p. 62, emphasis mine)

It is precisely, as standing against desires for imposing either a uniform culture or a mere motley of particular cultures that the ideal of European culture is conceived. And this cultural ideal is, as a result, anything but the idea of a self-contained or exclusively European formation. As an ideal image of a culture that aspires to gathered self-difference, the idea of a properly or authentically human culture belongs within it too.

It is, in fact, out of fidelity to the logic of this European cultural ideal that Derrida offers a qualification to his approval of Valéry's discourse on the disintegration of European culture in our time. Derrida "subscribes", he says, to the (in fact, very European) logic of Valéry's "ideal" capital, to the logic of value-maximising capitalisation that "de-limits itself…in order to open onto the infinite and gives rise to the universal" (OH, p. 68). But he does so, he says, "with one hand only" (OH, p. 68). The other hand he wants to keep free: "free to write or look for something else, perhaps outside Europe…which comes perhaps and perhaps comes from a completely other shore" (OH, p. 69). It looks like Derrida thinks Valéry is writing with one hand tied behind his back, assigning an exclusively European responsibility for world culture, for "the universality for which Europe is responsible" (OH, p. 69). Perhaps. But Derrida's free hand is also recapitulating something in Valéry, remaining faithful to something in the very text he has been reading. A key historical passage of Valéry's text, and one cited by Derrida, affirms the Mediterranean basin of ancient times as a "veritable machine for making civilization". Valéry regards the work of this spirit-machine as something "to which our culture owes practically everything, at least in its origins" (HP, p. 196). But this wealth was not the work of a single or self-sufficient people or culture, and, in particular, not the work of already identifiable Europeans. On the contrary, it grew from exchange, from trade all around the Mediterranean littoral. In virtue of "the vigorous trade that grew up around its shores", the Mediterranean became the "scene of both mixture and differentiation…each enriching the other with every kind of experience". And "in creating trade" it thus also created the conditions for the maximisation of cultural richness and diversity: "it created freedom of spirit" (HP, p. 196). The Mediterranean machine is like a "factory" says Valéry. But its product was not a commodity: it was Europeans. So the culture of the other was already and always inside Europe's culture and its "capital of immaterial riches" from the very beginning (HP, p. 209). Derrida wants then to keep to this culture of more than one culture, this culture that is not one, and to remain on the look-out for what might come from beyond the Europe so dear to Valéry and Eliot – from somewhere in himself perhaps (as an Algerian Jew) or perhaps from what he might find from altogether elsewhere. He resists with his free hand what would amount to setting up Chinese walls that would prevent the opening of that Europe (whose ancient canons, its ideal capital, are, we know, dear to Derrida too) "to the future" (OH, p. 69), which is to say not merely from here or there outside geographical Europe but from the wholly unanticipated, from the unprogrammed, and in that sense too "from a completely other shore".

III

It is no doubt tempting to see the "progress of disintegration" (HP, p. 201) that Eliot and Valéry bear witness to as belonging to the side of European cultural dispersion. But in our time, in a time of the mass market of a culture industry, it is not that at all, that is not what we are seeing at all. Today more than ever the processes of disintegration belong to a kind of levelling standardisation and homogenisation of European culture. The ideal of European culture as Eliot and Valéry champion it, is absolutely not about promoting the harmonisation or homogenisation of itself, still less exporting such homogeneity to the world. As we have seen, it is not about eradicating differences (or simply multiplying them) but of cultivating them, giving them solid value; the cultivation of a cultivated variety not a friction-free uniformity. For, as Valéry says too, "this very variety is a natural and *necessary* condition of vitality" (HP, p. 348, emphasis mine).

It is in view of this ideal of European culture, and the crucial role played in it by (let's name them again) lovers of responsible diversity, that Derrida, again like Eliot and Valéry, recalls with considerable anxiety attempts today to establish a new form of cultural domination among European minds through what Valéry calls "the harmony of uniformity" (HP, p. 348). Non-coincidentally, Derrida takes his bearings on this theme from a piece of "state talk" (OH, p. 50): an "official document coming out of the French Ministry of Foreign Affairs (the State Secretary of International Cultural Relations)" which itself cites a document from the "Congress on European Cultural Space" which had declared – in a grotesquely skewed Valérian spirit in fact – that "there is no political ambition that is not preceded by *a conquest of minds*: it is the task of culture to impose the feeling of unity, of European solidarity" (cited OH, p. 51). It is not just the jaw-droppingly crude instrumentalisation of "culture" that troubles Derrida here but the impetus one can see in it – just as much as in what he calls "the best intentioned European projects" beyond state-political initiatives – to "impose the homogeneity of a medium, of discursive norms and models" on European culture, where the ideal of European culture demands something else entirely (OH, p. 54).

Displaced by "democratic" platitudes of immediate accessibility and inclusivity, what the growing isolation and perhaps even disappearance of these lovers of responsible diversity announces is an increasingly serious two-handed threat to the European ideal of cultural identity-in-difference, a threat before which we simply cannot lie down. On the one (gathering) hand, we the guardians of this culture "cannot [logically] and must not [imperatively] accept...a centralizing authority" (OH, p. 39); a "hegemonic center", the "power center" or "power station" [*la centrale*] or "central switchboard" [*le central*] of some "new *imperium*" that would, precisely, "confuse" ideas of promoting a democratic cultural identity "with concentration, homogeneity or monopoly", all forces that would "control and standardise" culture in a "quasi-political" way (OH, p. 40). This kind of "monopoly" is one that (frankly speaking) despises what these lovers of responsible diversity love: namely, and especially, the most unpredictable, unprogrammable, in short, the most *untimely* – and hence at first "difficult", "inaccessible", "hard to read" – contributions to the material of culture, contributions which open a future. Levelling standardisation may dress itself in the garb of democratic pluralism but it cultivates, precisely, nothing new.

This is not to recommend a counter-to-gathering dispersion either. That is, on the other (dispersion) hand, and equally, we the guardians of this culture "[logically] cannot and [imperatively] must not [accept that European culture] be dispersed into a myriad of provinces, into a multiplicity of self-enclosed idioms or petty little nationalisms, each one jealous and untranslatable" (OH, p. 38–9). Or again, "it is necessary not to cultivate for their own sake minority differences, untranslatable idiolects, national antagonisms, or the chauvinisms of idiom" (OH, p. 44).

The theme is the cultivation of an ideal "law" of culture, and hence of responsibility for the *Dasein* of a culture that can only be gathered on its internal differences. The primary imperative here is to keep the space open for "difficult formulations" and "untimely developments" (writings whose timeliness for a culture lies precisely in their time being ahead of their time, the one's whose time is "not yet" and so today opens the future) against the supposedly democratic norms and models that impose a "grid of readability" on what counts as "*worth while*". Derrida rather wonderfully called the demand for such readability an "unacceptable obscenity": "It is as if I were being asked to capitulate or to subjugate myself—or else to die of stupidity" (LLF, p. 30).

This is about cultural work and its materials, but the terms of Derrida's cultural two-hander clearly draws on the language of politics and its institutions. A "hegemonic centre" and "new *imperium*" set over against "petty little nationalisms" and "chauvinisms": this is the language of the European-state-political drama. Indeed, the fact that Derrida sets off with "state talk" only heightens this parallelism between the quasi-politics of cultural monopoly, and contemporary political efforts to forge an altogether harmonised European Union. In the more straightforwardly political case, too, the questions for Europe are exactly the same. Will Europe confine itself to the gathered self-relation that erases the self-difference that makes it possible? Will it destroy itself in a counter-to-gathering dispersion? Or, alternatively, will Europe strive to be "an exemplary possibility of this law", gathering itself responsibly on its own difference-with-itself, forging a "self that is maintained and gathered in its own difference" (OH, p. 25)?

I will take these questions as political questions head-on in the second volume when we look at the idea and project of political and economic union in Europe. However, and now illustrating something at the core of the paradox outlined in the Introduction to this volume, we should see that being "gathered in its own difference" – being simultaneously transnational and national, for example – has never been far from the centre of thinking European cultural identity itself. Indeed, one finds it affirmed everywhere that it has been seriously thought, making of that (European) case more than a mere sample of cultural identity but something like the ideal concept of its concept. Tempted as Europe might sometimes be by centrifugal forces of dispersion or by centripetal forces of centralisation, the lovers of responsible diversity we are concerned with, and whose future we are concerned about, have consistently wanted to forge and form it as unified without uniformity, and diverse without fragmentation. This has not only been Europe's own particular call for itself as a regional culture but as a cultural ideal it necessarily opens onto human universality.

This is an image at the heart of the European ideal of culture. Indeed, it also the motto of the European Union (probably via the seventeenth century German philosopher G.W. Leibniz): "Unity in Diversity". At issue would be a culture that really *is* one because it really is not a culture that is *one*.

While liable (always) to be overwhelmed, disintegrated, by forces of both uniformity and dispersion, the ideal is conceived as one which wants to avoid both; cultivating itself (gathering itself) instead on, and with, and in view of its vital "frictions" ("the more the better"), and the "traces" of the culture of the other within the history of its culture ("there are always bits and traces"). As we have seen, however, this is not simply the European cultural ideal for Europe alone, but has an internal impetus that immediately carries it beyond any Chinese walls of political geography. It is not conceived as the regionally European way, but conceives itself as devoted to a universally fitting ideal of culture, and hence includes within it the idea of a gathered but still internally differentiated "world culture" as its "logical term of relations between cultures": not an undivided or unparted off-world, but a world gathered with its differences. The lovers of responsible diversity we have been following here conceive themselves as guardians of an ideal of culture – of a culture that really is one because it is not a culture that is one – that "Europe" is the very image of, a European ideal threatened today by forces or desires which throw it off towards ideals of cultural unity, a culture that would Be One, whether that is conceived in an international or national condition.

I got going in this chapter with four conceptions of what is proper to a culture. But perhaps, in the end, there are only two: two conceptions of a culture that really is one. First, a conception that supposes that for a culture properly to be one it should be one. And, second, a conception that supposes that for a culture to be one it should not be one. This contrast will, as we have already glimpsed, get fought out today over the inheritance of what we call "democracy", and within processes of democratisation that are underway. As should be clear, I am on the side of those who do not seek European unity in uniformity, but without thereby succumbing to nationalist or otherwise localised fragmentation; on the side, then, of those who resist movements towards a culture Being One, whether that is understood locally or globally, nationally or internationally.

This chapter has focused on what one might call the characteristic *form* of culture in general, and raised the question of Europe's own relation to that form, asking in particular whether we are only seeing the progress of disintegration of European culture in that regard, and not at all progress towards becoming "an exemplary possibility" of it (OH, p. 11). Positive progress seems a long way off today, and one might reasonably fear that it is all over for Europe as a culture that is worthwhile or worthy of the name. On the other hand, the idea of Europe's exemplarity has always been absolutely central to Europe's self-understanding, central to the idea of Europe's modernity and its promise. That self-understanding has rarely been unproblematic, rarely promising, and in our time it has become a problem: Europe, its Eurocentric heritage and history, called into question in an anti-Eurocentric recoil. However, over the course of these two volumes I hope to show that, beyond both Eurocentrism and anti-Eurocentrism, a new and more promising understanding of cultural exemplarity is, inside but under the radar of its dominant modern understanding, already making its way in Europe: not the idea of the best example of a universally compelling way to be for Man, not of Europe as the singular *avant garde* of a culture of universal humanity – but as the *avant garde* of a universalisable culture of singularities. This other heading for European cultural exemplarity also opens onto the possibility of a world culture: not a world of one culture, a world culture that is one, but a culture gathered on its differences, now projected "as the logical term of relations between cultures" (TDC, p. 62). In this volume, we will follow the history of Europe's modern sense of its cultural exemplarity into crisis; in the second we will consider its future beyond modernity. But how did this idea of exemplarity come to figure so centrally in Europe's self-understanding in the first place? How did it become so central to the *content* of a distinctively European cultural identity? In the next chapter, I will make a start in tracking down its basic sources.

2

GREEK, CHRISTIAN AND BEYOND

And the sons of Noah, that went forth of the ark, were Shem, and Ham, and Japheth
– Genesis

I

European cultural identity. How should we think about this? It pertains, first of all, to someone, a self. We tend to look at it as an element or part of some person's identity, a part which, in part at least, makes them the person, the "who", that they are. As such an element it will be a part among others: along with, for example, their sex, gender, ethnicity, nationality, region, town/country, religion, class, "values", language, and any other "markers" of this self. And other elements might bear on this identity too: musical taste, literary taste, culinary taste, dress sense, political preferences, and so on. It's like a collection of badges that I wear, expressed by what I repeatedly say and do.

European cultural identity. Is it one of these badges, one of the elements or parts of "my identity"? Or, alternatively, does it pervade my identity, as its more or less constant inflection? Could it be that I am, as it were, more or less Europeanised in every part? Could someone be European through and through? And is this something that can be verified or confirmed? Is it a truth about my being? Or is it something that must be affirmed: a commitment or promise or vow that must be avowed? Is it an identity that you simply "have" (like an objective property) or something you have to comport yourself towards and understand in some way as you go along? And can you have it (in some sense) and not know it?

European cultural identity. We can get captivated by the name, and can come to think that what is European is something that must be taken on or undertaken *in its name*. Something like this underlies the significance we attach to social

Greek, Christian and beyond **31**

survey type questions about cultural self-perceptions. Questions like *Do you see yourself as* [select one of the following]:

- European only
- European and National
- National and European
- National only

The Eurobarometer survey asks this question to already-identified-as-European individuals, with their national identity equally pre-supplied in the country-by-country questionnaire. Anna Ksiazczakova has worked through the survey responses for the last decade, and a summary of her "EU average" findings, commissioned for this book, are reproduced below. (In the second volume of this book, we will also look at the country-specific data Ksiazczakova collected for Germany, France and Britain in this Brexit-including period.) As will be seen from the table, the across-Europe results are fairly stable over the last decade, but they do show an intriguing decline in the "(NATIONALITY) only" responses, and a corresponding modest increase (mostly) in the "(NATIONALITY) and European" responses:

EB	Year	EU Average			
		European only	European and (NATIONALITY)	(NATIONALITY) and European	(NATIONALITY) only
EB73	2010/05	3	7	41	46
EB76.4	2011/12	4	8	46	39
EB77	2012/05	3	6	49	38
EB78.2	2012/12	3	7	49	38
EB79	2013/05	3	7	49	38
EB80	2013/11	2	5	47	42
EB81.2	2014/03	2	5	48	42
EB81	2014/05	2	6	51	39
EB82	2014/11	2	6	51	39
EB83	2015/05	2	6	52	38
EB84	2015/11	1	5	51	41
EB85	2016/05	2	6	51	39
EB86	2016/11	2	6	53	37
EB87	2017/05	2	7	54	35
EB88	2017/11	2	7	54	35
EB89	2018/03	2	6	55	35
EB90	2018/11	2	9	55	33
EB91	2019/06	2	8	55	33

The "analysis" in the Eurobarometer report for Spring 2015 headlines (in bold), something that is stressed by all the reports in one way or another; namely, that "**a stable majority of Europeans continue to see themselves as European citizens**" (which is the first three figures added together). The same analysis then concedes in the main text: "However, just under four in ten respondents define themselves solely by their nationality". That solely national number seems to be declining in recent years, moving towards three in ten. But to set a level analytic bar one might also add up the last three figures boldly to stress that **a stable (and massive) majority of Europeans see themselves as national citizens**.

Even with the decline already noted in view, it remains the case that a significant percentage of those the survey has pre-identified as Europeans do not self-identify as European at all. Are they Europeans, Europeans in any part? If we are captivated by the name or the avowal of the name, we might think not. However, this may be a very misleading assumption. Consider asking yourself whether there is such a thing as or something like a "European legacy in art", a "European legacy in literature", a "European legacy in law", a "European legacy in philosophy"? Would it be presumptuous of me to think that you think that there are such legacies? I doubt it. But I deliberately left one out. What about a European legacy in politics? And then one might wonder: is there anything more European than seeing oneself as…a national citizen? Isn't the nation-state and national-citizen status the most profound and still enduring legacy in European politics? Those "(NATIONALITY) only" respondents – they are also very European, even if not European through and through, not European in its name. And who *is* European through and through? That (currently) 2%? Who are they? Are they the "true" Europeans? If they are (which I do not believe), they are anyway not many. In fact, when the total is 2%, exactly half of the respondent countries give results somewhat *lower* than 2%. The overall figure is bolstered, especially, by Spain (and perhaps a little by little Luxembourg), but I am inclined to think that the Spanish numbers are swelled not by distinctively non-national-identifying European respondents but, for example, by Catalan nationalists who simply do not want to be pre-supplied with a Spanish identity in the first place. (I confess I don't really know anything about Luxembourg, but it has three languages and the percentage of its population that is "non-native" is unusually high.)

Perhaps more impressive than the still-large numbers of "(NATIONALITY) only" respondents, and the equally significant tiny number of "European only" respondents, are the middle two figures: the clear majority that regard themselves, in one way or the other, as *both* national and European. This belongs to the paradox of European identity that I am trying to keep track of as we go along: the avowal of what Derrida calls the European "national 'ego' or 'subject'" who declares "I am (we are) all the more national for being European, all the more European for being trans-European and international" (OH, p. 48).

European cultural identity. By the end of this two-part epic, I hope to have made a compelling case for thinking it is all-pervasive. And yet, *as such*, it also remains – with that pervasiveness it has to remain – as just one among other elements, leaving one with other elements beside it.

Some pervasively European minds find their Europeanness appearing as a part that weighs as an important and wanting-to-be-avowed part; for other Europeans, it may not show itself as a part at all. Moreover, as we shall see in this chapter, Europeans are not entirely single-minded about their European identity even as a part, though I will suggest that this many-sided, pervasively European, mind, in fact, has a certain centre of gravity.

II

To make our way towards this centre of gravity I want now to consider a short text in which a (British) European man speaks his mind ("my mind") about Europe; a text that stands, I think, as good an example as one might hope for of one such European mind speaking its mind. It is not a theoretical text but a "Letter to the Editor", a letter responding to an article that had outlined the case for Turkey to join the European Union in 2004. This was a case that divided European politicians, and threw up questions not just about European Union enlargement but the limits of Europe itself.

> *Oxford Today* (17.1 Michaelmas 2004)
> **Letters to the Editor**
> **European Dimensions**
> The proposal by Dr Anastasakis (*OT* 16.3, p. 15) that Turkey should join the European Union surely raises the question, where does Europe end?
> At school we learned that Europe was a peninsula west of the Urals and north of the Caucasus, otherwise bounded by water and including its offshore islands. On that basis, Turkey's claim to be European rests on its possession of Eastern Thrace, a mere 3 per cent of its total area. Adding it would extend the boundary of Europe well into the Middle East and include half the Kurds. If one half, why not the other half?
> Russia has a much more plausible claim, with the majority of its population in geographical Europe, but that would extend the boundary to Vladivostok. If geography does not matter, the cultural and historical associations of Australasia and the Americas are superior to those of Turkey. Obviously a line has to be drawn somewhere, and to my mind 50 miles from the Bosphorus is reasonable if untidy. Cyprus and Rhodes too are in Asia, the Canaries are in Africa, Martinique is in America, and so on, but these anomalies relate to islands with very small populations.
> Derek Bloom (St Edmund Hall, 1951)

Bloom is thinking about European limits, about setting and settling limits, and he supposes there should be limits, reasonable limits, that will gather together what belongs together by reason or right. And the reason in play that will settle matters is a logic of nearness, of proximity to what is already settled, and, above all, already known to be European. Within this logic some limits make more sense than others, better sense, good sense, and the properly adjusted mind should adjust itself to what is known, or obvious, or sure. Perhaps we honour the name of Europe, remain ourselves good Europeans, only by maintaining ourselves on such a firm basis, our own sense of good sense. This is a European text: Europe gathering itself by itself, by what shows itself as good sense to "my mind", according to and in accordance with my mind, with what my mind finds reasonable. As if this mind did not already belong to the very whereabouts it wants, by itself, to delimit.

So Bloom asks, "Where does Europe end?" the reasonable answer to which will settle unsettling questions, for example, the question of Turkish rights to membership of the EU – if only we can adjust our mind to what is reasonable.

He begins: "At school we learned…". Who is this "we"? Why the plural "we" in this letter signed by one man? There is an invocation of the authority of the school, and a common experience in the classroom – it is a question of common knowledge. He goes on to say that adding Turkey "would extend the boundary". Such an extension took place in 1730 when a Swedish officer in the Russian service suggested that Europe's boundary should be pushed east – from the River Don to the Ural Mountains (see Davies, p. 8); that is, extended to where it lay when Bloom learned at school that that was where it lay. But perhaps Bloom did not have a history teacher who was altogether comfortable with history – if history is a concern with what actually happens. The extension that would take in Turkey also raises the worry that it would "include half the Kurds", and if we did that "why not the other half?" Indeed, the Kurds, an Indo-Germanic group, why not? I'm not saying we should. I'm saying: Yes, why not?

The brief projection of an alternative non-geographical projection opens the discussion, however cursorily, to the suggestion (how could it even appear!) that all this talk of geography might be beside the point. Perhaps nearness was never simply spatial proximity. Perhaps Europe is not or not simply a regional site but a cultural formation. And here some claims are "superior" to others, some places closer, culturally closer, to the countries *known* (how?) to be European than others. I will come back to this.

But no. For this European mind, or for this side of the European mind, if Europe is to make good sense as the name of a place, geography must be respected, or rather a certain spatial reason must be respected: "Obviously a line has to be drawn somewhere". And here is better than there because it "minimises anomalies". Or at least it seems so. Is there an anomaly minimising definition of "off-shore" for the islands that are European because they are "off-shore" islands? Is Iceland an off-shore island? What are the limits of off-shore? Are they natural or rational? Bloom's anomalies are, fortunately, islands "with very small populations", little more than rocks. And who could reasonably suggest that it matters if a rock is in or out? Turkey, which is surely no rock, is out – obviously, clearly, reasonably, even if still untidily. Europe is fundamentally a bounded portion of the global surface. So it must end somewhere.

Here we have a first approach to Europe's identity, one that approaches it in terms of Europe's *final end* [*terminus*], its Land's End or Finisterre. But let's go back to the idea of cultural proximity that Bloom briefly invites but rapidly dismisses because it can't keep itself even remotely tidy. For there is another side of the European mind: one for which the space opened up when geography "does not matter" anymore matters most of all. In this case, as Bloom notes, what really matters are "cultural and historical associations": not spatial surfaces but what has gone on above the surface.

This draws us towards or flips over towards a quite different kind of analysis and understanding of Europe's "final end". Europe conceived not as the Western peninsula of Asia but as the centre of the unfolding of a distinctive culture. If we were writing a "Letter to the Editor" with this approach in mind we would not try to find Europe's proper territorial borders but stress that it has none. Instead of constructing walls, we would emphasise the emergence of a culture that understands itself not as a merely regional way of life, not just one regional sample of human culture among others, but as a culture cultivating the humanity of Man as such: Europe as the site of the emergence of a civilisation that aims at the cultivation, the progressive civilisation, the becoming-civilised, of Man as Man. On this telling, the letter would stress that European humanity is the advance guard in universal human cultural development: at the head of human history on its way towards its proper all-embracing "end". Here is a strictly non-geographical, non-superficial understanding of Europe's end: the *end* of Europe is not the border of a finite region [its *terminus*] but a universal destination, heading or goal for Man [its *telos*].

This second letter would find its words through a discourse of Europe's specificity conceived in terms of its cultural exemplarity. The spirit of this Europe is a spirit of self-responsibility, not just for itself but for the meaning of being human, for the meaning of what is called "Man". (For the sake of reading comfort I will try my best to drop the inverted commas around "Man", but will certainly come back to why we might not. Remember, however, that what we designate with that name is a distinctive understanding of *whatever it is* that we name with that name.) In that spirit, then:

> ***Only Today*** (16/6 2004)
> **Letters to the Editor**
> **European Dimensions**
> The proposal by Dr Anastasakis (*OT* 16/3, p. 15) that Turkey should join the European Union surely raises the question, where does Europe end?
> At school we learned that Europe was a peninsula west of the Urals and north of the Caucasus, otherwise bounded by water and including its offshore islands. But that eastern border had already shifted east from an earlier limit at the River Don. Adding Turkey would merely extend the boundary of Europe once more. And there is no reason why its borders should stop there either. The addition of Turkey would include half the Kurds, an Indo-Germanic group. If one half, why not the other half?

Russia also has a plausible claim, with the majority of its population already in geographical Europe. Is there any reason why we could not extend the boundary to Vladivostok? Geography does not matter. What matters are the cultural and historical associations. Australasia and the Americas are largely European settler colonies, with claims to be "European" that may even be superior to those of Turkey, a country whose claims are, however, already strong. Obviously the map of Europe's spreading out is untidy. But this is history, not geometry. The "area" of European culture today just is untidy. It has no definite frontiers: and you cannot build Chinese walls. Norway and Switzerland – and possibly the UK one day soon – are already geographical anomalies for the EU. Iceland is an island with a very small population. But why should that stand in its way should it one day wish to join? The end of Europe is not the border of a finite region, but a universal destination for Mankind. When we think of the ideal of "European culture" we are, as the poet T.S. Eliot put it, "pressed to maintain the ideal of a world culture".

Leo Bloom (St Stephen's, 1922)

III

On the way to seeing how these two European Blooms might yet belong together, let us pause for a moment with this idea of the unfolding destiny of Man in what amounts to a history of the world: the movement of Man from his primitive beginnings to his civilised end.

We begin, then, as an animal, an animal which starts out, like its fellow creatures, living a wild, raw. and wholly natural existence. But for some reason, and the reason here is fundamentally related to reason itself, this animal had special promise. Slowly and by stages, it began to raise itself out of mere (pure) animal ways and to develop, naturally enough, into something more than just a living thing. It was on a march, a forward march to a place of dreams. It sent itself away from its habitation with other creatures and set up on its own. This animal was going somewhere, it had its own special heading: the heading of Man.

Like all great stories for the not-so-young, this tale has always been told in terms appropriate to its own period and place: familiarly, and in homely ways. Indeed, the heading of Man has always been a heading home. Man ends up where he belongs, where he had belonged from the start when he set off that way from elsewhere, so that in the end he reaches a place where he can stop and rest, being at last where he should be. But the end is always also already seen, already known or anticipated in some way: it is already "close to home." There is no place like it, because it is utterly, properly one's own. Home from home.

Nearly there? Always only nearly there. Aristotle had an end in sight, and sent us on a two-thousand-plus year round trip:

> When several villages are united in a single community, large enough to be nearly or quite self-sufficient, the *polis* comes into existence, originating in the bare needs of life, and continuing in existence for the sake of the good life. And therefore, if the earlier forms of society are natural, so is the *polis*... Hence it is evident that the *polis* is a creation of nature, and that man is by nature a *zōon politikon*. (Politics: Book I, Chapter 2, 1253a2)

I retain and for a while won't translate "*polis*", nor the adjective qualifying a living thing as "*politikon*." While he insisted that we are not the only such living thing, Aristotle said that the "*zōon politikon*" that we are is, uniquely, a "*zōon logon echon*". I once more leave this too untranslated. All of this has been translated. We are, in part, that translation, in a history of translation, transposition and transformation that is not over.

And so the Greeks sent Man on for the sake of the good life. The Christian fathers saw this destiny in terms of life in the city of God. Much later Marx saw the social animal as off towards a communist end. And so, on: home and away, home and away…We trade and tread on stories from a past which is not simply past, inherited like old clothes (not as heritage pieces or heirlooms, but as hand-me-downs we find ourselves already wearing), and we push on. "Aristotle", "Augustine", "Marx", and so many ghosts whose sendings haunt each other. And haunt us, somewhere where we are. This story of Europe: it will always be a ghost story.

IV

With respect to Europe's "end", we find, side-by-side, two sides of the European mind, two Blooms of Europe's self-understanding: one side thinking of Europe territorially; the other thinking Europe teleologically. Could there be the calm assurance of this rational geography without the audacity of this kind of history? Without recourse to the distinctive understanding of the world and the significance of our lives that belongs to and spreads out from Europe, it would seem impossible not to experience a kind of radical arbitrariness of any territorial lines that must be drawn "somewhere", especially when "historical associations" all over the globe leave one with nothing more to stand on than what one learnt at school. Moreover, if the spirit of the modern Europe is a spirit of self-responsibility and rational inquiry, it is hard to see how anyone caught up in that spirit – anyone who wants their discourse to be governed by rational considerations – could avoid feeling that, theoretically at least, this spirit should triumph over forms of human life that are conceived as still mired in superstition, prejudice, mythology, and violence. I am not sure if this image of cultural exemplarity is readable in Derek Bloom's picture, it is not clear to me whether he would or could finally be happy to attest to a "superiority" of claims without implying any thought of differential levels of development measured in terms of that cultural nearness. But his line drawing is certainly anxiously protective;

and to modify the line from Sartre cited in the Introduction, one doesn't protect the worse.

In this chapter, we have so far been circling around two approaches to Europe's identity, approaches that conceive it in terms of its ends. However, both are caught up with a sense of Europe grasped through its cultural history – something that can then give rise to "associations" beyond geography – and hence ultimately to a discourse on Europe's cultural origins, its history and its genealogy. Genealogy seeks to identify what is fundamental to Europe's cultural identity in terms of the line that takes us back to "where it all began", in terms of historical roots that have most decisively configured its present formation. Here we find two more approaches to Europe's identity. And once again we can mark a contrast between something like an empirical orientation and a philosophical one, this time between empirical history and philosophical history. Both have a history within Europe's history, but very roughly one can say that the former conducts us back from our time seeking out its sources as one might try to follow a river back to its original *spring*, and the latter conducts us back inside our time seeking out its sources as one might try to disclose its originating *principles*. It is the latter that Heidegger has in view when he says that "the *archē* names that from which something proceeds. But this 'from where' is not left behind in the process of going out, but the beginning rather becomes that which governs" (WP, p. 81). In the archive of the word *archē*, we thus find stored the idea of both the commencement and the commandment: the opening up which holds sway, and whose "holding sway" may also "have a history".

While the writing of empirical history should be open to surprises and discoveries, writings on modern Europe's empirical history in fact displays a remarkably, indeed overwhelmingly, constant character in its overall picture. The historians business is always to identify something like a golden thread of developments that have brought Europe to where it is today. And it seems that there really is only one thread to follow. This (the only) golden thread history of Europe runs: *Greek-Roman-Christian-Modern*.

Nothing could be more European than this golden-thread history of Europe's history. Hence, even while Norman Davies will cite the historian A.J.P. Taylor playfully declaring that (given the vagaries of Europe's ends) "European History is whatever the historian wants it to be" (Davies, p. 45), Davies does not blink when he affirms what most historians want it to be. "Most historians", he says, want European history to be "found" in "each of the great epochs of Europe's past", so that what has "always featured prominently" in such accounts is a story that takes "the roots of the Christian world" to lie in "Greece and Rome", and "modern phenomena such as the Enlightenment, modernization" to emerge out of that Christian world (Davies, p. 15). We are in a space where the most decisive decisions on Europe's history have already been made.

Philosophical history has also had the time-line of this golden-thread history in view. But its own history is, as we shall see, more deeply marked by fairly radical ruptures and mutations. In its first and classical form, the form it takes in the work of Kant and Hegel above all, it was conceived as, fundamentally, a history of reason in its self-development. Europe's modernity is then represented there as belonging to a universal history of Man as a rational being: it belongs inside the history of the unfolding of the reason in Man, from a primitive origin, where reason is a mere potential in Man, to its civilised end, where reason finally realises itself. History is the movement of the self-development of reason in time. And the Greek origin of Europe is then understood to mark a new and higher stage in that overall human development. Perhaps the most significant ruptures in the history of philosophical history take place when the distinctively Christian character of the classical formation becomes an issue for it. In my own work, and the work I am most indebted to, another kind of turn is involved: philosophical history is no longer the attempt to account for the real development of Man in history, but an attempt to come to terms with the exhaustion of the world in which such an effort made sense. My interest is in the vicissitudes of a distinctively European self-understanding, its historical unfolding, and contemporary unravelling.

For sure empirical history does not have such grand philosophical designs in mind when it relates to the golden-thread history of Europe's history emerging into modernity. Norman Davies, for example, talks, at the start of his book, about the murky pre-historical beginnings of European history in what he calls the "Neolithic advance" (Davies, p. 74). And then, at the close of the book, he suggests, that an end of Europe is yet to be "established" (Davies, p. 1136). On the other hand, despite the vagaries of these origins and ends, Davies's narrative still belongs to the recognisably European self-understanding and self-elaboration, and the very one that is worked out in philosophical history too. In a passage that Kant and Hegel could have written themselves, and probably did, he declares that "Rome was built on Greek foundations, and Europe on the relics of Rome" (Davies, p. 94). This is the (only) European history of Europe. Indeed, once he has done with the vagaries of pre-history, Davies begins his telling of the non-murky history of Europe with a chapter entitled, simply, "Hellas: Ancient Greece".

But surely that's because what took place in Ancient Greece *is* the beginning of the history of Europe. Perhaps. The Hellenistic Greeks will have acknowledged the importance of Egyptian and Phoenician predecessors. And that would only push us back and back. Yet isn't there some justification in starting off with the starting off of what today we still call "antiquity" and "the classical age"? There is, I think, a clear justification in this sense: Europe will have called itself to appear within a self-understanding that wants to have its starting point with the emergence of philosophy and science (including historical science) in Ancient Greece.

In one way or another, philosophical history will also chart the movement of the opening up of modern Europe in the same genealogical terms. So one might be inclined to think that it is not really so different from what an historian of Europe like Norman Davies provides in his Greek-Roman-Christian-Modern golden-thread history of Europe. However, as an historian, Davies conceives what he is doing as identifying a series of causally connected "in the world" events: the historical event-line of happenings that happen to have taken us to where we are today. What (I think all) philosophical history will highlight and try to comprehend, by contrast, is the history of the world that such events belong to, and seeks the *archē* of that world.

The idea of empirical history is (for us) familiar, the idea of philosophical history much less so. The whole situation is complicated, however, by the fact that both have a history, and a tangled-together history at that. I will not attempt to get far into that tangle here, or relate anything about the way the discipline of empirical history has understood its own (for example, methodological) progress. (We will, however, get a picture of the emergence of the sciences, including humanistic sciences, as positive empirical sciences in Chapter 10.) I do suppose, however, that history as a discipline will understand itself as having made such progress, and that this is evidence of the tangle, evidence of its belonging to a cultural world whose history is marked by the kind of self-understanding that is given systematic form in philosophical history. Philosophical history has been, for most of its history, a discourse of the historical progress of Man, and of Europe's exemplary modernity. More specifically, it has been a discourse that conceives Europe as the most advanced stage in the *archeo-teleological* (beginning-to-end) progress or emancipation of Man: the history of the self-development of reason in Man. For most of its history, that is to say, it has elaborated a "metaphysical" conception of history, sometimes in an overtly religious form, sometimes in a more secular and supposedly scientific form. But over time the philosophical idea of the history of Europe's modernity has been confronted by the reality of Europe's own unravelling, an unravelling that is fundamentally inseparable from what I will call the exhaustion of its own *archeo-teleological* sense of world history, the exhaustion of the European understanding of ourselves as Man – the exhaustion of what, in the last chapter, I called the ideal of a world culture that is one because it is, finally, One.

In order to understand this development within a still-philosophical history, I will retain a sense of "European events" that is in some respects indebted to classical philosophical history, and it is a different sense to the familiar empirical-historical one. I want to affirm a sense of events that are not only empirical events and happenings *in* the world but which belong to the coming into being and holding sway *of* a world in which and in terms of which empirical events acquire their significance and meaning for us. Such "world-historical" events, as we might call them, open up the very world within which they appear.

The coming into being and holding sway of a world is itself an event. It might be called a *phenomenological* event. It is the event or happening of the historical presencing of the "somewhere where we are" that I invoked at the start of the last chapter. We *are* in the event of its presencing. We have our being in that "text", whether we like it or not, and indeed whether we know it or not – and, in the case of "Europeans" in this "spiritual" sense, even whether, geographically speaking, we are "in Europe" or not.

The events which matter most for me as an inheritor of philosophical history are, therefore, not over and in the past but constitute the *archē* of the "somewhere where we are" in which the worldly events that concern the empirical historian unfold. At issue for the philosophical historian who is a philosopher *of* Europe (and perhaps there is, as yet, no other kind) is not, then, the sequence of events that takes us from a distant past to a given European present, but rather the "event" that is the *becoming-European* of a world – a world which once was not, and which "we too now know" will one day be no more (HP, p. 23) – a world within which, for example, the style of historiography that provides a rational reconstruction of an historical causality becomes a matter of course for us. It is the opening up and holding sway of the European world.

Affirming this in no way compromises the legitimate authority of empirical historiography or evidence-based rational reconstructions of worldly events. However, I do want to insist that historiographical discourses on the origins of modern Europe are never arrived at by reflections in which empirical historical research on Europe – researches into the European archives – can be decisive. For where does the archive of European history begin or end? Like Eurobarometer questions about European identity that are asked to already identified Europeans, the question of Europe's archive is not itself settled or established independently of the inquiry that delimits it. Such inquiries are not purely empirical research into the truth of Europe's history. On the contrary, they depend upon a productive or performative dimension irreducible to an assessment in terms of truth, irreducible to rational reconstructions or empirical findings concerning a history of Europe. Facts about European history are not, in this view, fictions. They may even be "objective" in that interestingly complex historical sense of "objective". But here I will stick. What I will not back down from is the denial that these facts are decisive. To borrow from David Wiggins's discussion of "cognitive underdetermination" in judgements of value: "Such [facts] may be important to us. But they depend for their significance upon a framework that is a free construct, not upon something fashioned in a manner that is answerable to how anything really is....[It] is not something that we (as we say) found or discovered" (TIML, p. 124).

Moreover, such historical research is itself always also part of the very dossier, part of the very archive it seeks to disclose: it belongs to the movement through which a European heritage and archive, as it were, calls itself to be. It is never just a report on what was the case. Rendering, making known, selecting, choosing, de-selecting, discounting, this is what counts – beyond empirical discoveries or rational narrations – in the formation of the heritage and archive of thinking and feeling which forges and forms the fabric of what comes to call itself (to be) "Europe".

The dossier of debate on the history of Europe is inevitably a field of responsibility and decision, and the work of historians *of* Europe contributes to that dossier as much as it recalls it: it is not just a matter of telling the truth about a rich and independently identifiable or independently constituted data-set. It can make you giddy thinking about this construction site.

Think for a moment of the Pitt Rivers Museum in Oxford. The Museum was founded in 1884 when General Pitt Rivers, an influential figure in the development of European archaeology and evolutionary anthropology, gave his collection (mostly of weapons) from around the world to the University of Oxford. The General's founding gift contained more than 18,000 objects, but there are now over half a million. Many were donated by early European anthropologists and explorers. In beautiful and wonderfully cluttered Victorian display cases one can peruse "artifacts", both baffling and everyday, and the original, small handwritten labels still provide the visitor with a minimal context. But these labels are less significant than the rather larger labels often attached to the cases themselves, which identify the part of the world the items are from. Typically: "Africa", "Asia", "Europe" – although by 1844 "America" and "Australasia" are part of the divided off world too.

What struck me when I visited the museum again a few years ago (it has since been thoughtfully and still-beautifully revamped) is that the museum itself could be labelled, like one of the display cases, and labelled: "Europe". In this instance, the label would not function only as naming the place of origin of an artefact (a museum building) but indicates rather the site of an interpretation of the world. This non-empirical site is a structure and an articulation of a movement of understanding and feeling of what has come to call itself (to be) "European".

So the task of a philosophy of Europe today would be the analysis and history of this non-empirical site, this cultivated place, the historical localisation of the "Here I am" that belongs to the emergence of a distinctively European understanding of the world and the significance of our lives, the emergence of European *Dasein*.

There is no radical justification for a particular point of departure in such an investigation. As what is *most* familiar, it does not present itself as something "found", an object for a disinterested theoretical gaze, but as the "somewhere where we are" that we – *we the Europeans* (whoever that is) – already inhabit. While one might want to resist the idea that there is anything in the world that one might call "Europe as such", something that is given to be thought or represented by a science of Europe as such, there remain a thousand million traces of Europe to be read. We are left, that is to say, with the task of reading, with whatever flair or nose for the thing we can muster, the *archē* and not simply the archive, of the great "text" of Europe.

V

We are trying to home-in on what might be the basic "sources", the *archē*, of European *Dasein*. As we have seen, Valéry set his sights on the Mediterranean basin – though, in fact, he did not think it was the only site worthy of attention.

Greek, Christian and beyond 43

He also offers "another example" of such a "machine for making civilization" or a "factory" for producing Europeans: "Consider the Rhine basin, from Basel to the sea…" (HP, p. 196). He does not, but he could also have given the example of the trading world that grew up on the Atlantic coast, the extreme western edge of the Eurasian landmass. We will come back to these prototypically European places in greater detail in the second volume. However, I want to pick up here on Valéry noting at one point that the especially favourable position of the Mediterranean basin was due, in part, because the waters of that sea "washes the coasts of three very different parts of the world" (HP, p. 196).

Three? Before it all began were there three, already exactly *three* parts of the world? Perhaps – for the self-sketching European. Indeed, I think a clue to the *archē* of European *Dasein* can be found in something that has been in view for us for some time already: the names of parts of the world.

In the last chapter, we took our heading from the fifth century BC Greek historian, Herodotus, the writer often regarded as the "father" or "founder" of history (PH, p. 3), if not yet the beginning of "real history" (Kant (citing Hume's view), p. 52). In his writings, we find him wondering, since, he did not know, why the world – "which is one" – was considered to consist of three parts, and also why they bore the names of three women:

> Asia – Libya – Europa

From around the second century BC the part of the world that Herodotus called by the ethnonym "Libya" (the land of the Libu, the tribal inhabitants of the south-western shores of the Mediterranean), was renamed (by the Romans) "Africa" (the land of the Afri, probably derived from the Berber "ifri" meaning "cave"). The border of Africa also shifted east, to include Egypt.

Remarkably this is not the only tripartite division of the world found in *our* ancient texts. Another, which gave us a heading for this chapter, is found in the Bible. There the names are different, and it is three men or boys, the sons of Noah, commencing their dispersion after the flood, whose names name the parts of the one world:

> Shem – Ham – Japheth

We might remind ourselves of the relevant text:

> And the sons of Noah, that went forth of the ark, were Shem, and Ham, and Japheth: and Ham is the father of Canaan. (Genesis 9:18)

> God shall enlarge Japheth [יפת ליפת (*yapet le yapet*)], and he shall dwell in the tents of Shem; and Canaan shall be his servant. (Genesis 9:27)

Some four hundred years into Christian history, the Latin-speaking Roman-African Christian thinker St Augustine presented a reading of the Biblical story of Noah's sons that construed it as a piece of prophetic history, an allegory. For example, the Genesis narrative says that Japheth "shall dwell in the tents of Shem". The idea is that from the descendants of Shem, namely the Jews, the Messiah will be born. In the tents of Shem, that is from the dwelling place of the Jews, the peoples descending from Japheth, namely the Christians, will "enlarge" or, as we might more naturally say today, "spread out". Indeed, "Japheth" means just that: *yapet le yapet*.

Hold onto this two-fold tripartite division of the world for a moment. Before coming back to it, I want to turn briefly to a much more recent text, a text very much part of the modern European world, an essay by the cultural theorist Pim den Boer which forms part of a semi-official European history of the idea of Europe, published in 1995. In his contribution to that book, there is a claim to reproduce, in the spirit of disinterested European science and scholarship, "the oldest known maps of the world".

Pim den Boer confidently asserts that "the oldest known maps of the world are to be found in medieval manuscripts" (HIE, p. 22). The old maps in question, one of which is reproduced below, are called Noachide maps, named so because they present the dwelling places of the sons of Noah after the flood. The oldest extant Noachide map was found in a copy of an earlier text, a now lost early-seventh century manuscript by Isodore, Bishop of Seville (602–632). The crucial thing about this map is that its visual projection of the world is "entirely in accordance" with the description of the world provided by St Augustine some 200 years earlier (354–430). The Biblical names are there, naming the parts of the world. But, and here is the fascinating thing: it incorporates the Greek names too.

I want to make two quick points before turning to this map. First, no, these are not the oldest known maps of the world. The oldest known maps of the world are found on Babylonian clay tablets some 3,000 years before the medieval manuscripts cited in Pim den Boer's text. The tablets were found at a site south of Baghdad, in present-day Iraq. And there are other contenders that are older still, including some 6,200 BC engravings found at a site in present-day Turkey.

So, no, it's a transparently self-aggrandising claim, and one that doubtless will be learned at school by young Europeans some day. However, and second, I do wonder if this error covers over a much more interesting truth. Let's say they are the oldest known *European* maps of the world. If we take that as meaning they are the oldest known maps that were (as they were labelled) "made in Europe", that is not very interesting. But what if they are the first maps of the world that belong to the *becoming-European* world? What if, by forging and forming a certain tradition of more than one tradition, by bringing together in a single representation, into a single space, Greek resources and a Biblical, and here especially, Christian prophetic history, they project the projection of an understanding of the world-that-is-one that is distinctively European? What if the *Dasein* of Europe's culture has been, fundamentally, the holding sway of a gathered conjunction of this difference?

Greek, Christian and beyond   45

In one of his early essays, Derrida uses a passage from *Culture and Anarchy* by Matthew Arnold as an epigraph that frames this thought very clearly: "Hebraism and Hellenism, – between these two points of influence moves our world. At one time it feels more powerfully the attraction of one of them, at another time of the other; and it ought to be, though it never is, evenly and happily balanced between them" (VM, p. 79). The essay by Derrida was on Emmanuel Levinas, a Lithuanian-born naturalised French citizen from a culturally Jewish family, and focused on Levinas's engagement with the work of "two Greeks" named "Husserl and Heidegger" (VM, p. 83), for whom the entirety of philosophy, and by implication of Europe, is primarily "conceived on the basis of its Greek source" (VM, p. 81). Levinas, for his part, like Arnold, and Derrida too, wants to read "our world", as unfolding, still today, in the space opened up by not one but two fundamental *archē*: Greek and Biblical.

"Europe", Levinas says, "is the Bible and the Greeks" (RB, p. 182).

It is with this little protocol for reading the *archē* of "Europe" as my interpretive key that I will make my way into the becoming-European world. Let's take a look at this European map, this map *of* Europe: the Noachide Map.

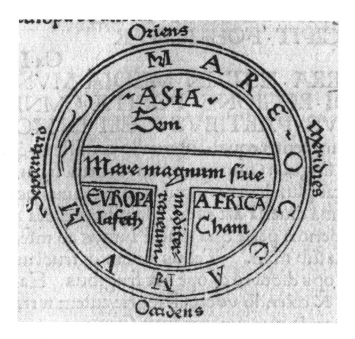

The orientation of the map may be unfamiliar since it is oriented to…the Orient. These maps are also called OT maps because of the letter-like geometry of their projection of the world and its division into three parts. The cross of the T is particularly interesting, representing two rivers which flow roughly north–south and roughly opposite each other, out of the seas which wash the shores. To the south, it is the River Nile. To the north, which one of our Blooms missed out learning about at school, is the River Don.

Europe is the space of Japheth's spreading out. But it (Europe) is given more significance than that. It is painful to read that God wished that Canaan, the son of Ham, the African, shall be Japheth's servant. Leaving the dwelling place of Shem behind him, and with the son of Ham as his recognised subaltern, "God shall enlarge Japheth" [יפת ליפת (*yapet le yapet*)]. The Isidore copy includes a Latin inscription "Lo: thus did the sons of Noah divide the world after the Flood". It was not a parting off and division without differences: this map of the world is Japheth's map, and belongs to Japheth's world, imprinting a "geography" which has, today, spread out and settled over the whole globe.

VI

The broad, and broadly phenomenological, direction of my approach to a philosophical history of Europe is to conceive "Europe" in the first instance, not as a geographical, political or even cultural region of the global surface but as the "event" of a movement. We can now specify that event more precisely: it takes place as the missionary spreading out of the world of the Greco-Biblical *archē*. Wherever we find a document or instrument or institution or discipline for which the basic and enduring "sources" are Greco-Biblical, *there* we always have something belonging to the European world in our sights, something belonging to what has called itself a "European" period and place. When the world in question is Japheth's world, the movement of its spreading out, its world-wide-isation or its "globalisation" already belongs to its programme.

The Levinasian formula (E = B+G) is not unproblematic. It may even be dangerous: belonging to a European self-understanding that threatens to be, precisely, narrow, exclusive and unified. And we know too that the Europe we inherited from yesterday often did, even most often did, forge and form itself by dedicating itself to remaining – that is to say to becoming – Greco-Biblical; dedicated to making it so that Europe *will have been* Greco-Biblical, intent on stripping out every other so that to be properly a European requires being (in the sense of "wanting to keep to being") Greco-Biblical.

The movement of this world, the movement so often un-critically referred to in geopolitical terms as the Europeanisation of the world or the globalisation of European civilisation, is not over. The Europe of the Greco-Biblical *archē* is not over. But it is, I believe, approaching its exhaustion. Moreover, in our time we know better than before that Europe will have rendered itself Greco-Biblical in the name of a monogenealogy (the golden thread) which will have always been constructed through selections, styles of selections, economies of assimilation, which are not only, and never were purely Greco-Biblical, from the start and each time never simply Greco-Biblical.

On the other hand, perhaps even the Levinasian conception of a European tradition of more than one tradition can belong to a cultivation of place that is more promising, exemplary perhaps, in its capacity for self-interruption, in its capacity to break with itself. This is why, while acknowledging the distinctive rootedness of the European heritage in Greek and Christian sources, I think Derrida is right to insist that one should not leave it there. Recall his prudence:

> One should more prudently say "Greek, Christian and beyond", to designate those places towards which we are still timorously advancing: Judaism and Islam, at the very least... [But], above all, starting from and still in Nietzsche's wake, [towards] the entire passage beyond whose movement bears his name. That is to say, everywhere where a tradition thus tends of itself to break with itself. (PF, p. 103)

The heritage and future of Europe are not simply disconnected in this thought of a tradition breaking with itself. The Nietzschean "passage beyond" is not a movement that simply rejects the European heritage or wants simply to destroy it, but which, and sometimes even in its name (for example in the name of what Nietzsche will call "we *good Europeans*"), aims to propel Europe in a new direction *out of* (i.e. both "from" and "beyond") its own sources: not to destroy its heritage but rather to give it a future. The "beyond" here is not simply the addition of further sources – though, as Derrida indicates, proper acknowledgement of Judaic and Islamic historical sources ought to be made "at the very least" – nor is it simply an addition of what comes "after", as an up-to-date variant of the old modern golden-thread history. Rather, it indicates an opening to alterity that was already available in Europe's heritage.

And so perhaps, finally, Levinas's formula also says the same thing, or can be made to say the same thing, in a kind of supplementary complication, installing the movement to the "beyond" right inside the Greco-Biblical event which (to use a term from computer programming) *initialized* Europe. As I say, the Levinasian formula can be dangerous and misleading, and then deserves to be criticised as such, requiring corrections to what Valéry called the "portrait of us Europeans" (HP, p. 319). We now have such portraits produced for us in ever-proliferating academic snapshots, each trying to outdo the others in penitent inclusivity of the other. Not simply to admit the Phoenician and Egyptian influences on Greece, or the Judaic and Islamic influences all over the place, not wanting better to include them so as to more prudently depict the European subject, or to encourage Europe to approach itself more prudently – but, in an anti-Eurocentric recoil, to blur the historical picture into what Valéry calls the "invisibility" of "indistinct equality" (HP, p. 27). In short, the interest in such snapshots today seems less about making contributions to an ongoing touching and retouching of the European portrait, and more about exhibiting "the humility of one who knows he is 'unacceptable'" (OG, p. 114): the only portrait sketched here is an apologetic sad-face selfie. Anti-Eurocentric gestures like this, as I suggested in the Introduction, also belong to the old programme of Europe's self-understanding. Without forgetting the risk of narrowness, the Levinasian formula should be heard as specifying the *archē* of a world that is distinctively hospitable to its own interruption and critique, especially in a time of its exhaustion.

We want to come to terms with this becoming-exhausted European world. Never simply the description of an object ("Europe") but, from the inside, an articulation of the fate of the sense-making sources of the world of modern European humanity, somewhere where we are, in a text already, where "we, the Europeans" believe ourselves to be.

The next part of this volume will go further into the fabric of this European whereabouts. We will see how a distinctively European (Greco-Biblical) understanding of the history of the being that we (human beings) are shimmers through the text of modern Europe's self-understanding and memory – and this will take us to the classical idea of philosophical history, to the idea of universal history, to the idea of the history of Man and his teleology – and its unravelling in our time.

PART II
Europe's modernity

3
FROM BARBARISM TO CIVILISATION

Civilization is the humanization of man in society

— Matthew Arnold

I

The orientation into European cultural identity presented in the first part opened onto a contrast between empirical and philosophical histories of Europe's origins and ends, and hence a contrast between two ways of conceiving the historical emergence of modern Europe: in terms of in the world events taking place within a finite region of the global surface, on the one hand, and, the becoming-European of a world, on the other. Focusing an investigation on the latter is not a matter of tracking a developing "idea" of Europe (the history of ideas) but of disclosing the *archē* of a distinctively European understanding of the world and the significance of our lives (the philosophy of Europe).

At issue in such an investigation is what Bernard Williams calls "a constellation of beliefs" (IBWD, p. 11) which not only "makes sense", but is the very sense-making structure through which "we Europeans" make sense of things. From the inside of any culture (any cultural "we"), how things are in the world, what we discover there, all empirical findings in the world as we find it, have the significance they have for us, the interest we take in them, by virtue of this constellation of beliefs. Any such constellation has its history; it is, as Williams puts it, a "complex" and "contingent" "historical deposit" (IBWD, p. 75), and, as Eliot stresses, it makes very little sense to speak of anyone consciously aiming at its creation. Nevertheless, such a framework of believing is, in Wiggins's words, still "a free construct" in the sense that it is not "answerable to how anything really is....[It] is not something that we (as we say) found or discovered" (TIML, p. 124). The word "free" is misleading here insofar as it suggests that it is something we might decide radically to alter or destroy at "will". ("Can we choose a style of painting at pleasure? The Egyptian, for instance?" asks a European philosopher (PI, p. 230).) No, as I put it earlier there is a profound "thrownness" of all believing: we find ourselves already inside such a construct, in a text already, and it supplies the resources for any new developments. Its holding sway (as long as it does) means that it is decisive for us – decisive in the sense that our lives are lived out in it and according to its terms. It is what is *most* familiar and matter-of-course: "somewhere where we are, in a text already, where we believe ourselves to be". And the "we" who have called ourselves (to be) "European" have our "native home" in just such a "text", there among the ghosts and traces of the past which is not past, and with a heading constantly being sketched and re-sketched out in advance.

On this understanding, it will always be questionable to suppose we can speak of "Europe" as the independent object for a detached scientific inquiry, or the object of a properly theoretical rationality. Unlike the rocks on the banks of the Soča river, the lizards warming themselves on them, and the men, women and children scrambling about among them, the European world is not something "there" or "outside us": it is the very inside of the inside, internal to the subjectivity of the "who" that "we, the Europeans" are. Of course, the great text of European *Dasein* has a history. But this "having a history" is not a supplementary addition to a sphere of sense-making we begin with "first", and then might subsequently add to, in history lessons at school, for example: for every *Dasein*, inhabiting this kind of construct is "first". Valéry spoke of the Mediterranean basin as an exemplary "machine for making civilization". But, as such, it was a machine for making sense, and a machine for making sense for the ones we ourselves are, including what we understand by "the ones we ourselves are", what we "believe ourselves to be", as Europeans.

For a being that does not just "have a past" but whose understanding of itself *is* historical, something like a working-understanding of its own historicality is always possible for it too. And this really is about the sort of thing "we learned at school". It is what gets elaborated and transmitted in a traditional understanding of our own being-in-history. For Europeans, the guiding thread of this is the golden thread: Greek-Roman-Christian-Modern. This provides us with a distinctive historical bloom regarding Europe: a history of the cultivation of place that has made its way, for the most part, on what our Blooms called that little "peninsula west of the Urals and north of the Caucasus, otherwise bounded by water and including its offshore islands": "our continent".

I am insufficiently knowledgeable even to review some of the seismic movements that belong to this history. But there is something wonderfully evocative just looking at maps of the shape-and-terrain-shifting empires that have settled it and settled (for now) its outline: in turn, the empires of Alexander the Great; Rome; Charlemagne; the Holy Roman Empire of the German nation; and so on. With respect to evocative territorial projections, however, it is hard not to be most impressed by maps of pre-Reformation Christendom from over 1000 years ago. There we see it, extending over the florid Western edge of a great landmass in the temperate zone of the planet's Northern Hemisphere, that little protrusion which, despite its not being a continent, strictly speaking, we Europeans have come to call our continent: Western Christendom *spread out* over almost exactly the same ground as today's *enlarged* European Union. Extraordinary.

As we are beginning to see, the discourse of Europe's history is never a simply or purely regional affair. It has also been comprehended within a discourse of the history of the world: a discourse of Europe as the avant-garde in the development – the progress or emancipation or de-alienation or self-realisation – of what it calls "Man". From the Neolithic "advance" towards an end "yet to be established", we still locate ourselves, even today, within a movement of transition for Man from a condition of primitive, human animality towards a condition of civilised, rational humanity. So we are also provided with another great historical bloom: one that understands what has taken place and is still taking place today in "our continent" as the emergence of a culture that has broken with itself as merely regional, a culture whose heading inscribes universal and not only regional significance to its *Dasein*. Europe's history belongs to the history and heading of (what we Europeans call) "Man". On this understanding, the "area" of European culture "has no definite frontiers: and you cannot build Chinese walls", and in the end, it opens onto, it cannot not open onto, an imagined future beyond any concrete imagining, of "the ideal of a world culture" (TDC, p. 62). And so the two blooms belong together: the discourse that frames the end of Europe [qua *terminus*] as a particular site of a regional history (it happened, for the most part, there) is inseparable from a discourse that frames its end [qua *telos*] in terms of a universal history of Man.

This is the discourse of Europe's modernity, and it all hangs on what we understand by, the sense that has been made of, "the ones we ourselves are", the ones "we believe ourselves to be". Derrida cites Valéry speaking about the French in a way that Derrida is sure "is *not* reserved for the French" (OH, p. 75): "to believe and to feel that we are universal – by which I mean, *men of universality*... Notice the paradox: to specialize in the sense of the universal" (cited from HP, p. 436, OH, p. 74). This paradox is, of course, the very heart of the paradox we have periodically returned to in "the European subject": that when it cultivates itself most intensely, when it relates itself to itself, it concerns itself above all with a subjectivity which is not merely its own.

At the heart of the European "text" is this double sense internal to what we understand by "the ones we ourselves are". Those who have called themselves (to be) "the Europeans" – with their unique regional history and culture – are people concerned above all with the fate or destiny of (what they call) "Man". The "who" that they understand themselves to be, the European subject, comprehends itself as belonging to the universal community of "Man" or "Mankind", in terms, then, of the meaning of (what they call) "Man".

With (what has been inherited as) the meaning of our own being as "Man" we reach what is really the centre around which the European understanding of the world and the significance of our lives turns. The paradigmatically European text *par excellence*, the "control" on all the rest, its motherboard, its operating system, the initialising programme of its programmes, is condensed in its anthropology. What, then, is the fundamental anthropological conception of European humanity?

II

While his approach always begins from a Greek philosophical *archē* in ontological questioning ("What *is*...?"), Heidegger's analytic of *Dasein* takes a remarkable turn when he turns this question on ourselves, the questioners, and asks "the basic question of *Dasein's* Being" (BT, p. 74). Remarkable because what becomes clear in the passage that immediately follows this basic question is that the *Dasein* he is investigating and interrogating is not just any old *Dasein*, and the understanding of its Being at issue is not just any old understanding. On the one hand, *Dasein*, as a name, is Heidegger's supposedly philosophically baggage-free word for the entity that *we* ourselves are: "Man himself" (BT, p. 32). *Dasein* is "Man" conceived through our pre-ontological familiarity with Being. That is, *Dasein* is defined as the entity which *is* at all only in so far as it has (already) an understanding of Being and of its own Being. So one can go a long way in Heidegger's great text *Being and Time* with the thought that the *Dasein* "that is in each case mine" is simply the *Dasein* of everyone and anyone. And so it is. However, and on the other hand, what "stands in the way" of *Dasein* attaining an ontologically adequate understanding of itself, "or leads it off the track" when "*we* come to the question of man's Being" (BT, p. 74) is not something that might block access for just anyone. Not at all:

> What stands in the way of the basic question of *Dasein's* Being (or leads it off the track) is an orientation thoroughly coloured by the anthropology of Christianity and the ancient world...There are two important elements in the traditional anthropology:
> 1. "Man" is here defined as a *zōon logon echon*, and this is interpreted to mean an *animal rationale,* something living that has reason...
> 2. The second clue for determining the nature of man's Being and essence is a *theological* one ["And God said, 'Let us make man in our image, after our likeness'"] – "*faciamus hominem ad imaginem nostram et similitudinem*". With this as its point of departure, the anthropology of Christian theology, taking with it the ancient definition, arrives at an interpretation of that entity which we call "Man".

The *Dasein* who undertakes the analytic of its own Being in *Being and Time*, the one who is engaged with the question of what "we call 'Man'", is not just anyone – even if what is at issue in that general question is. Following the Levinasian formula as our protocol for reading the *archē* of Europe, we can see that the *Dasein* whose understanding of itself leads it off the track is…*European Dasein*. A Greek and Biblical (or indeed, and Heidegger will want to emphasise this, a distinctively Romanised Greek and Christian) *Dasein* asks the basic question, and hence a distinctively European interpretation of "the entity that we are" is being identified here.

Heidegger introduces this traditional and paradigmatically European conception of Man as a problem. That is, Heidegger wants to suggest that we (Europeans) have kept to an understanding of our (human) Being which leads us astray. A characteristic German rivalry with (especially French) Romanity over what it means to be European is in play within Heidegger's diagnosis of the problem of the meaning of Man. The Latinisation of the Greek element in the "traditional anthropology" – the interpretative "translation" of *zōon logon echon* to mean an *animal rationale* – blocks our access, Heidegger thinks, to a more promising conception of Man that began in Greece. This leads Europeans off the track that the Greek beginning first opened up; a track which, were we to pick it up for our culture (we men of memory and repetition) would open onto a new and more authentically European future. Heidegger would want to out-do the French in being properly "*men of universality*", in being-authentically-European. And hence – and Derrida will call this "the paradox of the paradox" (OH, p. 75) – being specialised in something that is, in principle, not reserved for European humanity at all.

This scene of internal schism and quasi-national rivalry – and the theme of philosophical nationalism more generally – is not our problem in this book, and all I want to take from Heidegger's diagnosis for our Europe-focused purposes is his reading of the Greco-Biblical "elements" that make up the meaning of our (human) Being. These elements have guided, controlled, and programmed the modern European self-understanding and the Greek-Roman-Christian-Modern golden-thread self-portrait it hands down to itself. At issue is the understanding of "Man" that holds sway in an epoch formed and forged by Christian creationism as it appropriates Greek conceptual resources: the *archē* of the European understanding of our being as "Man".

III

In relating the sense or truth of its own history, the contingent "historical deposit" of the Greco-Biblical heritage is, in places, as stubbornly sedimented as it is elsewhere fluid and shifting. Nowhere is this more stubbornly so than with respect to the narrative structure internal to the European conception of "Man": a narrative that suggests the history of the human world can be related as a movement between an original "natural" or "animal" or "savage" or "barbarian" condition, and the final achievement of a distinctively "cultural" or "human" or "advanced" or "civilized" or "rational" condition. This is the idea of a transition for Man with respect to which European humanity has placed itself, invariably, at the head – either as the mark of its greatness (Eurocentrism) or as the principal sign of its darkness (anti-Eurocentrism).

It is here that we can begin to bring onto the stage the texts that will occupy us in the pages that follow in this volume and the next. For it is just this kind of "grand narrative" – in this case, an historical narrative that conceives itself as encompassing human history as a whole – which surges into the becoming-European world during the 1700s and 1800s in the proliferation of what was called philosophical or universal history, or the History of the World.

Immanuel Kant is often, and rightly, credited with having provided the first "serious effort" (EH, p. 57) and "outstanding example" (as Rauch observes in a footnote to his translation of Hegel's text on philosophical history, a footnote to which we will return (PH, p. 10)) of charting the movement of human history "construed according to thoughts, *a priori*" (PH. p. 10) in his short essay from 1784, "Idea for a Universal History with a Cosmopolitan Purpose". However, it was the post-Kantian philosopher G.W.F. Hegel who first attempted actually to write up rather than merely sketch such a history. Stunningly and (as we shall see) more or less continuously effacing his debt to Kant, Hegel wrote a history of the development of what he calls "Spirit" [*Geist*] which "fulfilled all the particulars of Kant's proposal for a universal history" (EH, p. 59). We will come to some of the fascinating and puzzling details of Hegel's philosophical history – and gain some clarity regarding his unbelievable resistance to acknowledging himself as standing on the shoulders of Kant – in due course, but I want to flag up one vital feature from Hegel's preliminary discussion of the very idea of philosophical history: namely, the connection he both recalls from Kant and affirms in his own way, between the rational intelligibility of the history of the world – its having this grand narrative structure – and what he calls "its religious truth" (PH, p. 13).

There are three tempting views of the intelligibility of history that Hegel wants decisively to reject when he acknowledges this "religious truth". First, is the idea that what happens in history is just one damn thing after another, with no overall significance beyond the sequence. Second, and in a slightly more sophisticated vein, that historical research could discover an intelligible development overall, but one whose significance can be fully grasped in wholly "secular" terms, in terms, for example, of "the passions of mankind, the genius, the active powers, that play their part on the great stage" (PH, p. 14). And, third, and most unsatisfactory for Hegel, the idea that despite supposing that a secular history is the best one can get, one should nevertheless console oneself with the "belief" that there is, nevertheless, a "concealed" Divine plan behind all these happenings (PH, p. 14, this could be Kant). Hegel is after something much stronger than all of that: he wants actually to show that the facts of history prove the "correctness" of the "truth" that "the world is not abandoned to chance and external contingent causes, but that a Providence controls it" (PH, p. 13). Pious gestures towards the "guiding hand of God" are as bad as leaving God out of it altogether – especially when such gestures are made to individuals to whom something genuinely terrible has just happened (PH, p. 14). For Hegel, the "subjects" of the history of the world are in any case not individual people and their largely unhappy fates but peoples and the development of their political States. And Hegel wants to find in the history of that development the resources for nothing short of an "intellectual comprehension" of the Christian conviction that God reveals Himself to Man. Hence Hegel's history of the world is, as he says, "a *Theodicaea*" (PH, p. 16). He wants history itself, its facts, to show or manifest that the unfolding of world history is presided over by God, and that the ultimate plan of God is nothing short of the "ultimate design of the world" (PH, p. 17). Hegel closes his account of the History of the World, some four-hundred pages later, with the following ringing paragraph (PH, p. 477):

> That the History of the World, with all the changing scenes which its annals present, is this process of development and the realization of Spirit – this is the true *Theodicaea*, the justification of God in History. Only this insight can reconcile Spirit with the History of the World – viz., that what has happened, and is happening every day, is not only not "without God", but is essentially His Work.
> The End

The philosophical idea of the History of the World is, first of all, the idea of a theological, providential history: the unfolding of God's plan for Man. Interestingly, Hegel conceives the development of political society that he is interested in comprehending as closely bound up with a movement in which religion itself comes to have an increasingly marginal role in the life of a State. As we shall see, later Hegelians, such as Karl Marx, came to see this process as one which would lead not only to the transcendence of theological residues (both in human societies themselves and in the narration of their history) but ultimately to the transcendence of the State form itself, especially the nation-state form. With Marx, as we shall see, philosophical history makes a profound turn from a standpoint that is philosophical and religious to one that conceives itself as philosophical and scientific. But the idea that world history has a rational intelligibility to be grasped as a movement towards an end, a "The End" which would bring about the final emancipation and de-alienation of humanity as a whole, this remained in Marx, just as it does in the "good news" of a coming end of history in the work of the liberal theorist Francis Fukuyama. Marxism may claim to overcome nationalism and providential history but there is no doubt that it is just as firmly installed as Fukuyama's evangelical liberalism in what we will get to know better in the next chapter as the *teleologism* and the *eschatologism* of Kant's and Hegel's religious-philosophical history.

We will explore those heady "isms" more explicitly soon, but I want for now to concentrate on, what seems to me, the most basic conceptuality of all narrative description and analysis in the tradition of European philosophical history: the distinction between civilisation and barbarism.

The distinction itself has a long and fluctuating history. And it is not just a distinction within history writing either. On the contrary, it has itself been historically world-forming: informing or imprinting itself on the lives of those who have celebrated the uninterrupted and unbroken golden thread of (singular) Civilization, and of course, the lives of those who, in the history of that history, were represented as lying outside of and as not measuring up to what the Europeans of the nineteenth century called the "Standard of Civilization". Something of its own history is uncannily visible in the definitions of "civilization" and "barbarism" in the *Oxford English Dictionary*:

Civilization:

1. Civilization; civilized condition or state; a developed or advanced state of human society; a particular stage or a particular type of this. Matthew Arnold "Civilization is the humanization of man in society".

Barbarism:

1. *orig.* Not Greek; *subseq.* not Greek nor Latin; hence, **a.** not classical or pure (Latin or Greek), abounding in "barbarisms". Hence, **b.** Unpolished, without literary culture; pertaining to an illiterate people.
2. Of people: Speaking a foreign language, foreign, outlandish; *orig.* non-Hellenic; *then*, not Roman, living outside the Roman Empire; *sometimes*, not Christian, heathen. (Often with a glance at sense 3.)
3. Uncultured, uncivilized, unpolished; rude, rough, wild, savage. (Said of men, their manners, customs, products.) The usual opposite of *civilized*.

The OED definition states that the term "barbarian" is *orig.* a Greek word. However, some etymological dictionaries suggest an earlier Indo-European root, and find variants of it in the Sanskrit word "barbara", meaning stammering, and in a different line from the Latin translation of the Greek, in Latin "balbus", and in Czech "blblati", both of which also mean stammering. All of which suggests that the OED assignment of a Greek *orig.* may itself be an example of just the sort of "stripping out" of other sources or origins that belongs to a Europe that has mostly forged itself by dedicating itself to remaining (becoming) Greco-Biblical. In any case, there is something both fantastic and fantastically telling to see the Greek-Roman-Christian thread appearing so visibly in the Modern history-telling history "of people", and their glances at others, in sense #2 of barbarism.

The word "barbarian" is generally regarded as having an echoic or onomatopoeic origin; a surely always somewhat pejorative animalistic expression for the speech of others: "bar-bar". With regard to the Greek use, the OED definition here indicates that the word was applied to what is "foreign". But it would be better (more refined) to say that it applied to anyone who did not share the refined Greek language and culture, i.e. someone who had not undergone a distinctive form of cultured education – what the Greeks called *paideia*. This was the process through which the young were prepared to become members of the *polis*, and included intellectual, moral and physical training aimed at cultivating properly human excellences. The Greeks cultivated cultivation – the acquisition of culture – embodied in a polished, refined, and literate individual.

The line from Matthew Arnold ("Civilization is the humanization of man in society") is thus particularly helpful to understanding the contrast. And with the golden thread in view, it is interesting to note its development beyond the Greek world and into the Roman world as it appropriated Greek thought. It was in the Roman Republic that the conception of this kind of "humanization" of Man through an enculturing education was first developed (the German concept of *Bildung* captures this better than any English word). The imitative appropriation of *paidea* by the Romans then marks a crucial historisation of the kind of development that had previously been individual. The transition of man from *homo barbarus* to *homo humanus* by way of cultivating the *humanitas* of *homo*, so that Man can become free for his humanity, so that Man can become properly himself, is what classical philosophical history of the world always relates for humanity at large, and what Europe's modernity within that is supposed, above all, to illustrate in an exemplary way. While we have to be on the watch for Heidegger's wanting to see the translation of everything Greek into Latin as a fateful transposition which sends Europe's history off the track, his summary of the history of this "humanism" is nevertheless helpful:

> *Humanitas*, explicitly so called, was first considered and striven for in the age of the Roman Republic. *Homo humanus* was opposed to *homo barbarus*. *Homo humanus* here means the Romans, who exalted and honored Roman *virtus* through the "embodiment" of the *paideia* taken over from the Greeks. These were the Greeks of the Hellenistic age, whose culture was acquired in the schools of philosophy. It was concerned with *eruditio et institutio in bonas artes* [scholarship and training in good conduct]. *Paideia* thus understood was translated as *humanitas*. The genuine *romanitas* of *homo romanus* consisted in such *humanitas*. We encounter the first humanism in Rome: it therefore remains in essence a specifically Roman phenomenon, which emerges from the encounter of Roman civilisation with the culture of late Greek civilisation. The so-called Renaissance of the fourteenth and fifteenth centuries in Italy is a *renascenetia romanitatis*. Because *romanitatis* is what matters, it is concerned with *humanitas* and therefore with Greek *paideia*. The *homo romanus* of the Renaissance also stands in opposition to *homo barbarus*. But now the in-humane is the supposed barbarism of gothic Scholasticism in the Middle Ages. (LH, p. 225)

Humanism is, as Heidegger says, an always "historically understood humanism" (LH, p. 225), which means that who the barbarian is can shift – the non-Greek, the non-Roman, the non-Christian, the non-secular-European, the terrorist…

But the golden thread is constructed or generated through this intertwining of developments over an historical, as it were intergenerational, stretch of handing down. Later employment of the contrast does not need to refer back to the Greeks. On the other hand, it will always retain certain conceptual affiliations to the Greek "*orig.*" we give ourselves. The crucial idea is that Man becomes free for his humanity, freed from his merely animal nature, freed from a merely natural condition to become in the movement of history fully in actuality what he already is in potentiality. This is the life and the history of the *zōon logon echon*, the *animal rationale*, or the *rational animal* made in the image of God. And in history thus understood, we see the figure of Europe, its history and identity, configured most decisively: as exemplary – whether we like it or not, or know it or not, or, indeed avow it only in "opposing denial" (UNSECO, p. 13).

It is still with us in our time. Writing in the *London Review of Books* (Vol. 29, No. 18, 20 September 2007), Perry Anderson cites the chair of political theory at Humboldt University in Berlin, Herfried Munkler, who describes the logic of empires, from ancient to modern times, as one in which "imperial power has been required to stabilise adjacent power vacuums or turbulent border zones, holding barbarians or terrorists at bay" (p. 18). Similarly, Anderson suggests that publicists for EU enlargement suppose that "without enlargement Eastern Europe would never have reached the safe harbour of democracy, foundering in new forms of totalitarianism and barbarism" (p. 15). The linkage stressed today between barbarism and terrorism or barbarism and totalitarianism can make us forget that the distinction between civilisation and barbarism has a long history. But it should help us remember that while it is always historically situated it is passed along too, and still current.

While it is undeniable that the distinction is still with us, it is equally undeniable that it is not the binary beast that it once was. Even those who think European politics and society today superior to those of other societies would be hard pushed to deny that times have changed, and that the idea of a basically linear history of the world, from a barbaric and savage origin to a civilised and rational end, with Europe at the front, is increasingly unbelievable. We will be taking a long march on the path of this unravelling, but in the next chapter, I want to get one of its most significant moments into view, a fundamental moment in the history of philosophical history that we have already noted: the transformation of universal history from a discourse that is philosophical and religious into a discourse that presents itself as philosophical and scientific, and the contributions there of Marx and of Freud.

4

THE EUROPEAN IDEA OF MAN

Eschatology, Teleology – that is Man

– Jacques Derrida

I

In the 1780s, forty years before Hegel wrote his theodical history of the becoming actual of Man's rational potential, Johann Gottfried Herder attempted a radically different account of the history of Man: one which construed human rationality in terms that, as his teacher, Immanuel Kant noted with some concern, presented it as "an acquired and learned" rather than "an inherent capacity" (Kant, p. 218). Human rationality is regarded by Herder as the result of "a natural effect" rather than "a predisposition in human nature" (Kant, p. 221). For this reason, Herder's work, though also deeply religious and unswervingly creationist, is a forerunner of what was to become the non-religious, scientific account of the origins of Man in the work of Darwin in the 1840s and 50s, and, the non-religious, scientific account of the history of Man in the work of Marx in the 1860s and 70s, and again in the work of Freud in the late 1920s.

I mention Herder here not only because he wants to give a natural account of the origins of rational capacities, but also because of the particular explanation he gives of the distinction between Man and animals, a distinction he does not give up on. In his view, the creature "Man" "became human because his head is adapted to an erect posture" (Kant, p. 204). Again, it should be noted how this breaks with the conventional Greco-Biblical (or, as we might say, onto-theological) point of departure in accounts of human life. As Kant clearly saw, for Herder, "it was not because [Man] was destined to be rational that he was endowed with the erect posture which allows him to make rational use of his limbs; on the contrary he acquired reason as a result of his erect posture" (Kant, p. 204). The explanation for Man's distinction is thus premised on a distinction of posture, a distinction which provides him with a decisive difference of sensory orientation: "elevated above the earth and the plants, it is no longer the sense of smell which predominates, but the eye" (Kant, p. 205).

This may look like a simple break from onto-theological conceptions – and modern scientific theory which likes to think that way will jump on it in that spirit – but the stress on the significance of vision is in fact entirely classical, identifying the distinction of human life in what the Greeks called, precisely, *theoria*. The rationality of Man is inseparable from the capacity for *a kind of seeing*: *thea* (a view) and *horan* (to see). The idea of the rational animal emerging as a theoretical spectator of the world, in contrast to a merely (purely) animal being that is sensibly steeped in it, takes shape around this classical vision of vision.

Understanding (or, as *we* also say, "seeing") human rational capacities as developing from this perceptual stand-point lends itself to a fully and not merely partially naturalistic account: providing a natural explanation of the origin of reason is far more challenging than a natural explanation of the erect posture. Indeed, a special interest in accounting for that upright adaptation has remained a mainstay of scientific-theoretical accounts of the early history of Man. However, and once again, the idea of this departure point for human development is not only entangled in a Greek root, but, as Heidegger noted, also a Christian one. The passage from *Being and Time* on "the elements of the traditional anthropology" that I cited in the last chapter continues:

> In modern times the Christian definition has been deprived of its theological character. But the idea of "transcendence" – that man is something that reaches beyond himself – is rooted in Christian dogmatics... The idea of transcendence, according to which man is more than a mere something endowed with intelligence, has worked itself out with different variations. The following quotations will illustrate how these have originated: "Man's first condition was excellent because of these outstanding endowments: that reason, intelligence, prudence, judgement should suffice not only for the government of this earthly life, but by them he might *ascend beyond*, even unto God and to eternal felicity" (Calvin). "Because man *looks up* to God and his Word, he indicates clearly that in his very nature he is born somewhat closer to God, is something more after his stamp, that he has something that *draws him to God* – all this comes beyond a doubt from his having been created in God's image" (Zwingli). (BT, p. 74)

Man *looking up* and *reaching upwards* – moving from worldly horizontality towards spiritual verticality (I will come back to this horizontal/vertical contrast in the final chapter of this volume) – is just as basic to the traditional anthropology as his rational endowments, and in the idea of the erect posture, these two roots come together perfectly. The different variations this can give rise to defy summary, but it is fascinating to find it to the fore in Sigmund Freud's great essay *Civilization and its Discontents* (1929–30). In that text, he too asserts that "the fateful process of civilization would thus have set in with man's adoption of an erect posture" (CD, p. 99). In Freud, as in Herder in fact, the erect posture is not only linked to "the diminution of olfactory stimuli" and the consequent privilege accorded to "visual stimuli" (CD, p. 99), but (as a result of both of these alterations) to the transformation in sexual habits that founds the family and ultimately establishes communal life with others beyond what Freud calls "the primal horde" (CD, p. 100).

I don't want to dig too far into the translation of philosophical history into psychoanalytic science. However, I do want to introduce an important and fascinating development that takes place in conceptions of philosophical history when it is "deprived of its theological character", something often taken for granted today but which is intimately connected to its becoming-scientific in the work of thinkers like Marx and Freud. While both Marx and Freud entirely rejected all talk of Providence (Freud regards it as a "patently infantile" idea (CD, p. 74)), they both treat human history as a movement towards some kind of world-wide unity as its proper end. Indeed, more definitively (and, I will suggest, far less plausibly) than either Kant or Hegel, both affirm that the fundamental processes of history move towards combining human beings "into one great unity" (as Freud puts it, CD, p. 122), a worldwide universal community in which "national differences" will "vanish" (as Marx puts it, CM, p. 23).

As we have seen in Eliot and will explore more closely in Kant and Hegel later, the thought of a universal community of Mankind is always the horizon idea in philosophical histories which take the "advanced" condition of European civilisation and its golden thread as their guiding thread. But something extraordinary happens when philosophical history thinks of itself as, in principle, non-religious and scientific. Kant and Hegel regard linguistic and religious differences among human beings as insurmountable limits to human community, forever parting off and dividing us, and hence conceive any ideas (however distant or fanciful) of a "world culture" to come as one that will remain "properly differentiated" even as the logical term of human development (DP, p. 252). When science takes over the task of relating human history, however, the thought of these limits become increasingly labile and ultimately subject to total elimination as politically differentiating factors that need to be respected in the projection of the human developmental horizon. The march of science itself would belong to that movement of de-differentiating: ridding us of patently infantile delusions of a pre-scientific sort, especially those concerning religion and nationality. In the shift to science, a shift to the most radically "theoretical spectator" perspective on whatever is, the in-the-swim conditions of human life that had hitherto been respected as primarily important lose that primary status. What scientist could tolerate anything so contingently historical – and irrationally atavistic – as, for example, national identity as a permanent barrier to the proper unity of Man?

In short, and here is the extraordinary thing, when philosophical history becomes (also) scientific, then, for the first time, it becomes radically amenable to calls for "the institution of the humanitarian ideal" (CD, p. 145), and a world without political borders. The trajectory of philosophical history, and the guiding ideal of its cosmo-politics, becomes the idea of a genuinely and fully united humanity, a humanity forged and formed "into one great unity": a human community that really *is* one because it is a human community that finally is *one*.

As we shall see, Freud was extremely suspicious of communist conceptions of Mankind as in principle or potentially "wholly good" – a potential that would be on the way to being realised once freed from the "corrupting" influence of a society based on "private property". Such a conception is, he thinks, a fundamentally "untenable illusion" (CD, p. 113). Nevertheless, he too thinks that "a real change" in the relations of human-beings to possessions "would be more help" in promoting the process of civilisation for the whole of Mankind, and would facilitate its eventual development into one great unity; it would protect human life at least somewhat from being overwhelmingly disturbed by "instincts of aggression and self-destruction" that he regarded as immutable (CD, p. 143–5).

National feeling certainly is historically contingent, and I think Nietzsche was right to suggest that the movement of becoming-European that belongs to the history of the old Europe of the nations will likely make its "old loves and narrowness", the tendency to find one's identity in "patriotic palpitations" (BGE, p. 152), less decisive in political life. When Kant, in 1784, projected the formation of "a great political body of the future" at the supra-national level in Europe, he conceived this as inseparable from the emergence of a new "feeling" among the peoples of Europe, a feeling connected not just to an interest in their own national existence, but also "an interest" in maintaining the existence of "the whole", of Europe as such (Kant, p. 51): they were becoming (also) Europeans. However, as we shall see, neither Kant nor Nietzsche projected a European future in which national politics and national feeling would simply disappear from the map. It would doubtless be absurd to suppose that there are any distinctions among humans not subject to cultural and historical variations and mutations in the way they are lived out. Does that mean we should follow Marx and Freud in finding Europe's promise in the horizon idea of the humanitarian ideal? Should we conceive humanity's best hope and future "end" in the idea of a politically borderless "global community" bound together above all by feelings connected to an interest in what we all have in common, our common humanity?

Scepticism about the humanitarian ideal must not be confused with hostility towards humanitarian agencies and organisations (see SM, p. 84). Moreover, in the closing chapters of the next volume, I will also want to affirm a new appeal to "the universal community", and the ambition to make a contribution to it. However, the humanitarian ideal that is affirmed in philosophical history once it has been freed from supposedly outmoded religious and pre-scientific convictions and feelings of national belonging, is, in my view, not only in some ways less realistic than the explicitly religious conception it displaces but, forgetting reality for a moment, even the realisation of its ideal would be, as thinkers from Kant to Eliot and beyond have urged us to appreciate (without much success I admit), "a nightmare" (TDC, p. 62). As I say, I will come back to that, but I want to mark my reluctance in endorsing the humanitarian ideal at this point with a further thought about historical contingency.

Philosophical history before Marx was philosophical and religious. The decisive and world-changing development we find for the first time in history in Marx is that it becomes philosophical and scientific. Derrida summarises (rather dramatically):

> All men and women, all over the earth, are today to a certain extent the heirs of Marx and Marxism. That is…they are the heirs of the absolute singularity of a project – or of a promise – which has a philosophical and scientific form. This form is in principle non-religious, in the sense of a positive religion; it is not mythological; it is therefore not national – for beyond even the alliance with a chosen people, there is no nationality or nationalism that is not religious or mythological, let us say "mystical" in the broad sense. The form of this promise or of this project remains absolutely unique. Its event is at once singular, total and uneffaceable. There is no precedent whatsoever for such an event. [For the first time] in the whole history of humanity, in the whole history of the world and of the earth…[we encounter] an event…bound, inseparably, to world-wide forms of social organization. (SM, p. 91)

This unprecedented event in the history of the world is, first of all, an event of decisive mutation within the discourse of the history of the world within which such an event might find a place: the first appearance in what we can think of as the history of the world of a discourse of the history of the world in philosophico-scientific form, a discourse which thus claims, as Derrida notes, "to break with myth, religion, and the nationalist 'mystique'" (SM, p. 91). The discourse does not only become properly "modern" in this moment, but by de-differentiating all the human differences which had governed all such discourses hitherto, it thus opens the way for a completely new and all-embracing politics as *geopolitics*. European politics had already been affected by Kant's and Hegel's discourses on the end of history as universal history, but their horizon remained fundamentally national even when it was cosmopolitan. With Marx and Marxism everything changes. "Communism", as Derrida notes, "was essentially distinguished from other labor movements by its [intrinsically] international character. No organized political movement in the history of humanity had ever yet presented itself as geopolitical, thereby inaugurating the space that is now ours" (SM, p. 38).

With Marxist internationalism, philosophical history becomes geopolitical through and through, and the very idea of "properly differentiated" cosmo-politics of the kind one finds in Kant and Hegel becomes increasingly experienced as sustaining, for example, an outdated "methodological nationalism": an anachronistic perspective hide-bound to a contingent, irrational and religious formation that is (it is supposed) already anyway "vanishing" in the movement of the "world-market" (CM, p. 23), and stands in the way of the proper universality anticipated by the geopolitical call for "working men", all over the world, to unite.

Derrida describes the event of this new geopolitical horizon as "uneffaceable". No thinking, in particular – no thinking about the future and our political future can go on as if nothing happened: the communist promise, the communist horizon, and the value it places on human equality and our common humanity, inaugurates a hope that the conflicts and miseries that plague our world might one day be healed, and healed in a form of social life that would have the chance of making real progress towards the permanent institution of the humanitarian ideal: freed from the perversions of interests (national, class, religious, gender, etc.) that are so clearly not "the interest of the immense majority" (CM, p. 14).

There is no doubting that our time is marked as "a time after Marx", a "since Marx" aspect haunts our thinking, as Derrida stresses (SM, p. 17). In the next volume, we will explore what, since Marx, has massively complicated this scene of the inheritance of a since Marx humanitarian ideal – call it the twentieth century. Freud was still writing then, and even if his humanitarian hopes were also, as we have seen, the hopes of a thinker "since Marx", he regarded Marxist communism as based on an illusion: namely, the illusion that "ill-will and hostility" among people would disappear from human life with the abolition of private property (CD, p. 113). Aggression had certainly not been wiped out in the Soviet Union, and Freud wondered "with concern", in 1929, "what the Soviets will do after they have wiped out their bourgeois" (CD, p. 115). There is a good deal of talk about the crisis of capitalism in our time, something whose periodic recurrence Marx anticipated better than most, conceiving each return as an event which would "put on its trial, each time more threateningly, the existence of the entire bourgeois society" (CM, p. 8). But such events, if they are really to amount to anything more than a temporary setback for a commercial market economy, are only (life/death) crises if its continued existence is actually threatened. And that requires the destructive power of a political movement capable of bringing about its "death" (CM, p. 9). One does not have to be Marxist to appreciate that in the time "since Marx", the most extensive crisis has been – its own.

I will say a little more about Freud's claim that communist hopes to forge a path "to deliverance from our evils" are based on "an untenable illusion" in a moment. But his own rather more pessimistic "science" shared Marx's nineteenth century conviction that science itself could oppose and disclose "religion as an illusion" (CD, p. 64). And it is here that I want to raise a new question of contingency. It is, I think, undeniable that no scientist of society could tolerate anything so contingently historical as, say, the nation-state form and its tie to religion ("in the sense of a positive religion"), as a radical limit to thinking the political future of humanity. But perhaps that is not all a scientist (at least one who is a scientist through and through) will not tolerate, and perhaps the scientific understanding of the world and the significance of our lives is marked by a contingency of its own, and one far more transient than the forms of understanding it finds so intolerable. Earlier, I cited Eliot's affirmation of "the ideal of European culture" as having its "logical term" in "the ideal of a world culture". While such an ideal end is, he thought, beyond imagination, he insisted that it should still be construed as a culture that maintained itself in its differences: as a "common culture" it would be actual *only* in "diverse local manifestations". The passage continues:

> And here, of course, we are finally up against religion, which so far in the consideration of local differences within the same area we have not had to face. Ultimately, antagonistic religions must mean antagonistic cultures; and ultimately, religions cannot be reconciled. (TDC, p. 62)

Which point of view would be more vulnerable to the charge of contingency? The one that takes seriously the continuing existence (as far as the eye can see) of religious differences or the one that thought religion's time, in the times of science, was nigh? One does not have to be by oneself, religious or anti-scientific to think that a discourse of the history of the world premised on the disappearance of religion has reached its sell-by date. And, with Kant and Nietzsche, one can say the same, I think, about the kind of "local manifestations" that are articulated by the fact that our primary existential involvements are with those who most closely share our lives. One has to speak in the first-person singular here to keep this in view. As Derrida acknowledges, "it is a fact" about (each) me that what matters most to (each) me is "my people, my family" and "those who speak my language or share my culture" (BS, p. 109).

II

Derrida carefully and more than once ("let us repeat") describes the new event which inaugurates our time, as a time "since Marx", as "the event of a discourse in the philosophico-scientific form claiming to break with myth, religion and the nationalist 'mystique'", breaking with religion "in the sense of a positive religion". Marx opens up the discourse of world history to a geopolitical end in a post-national and post-religious unity of Mankind. However, while the Marxist analysis wants to be scientific and geopolitical, its conception of history remains philosophical or geophilosophical, that is to say universal. And, one might wonder at that point whether the break with religion-as-positive-religion really breaks with religion altogether. Heidegger notes that modern conceptions of Man have been "deprived" of their theological character. But he insists that they nevertheless remain "rooted" in the traditional onto-theological anthropology. This idea raises sharply an issue that is in many ways central to how we should understand the modernity of our own time: its growing secularity. Bernard Williams notes, correctly I think, that there is general agreement that "modernity is marked by the decline of traditional patterns of authority, and by secularization" (IBWD, p. 42). However, there are two wholly distinct ways in which this has been understood, two distinct secularisation theses. Williams summarises the two, distinguishing, first, secularisation "in the sense of the substitution of secular for religious conceptions and institutions", and second, "in the sense…that the leading ideas of modernity are secular versions of religious ideas" (IBWD, p. 42). Do secular conceptions replace theological ones or is there a secularisation of theological concepts? The point of general agreement is that the world that has been spreading out from Europe for at least the last three hundred years has become remarkably secular. The "secularization thesis" that has dominated sociology – and which is undoubtedly a discipline that belongs to the world "since Marx" – conceives this developing condition in a new, if now familiar, story about European modernity: the story of a radical break from forms of society dominated by myth and superstition, of Western societies *en route* to a rational, scientific and, perhaps, Godless future. This familiar story is itself somewhat mythical, even magical. Nevertheless, sociologists such as Max Weber (1864–1920) and Emile Durkheim (1858–1917) certainly gave systematic and explicit expression to the idea that the European world had entered an historically distinctive modern age characterised by the marked and ongoing erosion of the social standing of magic, myth, superstition – and religion.

Of course, the point of general agreement shows that there is no denying that a profound secularising shift of the riverbed of thinking and believing has been taking place over the course of the last three hundred years in European societies. But the second "secularization thesis" can take on board the accelerating (and in virtue of the presence of secularists of the first kind sometimes, like Marx and Freud, sometimes aggressively anti-religious) spreading out of projects and institutions that are non-religious, in the sense of a positive religion. What the second thesis will insist on, however, is that the very discourse which promotes that spreading out, and which cleaves to the modern narrative of its likely future trajectory (towards the vanishing of mythology, the vanishing of religion, the vanishing of national "mystique", the ever more widespread institution of the humanitarian ideal, and so on) is itself the secularisation of an onto-theological conception. Perhaps there are some secular concepts that have come to replace religious ones, but it seems to me a genuine insight into our modernity to side with Carl Schmitt on this issue:

> All significant concepts of the modern theory of the state are secularized theological concepts, not only because of their historical development – in which they were transferred from theology to the theory of the state, whereby, for example, the omnipotent god became the omnipotent lawgiver – but also because of their systematic structure, the recognition of which is necessary for a sociological consideration of these concepts. (PT, p. 36)

When Marx writes with such passion about nearing the "decisive hour" (CM, p. 13) in the crisis of "the entire bourgeois society" (CM, p. 8), about the increasingly "universal inter-dependence of nations" (CM, p. 6), about "national one-sidedness" becoming "more and more impossible", of crises arriving "each time more threateningly" (CM, p. 8), about the bourgeoisie having "forged the weapons that bring death to itself" (CM, p. 9), about the "ever expanding union of the workers" (CM, p. 12), about "the revolutionary class that holds the future in its hands" (CM, p. 13), about the proletarian "mission" to "destroy all previous securities" (CM, p. 14) and create a society governed at last, indeed finally running itself at last, "in the interest of the immense majority" (CM, p. 14); when we read and hear all this, it is impossible not to be struck by its systematic continuity with the messianism of Christian eschatology.

Eschatology is that part of theology concerned with final things. The most well-known doctrine concerns the "last judgement" – which in the Greek means, equally, "the last crisis" – which settles the final destiny of the individual soul and of humankind. Christian hope is concerned with eschatology: the final events of history, the ultimate destiny of humanity, ideas of an "end time", of the perfection of God's creation, and of "apocalypse". We tend today to think of that last one in terms of complete destruction. That is not wrong but it is partial: the apocalypse is the final revelation, the end of all projects of clarification, and so insofar as worldly existence just is a sequence of such finite and partial projects, the arrival of complete clarity is also the end of worldly existence. I think it is undeniable that there is a messiano-eschatological vision of historical finality in Marx's secularised history of Man too, of Man on his way to becoming what he can be and where he truly can be – a fully de-alienated condition in which individuals can finally live at one with each other and the world in a communist society.

Of course, this end of Man has a history: the history of Man's developing being or nature in time towards a community that finally is one because it really is one. Marx's vision of all this development is from the point of view of the history of all "written" history (CM, p. 61). And at that point, stunningly, the "epochs" of the golden thread come back and simply fly from the first pages of the *Manifesto* (CM, p. 3): from the "freemen and slaves" of Greece, the "patricians, knights, plebeians, slaves" of "Ancient Rome", the "feudal lords, vassals, guild-masters, journeymen, serfs" of "the Middle Ages", and on to "our epoch", "the epoch of the bourgeoisie", and the increasingly simplified structure of social conflict, now played out between just "two great hostile camps" – an antagonistic struggle where the possibility of a "future" epoch is held in the hands of one of them, if it can only "overthrow" the "bourgeois supremacy" (CM, p. 17). Visible in the movement of this sequence is an historical trajectory towards an end of political antagonism, an end of the history of the world "as a history of class struggles". When we read and hear all this, it is impossible not to be struck by its systematic continuity with the Greek understanding of teleology.

Teleology is the philosophical doctrine of design and purpose in nature: a movement towards a definite end (*telos*). Marx was exultant when he read *The Origin of Species*, writing to Lassalle in 1861 that it dealt "the death-blow...for the first time to teleology in the natural sciences" (cited, RS, p. 345). We will see just such a science of nature (in the broad German sense of science, which will include work that is philosophical and religious) in the work of Kant, and in our time it will have become for us what it was for Marx: dead. But Marx retained, for all that, the teleological axis of a European history opening on to a universal end of Man.

This axis may be, in Marx, philosophical and scientific rather than philosophical and religious – but far from being more sober or sceptical than classical religious-philosophical history, and further still from being a death-blow to its spirit, it gathers Europe's modernity into a universal history in a way that had been previously thought fundamentally unimaginable: the whole horizon is blown open, gone are all the limits – especially national and religious limits – that had seemed to stretch ahead as far as the eye can see, and a new, new, new world end is announced as coming. Philosophical history had always been a history of the movement of de-alienation, emancipation and progress of Man towards his proper end – Man finally attaining to himself at the far end of a history of antagonisms that is his proper history, the historical passage that he is. In Marx, the globalisation of Europe's Modern economy, capitalism, draws everything to a head. Simplifying down to the field of a geopolitical battle between just two great classes, the bourgeoisie and the proletariat, the coming victory of the latter heralds "men of universality" in its final, and no longer paradoxical sense: precisely as a universal class, the proletarian revolution in Europe (and first of all Germany) promises a victory for all men and women all over the globe, and the final attainment of one great unity.

"Eschatology, Teleology – *that is Man*", says Derrida (OH, p. 14). Yes. That is Man. But not just any Man. This is Europe's (Greco-Biblical) Man. And in the victory Marx sees coming, or wants to see coming and wants more than anything to hasten to its arrival, this Man will have finally gone global, absolutely enlarged, totally spread out across the entire planet, uniting mankind in a universal human community that erases the hostile borders of all the old parts of the parted off and divided world. The final end of the paradox, the final end even of the paradox of the paradox: the geophilosophical task of European Man – to specialise in the sense of the universal – is not reserved for European Man because European Man is absolutely de-Europeanised in the geopolitical movement of his own becoming-planetary; radically humanised in his final spreading out. It didn't end well. Perhaps that is because it did not begin well. I will come back to that.

III

For Marx, history would chart a series of epochal transitions that take human beings, in stages, out of conditions of rivalrous conflict towards an altogether different condition, an ideally civilised, fully human, de-alienated and peaceful condition beyond all class struggles. In some ways, Freud goes further with Marx than might be thought. While he is strikingly less optimistic than Marx, and is clearly very sceptical about the Soviet Union and communist accounts of Man in general, he too writes about human history in a form that is both philosophical and scientific, and he is led, he acknowledges, to affirm a conception of universal history as the "special process" of civilisation "which mankind undergoes". It is an historical movement that is, for Freud, "in the service of Eros", giving human history both a profoundly teleological "programme" and an eschatological "end", an end which, with obscure necessity, he suggests "has to happen" (CD, p. 122). Indeed, the history of human civilisation is the movement of this happening:

> Civilization is a process in the service of Eros, whose purpose is to combine single human individuals, and after that families, then races, peoples and nations, into one great unity, the unity of mankind. Why this has to happen, we do not know; the work of Eros is precisely this...programme of civilization. (CD, p. 122)

As we have seen, Freud will also affirm something of Marx's emphasis on the need for a real transformation of property relations: "I too think it quite certain that a real change in the relations of human beings to possessions would be of more help [in overcoming obstacles to the process of civilization] than any ethical commands" (CD, p. 143). But there is a "but" coming. Freud hesitates: "... but the recognition of this fact among socialists has been obscured and made useless for practical purposes by a fresh idealistic misconception of human nature" (CD, p. 143). His concern is summarised as follows:

> The Communists believe they have found the path of deliverance from our evils. Man is wholly good and is well-disposed to his neighbour; but the institution of private property has corrupted his nature. The possession of private property gives power to the individual and thence the temptation arises to ill-treat his neighbour; while the man who is excluded from the possession of property is bound to rebel in hostility against his oppressor. If private property were abolished, all wealth held in common, and all allowed to share in the enjoyment of it, ill-will and enmity would disappear among men. Since the needs of all would be satisfied, none would have any reason to regard another as his enemy; all would willingly undertake the work which is necessary. I have no concern with any economic criticisms of the communist system; I cannot enquire into whether the abolition of private property is advantageous and expedient [though I am among those who have good will towards endeavours to fight against the inequality of wealth among men and all the miseries that it leads to]. But I am able to recognize that the psychological premises on which the system is based are an untenable illusion. (CD, p. 143)

One might want to place a great big counter-but to this Freudian "but". Marx certainly had a "fresh" conception of Man with respect to traditional views of his "nature"; but far from affirming that this nature was "wholly good", he (Marx) altogether rejected the "old legend" that Man has one "nature" that is "wholly" anything at all, wholly good, wholly bad or anywhere in-between. History for Marx involves a "continuous transformation" of human nature: what our "nature" is (what we need, what we desire, and so on), is not, perhaps excepting some very general animal constraints, fixed.

There is, nevertheless, something right about Freud's scrupulous "but". There is or remains for Marx an idea of the end of Man in the possibility of full self-actualisation, a possibility which is not realised in just any mode of human existence, but towards which human history is directed. And it seems to me inconceivable that Marx did not see communist society as the form of individual and social life in which, finally and for the first time, this possibility would become actual for human beings. History is the history of alienated humanity, and opens onto the possibility of the radical de-alienation of human beings in the communist future in which the class struggles of history had worked themselves out in a final way. And this is the real point of Freud's worry. In his view the "struggle for life of the human species" is never over, consisting in a "battle of the giants" between "man's natural aggressive instinct", which is expressed in hostile enmity between people, and the "programme of civilization" which binds human beings together in a "libidinal" way in a community of friends (CD, p. 122). The naïve belief of the communist is that human beings are such that they can produce conditions of living together in which "ill-will and enmity would disappear among men". And for Freud this is simply inconceivable: we are not "gentle creatures" (CD, p. 111), and whatever revolutions and reforms we succeed in bringing about in human life – whose general effects cannot, in any case, be foreseen – there is one thing we can expect with certainty: wherever human life takes itself "this indestructible feature of human nature will follow it there" (CD, p. 114).

There is still an idea here of a radical shift from nature to culture in Freud's vision of the process of civilisation, and the shift remains one that takes human beings from a wild, untamed condition to what is called a civilised one. However, for Freud, the barbarian, savage man is not transcended or transformed through a history of the civilisation of Man. On the contrary "what is primitive is…preserved alongside the transformed version which has arisen from it" (CD, p. 5). The only issue for Freud is whether our aggressive instincts can be made more or less "innocuous" (CD, p. 123), which to some extent he thinks they can – but at the cost of making us mostly neurotic in the process. Freud seems even to wonder whether the unity of mankind that Eros promises as the final outcome of the process of civilisation might be a situation in which "the whole of mankind – have become neurotic" (CD, p. 144).

So while he retains the distinction between barbarism and civilisation, Freud replaces a classical "OED" understanding of that with what Carl Schmitt calls a "realistic" one: the barbarian is no longer only the other that I am not (the savage beyond the walls of civilised society) – but the other within the civilised man that I am. *Homo humanus* is *homo barbarus* sublimated and repressed: "*homo homini lupus* [man is a wolf to man]" (CD, p. 111). The institution of monogamous heterosexual marriage and the commandment of universal friendship ("love thy neighbour") that structure European civilisation are both conceived as basic to our "advanced" contemporary condition but as also threatening its collapse, and produce all sorts of psychopathologies to individuals who live within it. Freud clearly thinks we can at least do somewhat better at ameliorating human misery and human violence, and recommends his quasi-communist reforms in that spirit. But he does not imagine an end of human history that would be an end of human misery or human violence.

There is another and in some ways more dramatic development in Freud's approach to human history. What he describes as "the high-water mark...reached in our Western European civilization" (CD, p. 105) was a time when there was a general acceptance among Europeans that the ways of life of non-European cultures should be understood (whether preferable to our own or the opposite) with reference to "the absence of the complicated cultural demands" of the sort supposed to characterise our own (CD, p. 87). Freud regarded this attribution as "mistaken". And it is important to note that the work of thinkers like Marx and Freud, and many other thinkers of the nineteenth and early twentieth century, has contributed to calling into question many of the preconceptions and prejudiced evaluations of not only our own complicated cultural heading but also that which belongs to what Derrida calls "the heading of the other" (OH, p. p. 15), including the cultural ways of life of human societies that are historically "primitive". Today, in part, precisely because of their work, the self-understanding of European humanity in which the opposition between civilisation and barbarism had its world-forming place, is no longer so matter of course.

An uncritical adherence to the ethnocentric and Eurocentric civilisation/barbarism distinction is now increasingly felt old-fashioned, prejudiced and ignorant. Indeed, as Derrida had already suggested in 1967, the old self-understanding, the understanding of European humanity in which that distinction had a central and powerfully world-forming place, "seems to be approaching what is really its own *exhaustion*" (OG, p. 8). In view of what he calls "a slow movement whose necessity is hardly perceptible", we are, he suggests, witnessing in our time, something that was a long time coming: nothing less than "a new mutation" in our understanding of ourselves and of the history of the world (OG, p. 8). Racism, xenophobia, ethnocentrism and Eurocentrism have not gone away, and a recoil against the idea of a de-differentiated "post-national" condition is certainly asserting itself too. But that recoil is not everywhere racist, xenophobic, ethnocentric or Eurocentric. Indeed, as part of an intellectually modest and entirely non-utopian politics, descending, as we shall see in the next chapter, most decisively from Kant's cosmopolitical writings, it has been a mainstay of European liberalism. Here is J.S. Mill, for example, writing in 1861:

> If it be said that a broadly marked distinction between what is due to a fellow-countryman and what is due merely to a human creature is more worthy of savages than of civilized beings, and ought, with the utmost energy,

to be contended against, no one holds that opinion more strongly than myself. But this object, one of the worthiest to which human endeavor can be directed, can never, in the present state of civilization, be promoted by keeping different nationalities of anything like equivalent strength under the same government. (RG, p. 291)

Whether it has been in the name of a humanitarian ideal or simply a more humane politics, it is undeniable that, with plenty of bumps and bruises, European societies and European institutions have made considerable efforts to make Europe a home fit for a far more diverse, multi-faith, multi-cultural, and even pluri-sexual society. The European world is in mutation. We will be tracking this. And central to what we will be tracking is the European world overcoming of what Mill says he objects to through and through: "a broadly marked distinction between what is due to a fellow-countryman and what is due merely to a human creature". Nevertheless, as Mill insists, this does not have to be conceived as something that would be "promoted" by an overcoming of the "different nationalities" that still differentiate our world. In view here is the bumpy development of Man as a national political animal into a still differentiated but now also international cosmopolitical one, the emergence in the Europe of nations of a radical cosmopolitan hope. In the next chapter, I will introduce this distinctively European development.

5

THE COSMOPOLITICAL ANIMAL

The means...to bring about the development of [Man's] capacities is that of antagonism within society

— Immanuel Kant

I

The philosophical discourse of world history, the "grand narrative" of the spiritual/cultural development of Man in time, from a primitive origin to a civilised end, is also a discourse of Europe's exemplary modernity. It is a discourse of Europe's historical development into a distinctively rational and scientific culture, breaking with ways of understanding the world and the significance of our lives through myth, magic, and superstition. We have identified a particularly decisive event in the history of the world within the historical development of the philosophy of the history of the world itself: the characteristically modern break from religious (Kant, Hegel) to scientific (Marx, Freud) forms of such philosophical history. In a general way, every rational philosophical history of the world will have always conceived itself as a scientific achievement, and simply to call it philosophical history will already have been to conceive it as in some sense "scientific". But in the break I am concerned with, the position of religion (as "positive religion") shifts from one whose significance is being understood internally, to one whose presence – and (likely) increasingly negligible presence – is being explained (away) externally. This break has a seismic impact on the human future projected by philosophical history. "Since Marx", the most basic differentiating structures of human cultural differences – especially interconnected national and religious differences – have become increasingly regarded as both historically contingent and irrational, rather than natural and permanently compelling. With that shift, the idea of the end of history is transformed from one in which humanity would remain, even in its final form, in some way or to some extent, properly differentiated, parted and divided off, into one which on the face of it may seem more not less religious, or at least more radically cosmopolitan: the end of history in a (politically) undifferentiated universal human community of the future, a community where all human differentiation has ceased to be politically salient.

That the appearance of a supposedly objective and scientific discourse in this field may itself be more historically contingent and short-lived than the forms of individual and social life; it regards as withering in our time is something I think we need to take very seriously today. Even a non-religious thinker "since Marx" might affirm that as far as the eye can see religious and national differences, everything that parts off and divides the world politically, are not going away, even if they are no longer to be regarded as natural and immutable. And we need to think through the implications of that.

In the second volume, I will do what I can to address and reassess the, "since Marx", assumptions about our post-national and post-religious future, and will consider the fate of the humanitarian ideal in our time in the light of that reassessment. But the fact that we need to do so is itself evidence of a more general development that I want to be able to address: an overall sense, in our time, of a loss of a sense of direction of historical developments, and, no doubt, a lingering desire to bring it all back, a nostalgia for a past of redemptive futures.

The break in the history of philosophical history into a form that is philosophical and scientific presents itself as belonging to a history of the world in terms of which just such a break makes sense: it makes sense as a great philosophico-scientific achievement and advance within the unfolding history of "Man". I think it is undeniable that the hold of that progressive vision of history, indeed the very idea of that history, the history of the world as the emancipation or progress of "Man", is severely weakening in our time. And this is something we need to try to understand today: the promise of Europe's modernity is losing its effective power as the framework of sense-making that is "decisive for us" in the sense that I outlined at the start of Chapter 3. We are, I believe, living in a time of the exhaustion of the old modern understanding. We inhabit its ruins. Reassessing the "since Marx" assumptions about a post-national and post-religious future thus belongs to a far more wide-ranging task of coming to terms with our time, a task to which this book, in both its volumes, is dedicated. It is a long march. In the second volume, I will explore the idea of an exhausted-Europe condition in detail. In this volume, we will set the scene by showing how the classic philosophical discourse of world history (whether religious or scientific) reaches a condition experienced as its "crisis" in the first half of the twentieth century.

What we are heading towards in these volumes is the illumination of a distinctively contemporary perplexity. I am attempting to make sense of the not-making-much-sense that marks our current condition. It is a time in which, increasingly, we no longer know where we are heading or even if we are heading anywhere at all. We are, it seems, becoming mere occupants of a (sometimes barely sustainable and certainly increasingly fragile) life-support system with no higher heading than continued functioning, or rather no higher heading than the optimising of its performative functioning; as if our heading today was simply to transform the world into a 24/7 convenience store and petrol station – and the world's ancient and holy places made into heritage sites and visitor attractions. Europe, for example. The possibilities are endless, but I can only recommend the reader explore the website of the Association for Convenience & Fuel Retailing, NACS. Among its "popular" awards at its annual "'must attend event'" is the "International Convenience Retailer of the Year Award" which "honors" the most innovative and successful international convenience and petroleum retail store of the year with the accolade of "the best convenience store in the world". In 2014, the "home-grown" York County firm "*Rutters*" in the USA won the award. To order "fresh food on the go", their customers encounter a diverse "array of screens" giving them "many options" while still showing a concern to "improve and simplify" their experience, and, "at the *highest* level, their lives". Sponsored by Imperial Tobacco, the must watch post-award video is online here: https://www.youtube.com/watch?v=oYxy9DBEMvU)

How did we get into this rut? Perhaps no one has described the early stages of the onset of this condition better than Marx. Running straight out of his history of the golden thread that we have already cited, Marx continues:

> From the serfs of the Middle Ages sprang the chartered burghers of the earliest towns. From these burgesses the first elements of the bourgeoisie were developed. The discovery of America, the rounding the Cape, opened up fresh ground for the rising bourgeoisie. The East-Indian and Chinese markets, the colonization of America, trade with the colonies… gave to commerce, to navigation, to industry an impulse never known before…The markets kept ever growing…The place of manufacture was taken by the giant, Modern Industry…Large-scale industry has established the world market [leading to] immense development to commerce, to navigation, to communication by land…All fixed, fast-frozen relations, with their train of ancient and venerable prejudices and opinions are swept away, all new-formed ones become antiquated before they can ossify. All that is solid melts into air, all that is holy is profaned…The need of a constantly expanding market for its products chases the bourgeoisie over the surface of the globe. It must nestle everywhere, settle everywhere, establish connections everywhere. The bourgeoisie has through its exploitation of the world market given a cosmopolitan character to production and consumption in every country. (CM, pp. 4–6)

One might wonder if we should be doing political economy rather than philosophy. But I think philosophy can make a contribution, perhaps a singular contribution, in helping us make sense of this geopolitical development as a geophilosophical one. And, as we have already begun to see, from the point of view of an investigation of philosophical history, it takes in Marx too.

"All that's solid melts into air". Indeed. We are coming to terms with the coming to an end of a world, a European world reaching its exhaustion, but now including in that Marx's solid idea of a new world to come which would occupy the still-differentiated space that he supposed was being swept clear by its melting. As I say, an exhausted-Europe problem will be the major theme of the second volume. For now Marx's somewhat casual description of this development as having "a cosmopolitan character" will provide a first step in a step-by-step understanding of the unfolding and unravelling of the promise of Europe's modernity. At issue in our time is, I will argue, the accelerating movement of the Greco-Biblical world in deconstruction.

Geophilosophically speaking, this might be called the coming to an end of the world made with "Man" in mind. Writing towards the end of the Cold War, writing before the unpredictable acceleration that led, in a blink of an eye, to what we call "the fall of the Berlin wall", and writing, with another lens, in what he identifies as a time "after Darwin", the British philosopher David Wiggins offers the following summary:

> Unless we are Marxists, we are more resistant [today] than the eighteenth- or nineteenth-centuries knew how to be [to] attempts to locate the meaning of human life or human history in mystical or metaphysical conceptions – in the emancipation of mankind, or progress, or the onward advance of Absolute Spirit. It is not that we have lost interest in emancipation or progress themselves. But whether temporarily or permanently, we have more or less abandoned the idea that the importance of emancipation or progress (or a correct conception of spiritual advance) is that these are marks by which our minute speck in the universe can distinguish itself as the spiritual focus of the cosmos. (TIML, p. 91)

If this is a time after Darwin, then it is also, quite clearly, a time after Copernicus too. Moreover, since Wiggins says that the formation of the framework articulating our understanding of the world and the significance of our lives is a "largely unconscious" development (TIML, p. 124), perhaps this is also a time after Freud. But writing during the Cold War it is also both a time after Marx (so that there can be Marxists among us) and a time in which another event inseparable from his name – what I am calling the twentieth century but which Derrida calls "the Marxist blow" (SM, p. 98) – is still ongoing. In this very complicated complex of spirits, Wiggins says that the non-Marxists today are not only more resistant to attempts to locate the meaning of our lives in mystical or metaphysical conceptions of emancipation or progress than our forebears – but also that we have *not* lost interest in "emancipation or progress themselves". We who are not Marxists retain that classic interest – and yet something has, for us, worn away. Whether what survives here can hang on without a certain survival of Marx (so that, equally, we are all Marxists) is extremely questionable. In the next volume, I will return to this passage from Wiggins, and try to clarify this spectral survival of Marx, since Marx, with and without Marx. But this is not what Wiggins's initial qualification "Unless we are Marxists" points towards. What he has in view, quite rightly I think, is the hanging on, as a still-yet-to-melt but no-longer-so-solid vestige in our time of a discourse in which the classic interest could be more unproblematically "ours". Unless we are messiano-eschatological Marxists things are far more complicated for us.

The mystical and metaphysical conceptions that Wiggins mentions are ways of thinking about some kind of ultimate unity of Man, a unity which will also be a unity of Man and the Cosmos, or Man and the World. In mystical thought attaining such a unity with the One is something that can, in principle, be attained in *any* "now". In philosophy, by contrast, this unity has been posited as a spiritual finality in which Man attains a proper relation to himself and to the world as the historical end of a movement of self-emancipation and de-alienation. It is the metaphysics of the epoch of Greco-Biblical – and hence European – *archeo-teleo-eschatologism*; an epoch that dreams of the future attainment of a form of individual and social life in which the full potential of Man could be realised. This is the epoch of history as universal history, a history in which the most "advanced" developments have taken shape first in Europe, but concern an end that embraces all humanity – whether in a properly differentiated way or a fundamentally (politically) undifferentiated way. In either case, Man is conceived as a creature with a historical nature in the strictest sense: he is the being whose own being unfolds in time in a movement of history from a primitive origin towards his properly civilised end. What we should now add to this picture is the thought that this is a movement towards the attainment of an increasingly cosmopolitan existence; where (differentiated or undifferentiated) every other is my fellow, and not just "my fellow Germans" or "my fellow Europeans".

These fellows – all of them – they are all, of course, human, and first of all men (males): my fellow is, first of all, my brother. Hence, we might also speak of this epoch as an epoch of androcentric cosmopolitanism. This is not merely one political idea among others in this epoch. Indeed, there is reason to consider it the European political idea *par excellence*. Here is Derrida summarising the cosmopolitan tradition, in a lecture given in English in 1997 (http://www.livingphilosophy.org/Derrida-politics-friendship.htm):

> [The] tradition of cosmopolitanism…comes to us from, on the one hand, *Greek* thought with the Stoics, who have a concept of the "citizen of the world". [But] you also have [in] St. Paul, in the *Christian* tradition, a certain call for a citizen of the world as, precisely, a brother. St. Paul says that we are all brothers, that is sons of God, so we are not foreigners, we belong to the world as citizens of the world; and it is this tradition that we could follow up until Kant…

Having traversed the field of formation of a distinctively European cultural identity, having rooted up its *archē*, we can now start tracking its development into Kant's thought on history and the cosmopolitan hope he cleaves to as its truth. Across two volumes, we will follow the vicissitudes of this hope across the centuries, and into our time. After Kant, we will be exploring a line of development that decisively follows Kant, "in the very skull of Kant" (SM, p. 5), in this Greco-Biblical cosmopolitan tradition of more than one tradition, a tradition that Kant carries and sends on right here, somewhere where we are.

II

While the Greeks developed a concept of the citizen of the world, and produced what we Europeans still regard as the first efforts at narrative history, the narratives the Greeks produced were never, as Hegel noted, "very comprehensive in their range" (PH, p. 2). Man, like everything that is, is regarded as having a *telos*, and political questions relate centrally to the social conditions of its possible fulfilment, which are, for Aristotle at least, necessary conditions: individual men cannot "live well" (cannot fulfil the *telos* of their nature) on their own. As we have seen, the *zōon logon echon* is a *zōon politikon*, although it is not the only one. In his *History of Animals*, Aristotle maintained that some gregarious animals – not those that merely herd or flock together or swim together in shoals – should be called *zōon politikon*: "Animals that live politically are those that have any kind of activity in common, which is not true of all gregarious animals. Of this sort are: man, bee, wasp and crane" (History, 488a). With the idea of having some kind of "activity in common", Aristotle is highlighting a certain way of doing-a-thing-together, rather than simply doing things at the same time or in the same place. At issue, then, is a mode of collective self-organisation in which what gets done gets done only by working together. So Man and bee are both political animals, even though their ways of being such are, naturally, very different. Individual human beings, for Aristotle, can only fulfil their *telos* in this social way, and there is, as a consequence, a certain natural home for Man too: an environment in which individuals can "live well". This is the *polis*, the city: "the city is their end". We are, as it were, destined to be citizens: "Every city, therefore, exists by nature, if such also are the first partnerships. For the city is their end...[T]he city belongs among the things that exist by nature, and...man is by nature a political animal" (Politics, 1252b30–1253a3).

So, the *zōon politikon* that are human (the *zōon logon echon*) are the ones who find their proper home in the *polis*. But what about the idea of a *zōon cosmopolitikon*? Greek philosophy seems never to have given this philosophical attribute, the attribute of the philosopher, to Man as such, or as part of the *telos* of Mankind.

In the epoch of the becoming-European of the world, when Christian creationism appropriates Greek conceptual resources, there is a crucial change. With the introduction of ideas of equality before God (which will later become secularised as equality before the law), the Greek concept of the universal – *katholikos* – is drawn into the universalism of the, in principle, all-embracing (Roman) Church, where "church" here means "the body of all believers", the assembly or *ecclesia*, from the Greek *ekklēsía* ("gathering"). The Church is the gathering or binding of all the believers into a distinct but potentially universal institution. The interest in history in the Greek sense (*historia*) is then tied to Christian (or Greco-Biblical or onto-theological) anthropology, with Man, theomorphic rational subjectivity, as the centre of God's creation in an earthly horizon that spans a beginning (creation) and an end (final judgement). Historical time becomes both finite and linear. It also becomes providential and redemptive: universal history, the history of the world, is inscribed within the conceptuality of the world after the Fall of Man, and hence has a Fall/Redemption structure. Covenant theology, as we have seen, understands the whole of human history after Man's fall into sin as unifying under the provisions of the covenant of redemption. It is the world made with men in mind, and history is the movement towards the perfection of God's creation, and the end of (in-the-world) time.

On this understanding, Europe itself unfolds in the space opened up by Greek philosophy and Biblical Christianity, the site of the unfolding of the understanding of ourselves as Man, where Man, the being that we ourselves are, is understood in terms of the historical development of his being towards the ultimate destiny of Mankind. The history of the world is a history of a redemptive emancipation of theomorphic rational subjectivity, the true *Theodicea*, as Hegel will say, with Greco-Roman-(Catholic)–(Protestant)–Christian-Modern Europe at the head, both the centre of the centre of God's creation and the site of the opening of history onto universal history. Every other cultural heading will be and will have always been part of this history, but the truth of *political* animality as *cosmopolitical* animality, and the religious truth that its history reveals, is disclosed as such, first, from what has taken place in "our continent". Out of its opening in Greek history, Europe's modernity bears witness to this break from forms of life dominated by magic, myth and superstition, exemplary evidence of humanity *en route* to its proper end, every other part of the world likely to take its course in turn from Europe's heading. This is Europe's promise, the promise of Europe's modernity.

Like a force of nature entering Europe's history – writing with a conceptual flair and lucidity that seems to make him an intensifying prism of the entire spectrum of tendencies of his past, and without reference to whom the spectrum of practically everything in philosophy since seems barely comprehensible – these becoming-European ideas found their most systematic synthesis in the writings of Immanuel Kant.

Kant was born in 1724 in Königsberg in what was then East Prussia (now Kaliningrad, Russia). He lived for eighty years and hardly ever left the city, never going more than ten miles from it. And yet, despite the fact that he never really went anywhere, Kant became the thinker of the most ambitiously universal form of social and political philosophy: a philosophy of a global humanity living a "universal cosmopolitan existence" (Kant, p. 51). There is some justification in referring to Kant's writings on this theme as "late texts": his earlier writings did not show the cosmopolitan sympathy of his late years. Indeed, his early *Observations on the Feeling of the Beautiful and Sublime*, written in 1764, when he was 40, while often very funny about nationalities in Europe has comments on people from Africa that are horribly and continuously derogatory, and his work in anthropology has a similarly pervasive racist undercurrent. How could it be that Kant, of all people, could become, seventeen years later, such a cosmopolitan thinker? I am sure his observation of the French Revolution was decisive in this transformation, but we do not know for sure. But whatever the reason it seems undeniable: change he did.

It is not just Kant's cosmopolitanism that is ambitious. Indeed, his very inquiry and its guiding question are likely to strike us as the most unlikely to find a philosophically compelling answer (other than "nothing"): asking what "a philosophical mind" might be able to say about history. History: the domain of what has actually happened; not merely a domain of matters of fact rather than logical relations of ideas, but the domain of the apparently "senseless course" of contingent human events, so much of which is "made up of folly and childish vanity" (Kant, p. 42); all-in-all a seemingly "planless aggregate of human actions" (Kant, p. 52). How on earth could one say anything at all about history in an *a priori* rather than empirical form? Space and time may be conceived as having an *a priori* character, but what takes place in space and time – history – that would seem beyond the proper limits of philosophical inquiry.

There is an anxiety here to which Kant is alive, and which will only get more overwhelmingly intense as the kind of history Kant announces "*as possible*" unfolds into our time:

> It is admittedly a strange and at first sight absurd proposition to write a history according to an idea of how world events must develop if they are to conform to certain rational ends; it would seem that only a *novel* could result from such premises. (Kant, p. 52)

Philosophical history: a rational inquiry or just an inventive fiction and delusion? We'll come back to this worry again and again as we follow the chain of thinkers who have picked up the Kantian baton.

In 1997, in the first of what was to become a series of public talks he gave at UNESCO in Paris, Derrida addressed that institution's commitment to a universal "right to philosophy". He spoke on this theme not only to speak up for such a right but to draw attention to the way in which the institution in which he was speaking, and from which such a right now emanates, is itself an emanation from philosophy: it is itself a "philosophical act", a "philosophical production and product", it is a "properly philosophical place" (UNESCO, p. 4). Like Europe itself, in its Greek memory and universalist specialism, it is a "philosopheme": a philosophical thing (UNESCO, p. 2). And at this point Derrida turns to "a great short text by Kant" entitled "*Idee zu einer allgeneinen Geschichte in weltbürgerlicher Absicht*":

> This brief and difficult text belongs to the ensemble of Kant's writing that can be described as *announcing*, that is to say predicting, prefiguring and prescribing a certain number of institutions which only came into being in this century, for the most part after the Second World War. These institutions are already philosophemes.

In the next volume, I will explore the founding memory and institutional structure of what has become the European Union in terms of Kant's prediction/prescription, his *teleo-poetic* projection of what, in that great essay, Kant calls (to be) "a great political body of the future, without precedent in the past" in "our continent" (Kant, p. 51). Setting that aside for the moment, it nevertheless brings into prominence that while Kant's "idea" is universal in its scope, it is in its orientation and focus fundamentally European. Indeed, it is, as Derrida remarks, "the most strongly eurocentred text that can be" (UNESCO, p. 5). The emanation and projection of a history that would be a universal history, an *allgeneinen Geschichte*, not only comes from Europe but passes through it, is carried by it and disclosed by it from the history of its actual history. This is nowhere more tellingly insistent than when Kant appeals to the actuality of the uninterrupted golden thread of the history of our continent precisely to head off the threatening possibility that the idea of a universal history is just an inventive fiction:

> For if we start from *Greek* history as that in which all other earlier or contemporary histories are preserved or at least authenticated, if we next trace the influence of the Greeks upon the shaping and mis-shaping of the body politic of *Rome*, which engulfed the Greek state, and follow down to our own times the influence of Rome upon the *Barbarians* [i.e. the Germanic peoples SG] who in turn destroyed it, and if we finally add the political history of other peoples episodically, in so far as knowledge of them has gradually come down to us through these enlightened nations, we shall discover a regular process of improvement in the political constitutions of our continent (which will probably legislate eventually for all other continents)… All this, I believe, should give us some guidance in explaining the thoroughly confusing interplay of human affairs and in prophesying future political changes. (Kant, p. 52)

In Hegel's massive *Philosophy of History*, the seismic upheaval-continuities of the golden thread are re-iterated step-by-Greek-Roman-German-step, adding the (implicit in Kant) thought that while this German "Europe is absolutely the end of History", "Asia" is "the beginning" (PH, p. 109). In both cases, however, Europe's actual history – which I am suggesting cannot in fact finally be distinguished from a discourse that strives to make it so that universal history (really) will have been the sense of Europe's history – is "the real test" (Kant, p. 50) for the claim that a movement of universal world history is (and here is the anxiety again) "anything but overfanciful" (Kant, p. 50). Hegel worried in turn, that philosophy would only succeed in approaching history in such a way as to "force it into conformity with a tyrannous idea., a process *diametrically opposed* to that of the historiographer" (PH, p. 9, emphasis mine). But, like Kant, Hegel supposed that political developments in Europe (and especially in Germany) could quiet the anxiety that the "historical" portrait produced was just spinning a golden yarn.

As far as "prophesying future political changes" is concerned, this history of the golden thread also opens out onto the dawning of a golden age to come. Kant's brief text and Hegel's lengthy *Theodicaea* both have, as Kant explicitly accepts his own to have, "*chiliastic* expectations" (Kant, p. 50) – that is to say the coming of a time on earth (often called "a golden age" in fact) in which a certain "perfection" of Man will have been attained, something that Kant also calls "the fulfilment of man's destiny here on earth" (Kant, p. 52). In the work of Kant and Hegel, this is a destiny which, from the start, will have been God's plan for Man, the providential "design of a wise creator" (Kant, p. 45): the realisation on earth (as Marx could have said too, without God and against religion) of Man's "ownmost" potential for being what he is. For Kant, this will lead to a time "(as far as is possible on earth)" of "happiness" (Kant, p. 43). (I will come back to Kant's cautious, parenthetical qualification.)

III

The fact that Marx could have affirmed something of this philosophical history belongs with his own secularised inheritance of the classic theological *archeo-teleo-eschatological* conception. Having said this, while the theological horizon of their analysis is not just something they want to accept but belongs essentially to their sense of its meaning and truth, neither Kant nor Hegel appeals to God to "explain" human deeds regarded as "secular events" (Kant, p. 109), and it is striking that Kant's explanatory accounting of the development of human capacities in history is, precisely, and foreshadowing both Hegel and Marx, "*antagonism* within society*"* (Kant, p. 44). Moreover (though, as we have seen, this is something Marx thought had been dealt a "death-blow" by Darwin), Kant affirms that a thoughtful "modesty forbids us to speak of providence as something we can recognise", and in his theoretical work, he regards it as "more in keeping…to speak of *nature*" (Kant, p. 109). So the set-up is already and overtly de-theologised in its theoretical content. Indeed, anticipating Hegel, the only thing that Kant begins with, or brings *a priori* into his inquiry into history is "reason" (cp. PH, p. 9). Having affirmed that natural capacities are naturally destined to be developed to their full potential, Kant notes that "in man" the natural capacities at issue are those which are "directed towards the use of his reason" (Kant, p. 42). It is thus, first of all, an idea of Man, a conception of the being that we ourselves are, which is the point of departure for an account of history that will be singularly philosophical, that is to say, universal. As such, it will remain onto-theological through and through, as it does in Marx, and as it does in any number of other secularising approaches which "deprive" the classic definition of Man as a being that reaches beyond itself of its Christian character. History, for the classics of philosophical history, *is* that ongoing "transcendence" or the "looking up" of the becoming-vertical of Man. In Kant, it is the self-development of reason in time. (And who is to say that is not basically what it is for Hegel and Marx too, whatever their differences, and Husserl too as we shall see at the end of this volume.) In a successive and interconnected series of generations, human beings pass down whatever understanding and insight is granted their time until "the germs implanted by nature in our species can be developed to that degree which corresponds to nature's original intention" (Kant, p. 43). In this way, Man slowly, and perhaps after many, many revolutions, upheavals, setbacks, and reversals (as Derrida stresses Kant's "hope" for a "cosmopolitan end" – which, Derrida adds, "remains a hope" – "is anything but the expression of a confident optimism" (RP, p. 3)), "*work[s] his way up* from the uttermost barbarism to the highest degree of skill, to inner perfection of thought and thence (as far as is possible on earth) to happiness" (Kant, p. 43).

When this history of Man becomes conscious of itself in this way, this very event – this enlightened seeing – becomes part of the development it describes, becoming in that event a "normative-practical" contribution to it, so that "their fulfilment can be hastened, if only indirectly" by the work of philosophy, which can thus "accelerate the coming of this period" (Kant, p. 50; cp. DP, p. 247 where we find a related claim for Hegel. Again, as we shall see, one can say the same for Marx's "theoretical" work, and Husserl's too.)

Here we have, in a setting where the normative-practical first arises on the back of a claim to "knowledge of the idea [of Man]" (Kant, p. 50), a classic cognitivist expression of the potential contribution of philosophy to history's unfolding. Ultimately, it will be resistance to that cognitivism – resistance to the idea that there is a final "truth of Man" to be known – that will overwhelm the classic project of philosophical history. Recall that a contemporary non-cognitivist like Wiggins would not want to take no account of historical or scientific discoveries about ourselves, and would in fact respect their objectivity. Nevertheless, the decisive difference of the non-cognitivist about life's meaning is the insistence that such facts are not decisive *for us* but depend for their significance on a framework of sense-making that has an irreducible autonomy. What we mean by *"us"*, our understanding of our own being, does not escape this logic, disclosing an irreducible responsibility, up to and including what Nietzsche called "the most comprehensive responsibility" (one internal to philosophy itself) (BGE, p. 67): responsibility, that is to say, for the meaning of our own being (which will therefore always be "political", affecting what we mean by being a "political animal") – in the understanding of the world and the significance of our lives that most makes sense to us as "ours".

Acknowledging this autonomy and responsibility does not make thought on the meaning of our own being something simply in the service of a given political motivation, but it does entail a resistance to a "positivism" or "scientism" which acknowledge no such responsibility, announcing what one might call a "politics of thought" invisible to modern cognitivist ideas of basing philosophical history on a claim to knowledge concerning our being (UNESCO, p. 10). Our thinking concerning our own being belongs, as one might put it, to a conversation that is not a one-way street from science to philosophy but "would be at once provocation or reciprocal respect", a conversation that would not be marked by philosophy's antagonism towards science – or indeed religion – but would not be simply subordinate to it either, philosophy also asserting its "irreducible autonomy" (UNESCO, p. 10). I will return to this theme in the second volume but it will become especially sharply in view in this one when we explore Husserl's concern with a "crisis of the sciences" in a time of "portentous upheavals" following the rise to power of Nazism in Germany, a situation that Husserl will present as a "crisis of European humanity" as such.

To help us traverse the time that takes us to that condition of European crisis, an historical passage that will track the development of philosophical history from Kant to Hegel to Marx and beyond, I want to introduce an essay by Paul Valéry which also deals with a European crisis condition: "The Crisis of Spirit". Valéry's essay is composed of two "letters" written for publication in English in 1919, and thus at the close of the most devastating war in Europe's bloody history, which brought the death of millions. We will look at the details of this text later in this volume, but for now, I simply want to set the stage with Valéry's own stage-setting of the history of philosophical history that concerns us. The text is written with the melancholy sadness, a sort of mourning-before-the-fact, of someone who though feeling "everything has not been lost", felt too that "everything has sensed that it might perish" (HP, p. 24). "The military crisis may be over. The economic crisis is still with us in all its force. But the intellectual crisis, being more subtle, and by its nature, assuming the most deceptive appearances…this crisis will hardly allow us to grasp its true extent, its *phase*" (HP, p. 25).

He looks back to the Europe before the war, to Europe in 1914, and sees "the most perfect state of *disorder*" (HP, p. 27). Disorder is not a state he entirely shies from. He calls it, precisely, "modern", and speaks in the name of "*we moderns*", using that in a boldly generic sense concerning any time (whenever it happens) of "formidable" intellectual energy and "the free coexistence, in all…cultivated minds, of the most dissimilar ideas, the most contradictory principles of life"; a time then of intense cultural vitality, and, in pre-War Europe, of near "infinite potential" (HP, p. 27). The contrast to a modern period (and he gives examples of other "modernisms" from periods in ancient Egypt and in ancient Rome) is a time when a culture is characterised more by its uniformity and order: "more specialized in a single type of manners and entirely given over to a single race, a single culture, and a single system of life" (HP, p. 28).

As we have seen already, such a mono-culture is hardly a culture at all. And for Valéry, Europe's pre-War world was the dangerous opposite of that: the Europe of 1914 is presented as having "reached the limit of modernism"; its "wealth of contrasts and contradictory tendencies was like the insane displays of light in the capitals of those days: eyes were fatigued, scorched..." (HP, p. 28). "The most perfect state of disorder" just as much as "the most perfect state of order" threatens culture (it has limits at both ends). That the upshot of Europe's radical disorder was disorder itself, war, which left Europe in ruins, is perfectly fitting.

Following the striking impression of Europe before the War, in 1914, Valéry develops a Shakespearean image of the situation facing Europe after the War, Europe in 1919. Here is Valéry's "Hamlet of Europe". For reasons that will be significant later in this volume, I reproduce it here in its entirety, with no omissions and all ellipses in the original:

> Standing, now, on an immense sort of terrace of Elsinore that stretches from Basel to Cologne, bordered by the sands of Nieuport, the marshes of the Somme, the limestone of Champagne, the granites of Alsace...our Hamlet of Europe is watching millions of ghosts.
>
> But he is an intellectual Hamlet, meditating on the life and death of truths; for ghosts, he has all the subjects of our controversies; for remorse, all the titles of our fame. He is bowed under the weight of all the discoveries and varieties of knowledge, incapable of resuming this endless activity; he broods on the tedium of rehearsing the past and the folly of always trying to innovate. He staggers between two abysses – for two dangers never cease threatening the world: order and disorder.
>
> Every skull he picks up is an illustrious skull. *Whose was it?* This one was *Lionardo*. He invented the flying man, but the flying man has not exactly served his inventor's purposes. We know that, mounted on his great swan (*il grande Uccello sopra del dosso del suo magnio cicero*) he has other tasks in our day than fetching snow from the mountain peaks during the hot season to scatter it on the streets of towns. And that other skull was *Leibnitz*, who dreamed of universal peace. And this one was *Kant...and Kant begat Hegel, and Hegel begat Marx, and Marx begat...*
>
> Hamlet hardly knows what to make of so many skulls. But suppose he forgets them! Will he still be himself?... His terribly lucid mind contemplates the passage from war to peace: darker, more dangerous that the passage from peace to war; all peoples are troubled by it..."What about Me," he says, "what is to become of Me, the European intellect?...And what is peace?...*Peace is perhaps that state of things in which the natural hostility between men is manifested in creation, rather than destruction as in war.* Peace is a time of creative rivalry and the battle of production; but am I not tired of producing?... Have I not exhausted my desire for radical experiment, indulged too much in cunning compounds?...ambitions?... Perhaps follow the trend and do like Polonius who is now director of a great newspaper;

like Laertes, who is something in aviation; like Rosencrantz, who is doing God knows what under a Russian name?

"Farewell, ghosts! The world no longer needs you – or me. By giving the name of progress to its own tendency to a fatal precision, the world is seeking to add to the benefits of life the advantages of death. A certain confusion still reigns; but in a little while all will be made clear, and we shall witness at last the miracle of an animal society, the perfect and ultimate anthill."

The wording of Valéry's list of the generations of Kant in his (not entirely in French) French text made it more transparent that the ghosts were generated from each other (although he obviously did not think they were generated only by each other), and this will be important to me later. Valéry had written: "*...Kant qui genuit Hegel, et Hegel qui genuit Marx, et Marx qui genuit...*".

And Marx *qui genuit... What? Whom?* Perhaps, as I have said, the twentieth century, and perhaps, first of all, a Rosencrantz who did God knows what under a Russian name. In 1919, the magnificent ghosts proceeding from the skull of Kant, like the invention of Lionardo, and the dream of Leibnitz, seem to be on a precipitous, heading into disaster in a European world that is increasingly following a trend of *giving up the ghost* – and becoming "the perfect and ultimate anthill".

I shall not say "Farewell" to the ghosts. Indeed, I want to follow them closely, and to track the fate of the discourse of Europe's modernity as it passes through Kant, the begetting of Hegel, the begetting of Marx, and (in one line of its unfolding) the begetting of something from that line of ghosts that Valéry may have anticipated when he noted, in 1919, a "paradox suddenly become fact": namely, that "the great virtues of the German peoples have begotten more evils, than idleness ever bred vices" (HP, p. 24) – the begetting of Lenin. The next part of this book will follow the development of philosophical history from Kant's geophilosophical, cosmo-nationalist hope through to the geopolitical, communist and internationalist vision of a united humanity in Marx and Lenin. As we proceed through our line of ghostly variations we will see how philosophical history, the history of the world, is invariably elaborated as a discourse of Europe's modernity and Europe's promise for humanity. "The archeo-teleological program" of world history is, at the same time, the basic form of "all European discourse about Europe" (OH, p. 27). However, as the disjunction between Europe's promise and Europe's actual history grows ever more acute, we will also begin to see this programme's unravelling – as the old discourse of Europe's modernity becomes a discourse of modern Europe's crisis.

"Et celui-ci fut *Kant...et Kant qui genuit Hegel, et Hegel qui genuit Marx, et Marx qui genuit...*". Did I say I was following a chain of thinkers who picked up a Kantian baton? It wasn't a baton, it was a weapon, a cudgel. Let's follow our ghosts as they smash the skulls of those who generated them.

PART III
The history of the world

6

PERPETUAL PEACE

The peoples of the earth have thus entered in varying degrees into a universal community
– Immanuel Kant

I

I am not calling for the revival of a religious form of philosophical history. But nor am I following the progressive scientific spirit in Marx that dreams of putting an end to religion and promises a politically de-differentiated humanity to come. In this regard, we might note that when Derrida reaffirmed Kant's cosmopolitan hope, and reminded us that this hope was anything but the expression of "a confident optimism" that so often attends criticism of it, he went on to say that this hope was "above all" anything but the expression "of an abstract universalism" (UNESCO, p. 4). The charge of abstraction from concrete reality, and especially, as we shall see, the sneering charge of a conception as "*merely formal*", is a mainstay of Marxist criticism of whatever it does not like. But here (and not only here as we shall see) the charge can be turned against Marx and Marxism. On the other side of communist revolutions which will have changed the world, Lenin predicted ("scientifically") the emergence in the old nation-states of what he called the "non-political state" (SR, p. 66). Their appearance would sweep-clear the world of its (supposedly) already "vanishing" "national differences and antagonisms between peoples" (CM, p. 23), leading ultimately to the specifically humanitarian construal of universal freedom, peace, and well-being as the final end of history. As our sense of what is most contingent alters, it is now the "scientific" belief in a worldwide order without politically salient differentiation, "proletarian internationalism", and not the "religious" assumption of ongoing parting off and division that looks today, "above all", like an abstract universalism (RC, p. 255, see CM, p. 23).

There is, I believe, something akin to "abstract universalism" to be affirmed. But it is an abstraction that brings into view not what is most general and common, but what is most concrete and singular: an abstraction that attends as far as possible, as a friend might, to *the one who lives a life* in some specific way of life, whatever that way of life might be. It is not that there is some singular presence or "soul" beyond or behind any "cultural identity". However, attending to another in this friend-like way (rather than attending, for example, only to the role people have in society or the titles their social position grants them), means bearing witness to a relation of identity with the other based only on our irreducible difference as singular life-livers, and not what we may have in common. Along with the old humanitarian ideal, I will explore this further at the end of the second volume of this study. Suffice to note at this point that while it is not the abstraction of a universal common humanity that would ground a common cultural or political heading for all, it does raise the possibility of universalising this relation in a renewed politics of friendship that does not aspire or hope for a "world culture" in which social or cultural antagonisms (for example, in the form of irreconcilable religious differences) have been simply and finally eliminated. We need to call into question the scientism that took Marx to his abstract internationalism and a "secularization thesis" that imagines a future without the "ideological illusion" of religion. This is an illusion of a world without illusion which is still heard, today, in the activist voices of what Eliot rather testily calls the "zealots" of "the humanitarian type" who think cultural differences that produce conflict should be abolished (TDC, p. 60). Bernard Williams calls this, rather more politely but no less pointedly, "humanitarianism in the passive voice" (IBWD, p. 148). In Kant, we find the first, and I think unforgettably brilliant, attempt to forge a humane politics in which a respect that is owed to each person is recognised for all humanity: a universal cosmopolitan (small-s) state cultivating "mutual understanding and peace", but without a world (capital-S) State or indeed a world no-State (Kant, p. 114).

In his UNESCO lecture, Derrida explicitly linked the international institution in which he was speaking, to Kant's philosophy of the history of the world, and Kant's prophetic announcement of cosmopolitan political institutions to come. For Kant, these "announcements" are not "predictions" in the sense of empirical hypotheses based on empirical evidence. Rather, they are based on what in French would be, to the ear, an immediately ambiguous project: "*une histoire philosophique*", a philosophical (hi)story. That ambiguity is, of course, heightened by the fact that philosophical history is supposed to say something *a priori* about the movement of world history. Despite taking a non-teleological view of actual history, Derrida still finds Kant's announcements astonishing: even if not accelerating a movement based on knowledge of an idea of Man (a non-novel-like science of a teleology of nature and human nature), they have been undeniably *future-producing*, conjuring institutions like UNESCO from a distance of nearly 200 years, making it so that there will have been a philosophical (hi)story inscribed in their charters and treaties, including the demand for a universal "right to philosophy".

If Kant's writings can be described as inscribing a philosophical (hi)story into UNESCO's charter, how much more so can we attribute to Kant's work a sort of future-producing event (still not over) with respect to the project of what is now called the European Union? When Kant anticipates the emergence in "our continent" of "a great political body of the future without precedent in the past" (Kant, p. 51), it is impossible not to be impressed by the extent to which his anticipatory descriptions map on to that still developing (and faltering) project. As I say, we will come back to that in the next volume.

So influential is Kant that he can sometimes end up being "responsible" for everything. Adolf Eichmann explicitly appealed to "Kantian" notions of "duty" at his trial in Jerusalem. Emmanuel Levinas said that a dog called Bobby at Auschwitz was "the last Kantian in Germany" for treating the Jews there with respect, as fully human. The second, though obviously appealing, is as spurious as the first: Kant restricts moral feelings of respect to rational animals, to humans.

We might see here, however, a sort of powerful generative openness (*Kant qui genuit…*) internal to Kant's thought. We will see this in a more consequential and decisive context when we examine Isaiah Berlin's essay "Two Concepts of Liberty" in the second volume. Berlin's essay is justly famous for giving a strictly philosophical reading of the geopolitical conflict that raged through the twentieth century, and especially the Cold War. But it is also an essay on the ambiguous legacy of Kant, because Kant's ideas are massively formative of *both* of the concepts of liberty that Berlin sees at stake in that conflict.

We Europeans of today, we are all, to some extent at least, post-Kantian, all issuing from the skull of Kant. Derrida invites us to wonder at just how much Kant's conception of world history and the conception of Europe's modernity that belongs to it prefigures the "tasks and problems of our time" (UNESCO, p. 4). But he will also ask and try to specify "what they do not prefigure", and what "in our time" calls for us to go beyond Kant's "most modern" and "most richly instructive" text (PR, p. 4). We will return to that towards the end of this chapter. First, however, we should present some of the outlines of Kant's still-differentiated vision of the cosmopolitan end of Man.

II

In an essay on the idea of moral progress, Kant identifies what he calls a world-encompassing "cosmopolitan society" or "cosmopolitan [small-s] state" as the ultimate achievement of human social and moral development (Kant, p. 188). In perhaps his best known, and most experimentally written, essay on this theme, "Perpetual Peace: A Philosophical Sketch", he outlines, in the form of a quasi-legal document, conditions under which "the human race" can be brought "nearer and nearer to a cosmopolitan constitution" (Kant, p. 106). In all his discussions of this development, his basic thought is really quite simple: it is an application of the idea of a *national* "social contract" to an *international* context. It is the internationalisation of constitutional (rightful) government.

The social contract idea relates to a way of conceptualising the kind of shift that takes place when human beings move from a primitive condition of "lawless freedom" into a life in "civil states" within a framework of formal law. This is conceived by Kant (following earlier thinkers such as Hobbes and Rousseau) as a move from a state of nature, which is "a state of war", to the "formal institution" of a state of relative peace in a "legal civil state" (Kant, p. 98). There is a kind of fiction internal to the idea of this transition, at least for Kant, because no actual "social contract" was ever made or entered into. Nevertheless, and this is one of his truly great contributions to social contract thinking, Kant supposes that there comes a point when a society (by and large) cannot be coherently described as the society that it actually is, except with reference to the "*idea* of an original contract" (Kant, p. 94, and p. 100): it is *as if* such a contract had been formally entered into. I think this suggests that when we see social breakdowns (either of the "rule of law" kind by corrupt governments or State powers, or of the "law and order" kind in social violence beyond civil disobedience), we should not say the social contract is breaking down but that a society cannot be or can no longer be wholly captured with reference to that idea. With this idea of an original contract, we conceive society as, in principle, a community of friends rather than one in which every neighbour may be treated as "an enemy" or at least "a permanent threat to me" (Kant, p. 98). Where and when it can be thus described, what we are invited to see is a society where there is consent to submit to coercive laws that restrict (for each and every one) "my freedom" in order to maximise the freedom of each and every one. This is the principle of what Kant calls "rightful government", and he set out its necessary constitutional form in his masterwork, *The Critique of Pure Reason*, written in 1781:

> A constitution allowing *the greatest possible human freedom* in accordance with laws by which *the freedom of each is made to be consistent with that of all the others* – I do not speak of the greatest happiness, for this will follow of itself – is a necessary idea, which must be taken as fundamental not only in first projecting a constitution but in all its laws. (CPR, p. 312)

The upshot is a (capital-S) State with legal hindrances (perfectible laws) on individual freedom that, consequently, optimally maximise each person's freedom from hindrances. Such is the ideal law in an ideal civil (small-s) state. In this context, each individual (along, therefore, with their neighbours) shifts from a barbaric condition to a civilised condition: the state becomes the State in the transition from "barbarism to civilization" (Kant, p. 44).

The achievement of optimally maximum freedom for all through a framework of self-imposed law within a State is not thereby guaranteed, however, since such States do not exist in isolation from other human groups outside them. A "just civil constitution" (Kant, p.46) attained in one State will be threatened as long as there are other human societies that threaten it. So the imperative that we attain a condition of the greatest possible freedom for all in society, presupposes not only that our own society is rightfully constituted but that every other society becomes so too. In other words exactly parallel considerations that Kant relates concerning the individuals and their neighbours in any particular society apply to considerations concerning individual societies and their neighbours. Here too, we should expect to enter into legal relations; one with each other "similar to a civil one within which the rights of each can be secured" (Kant, p. 102). Rightful international relations thus belong to the necessary conditions of rightful national government. In formal terms, States, like individuals within States, must consent to submit to coercive laws (binding international treaties) which imply that their sovereignty is both *limited* and *maximised*. Limited national sovereignty, far from being a renunciation of freedom, optimises it by securing universal conditions which make international peace more likely.

For Kant then, the movement that aims at optimising freedom for all members of a society as citizens of a nation-state leads ultimately to a recognition of the rightfulness of a truly global but still differentiated order in which each nation-state becomes also a member-state of an international world-community, a league of nations that he calls "a pacific federation" (Kant, p. 104). It is within this federation set-up that each individual in a nation comes to obtain not just equal political rights as a citizen of a nation but also (certain) cosmopolitical rights (*Weltbürgerrecht*) as a citizen of the world.

Kant's central points on this theme are made when he is discussing the right of strangers to visit the society of others: a right to hospitality, or as Kant puts it, negatively, "the right of a stranger not to be treated with hostility when he arrives on someone else's territory...so long as he behaves in a peaceable manner" (Kant, p. 105). Kant's view is that everyone is entitled to present themselves in the society of others "by virtue of their right to communal possession of the earth's surface" (Kant, p. 105). We should be clear on what Kant is and is not expecting here. For example, he circumscribes the limits and conditions for this international cosmopolitan right in cautious, and in what some regard as problematic, ways. First, since Kant is considering a situation of a worldwide-federation of nation-states, it is a right that is accorded only to citizens of such nation-states, in the movement of citizens from one nation-state to another, and thus does not touch on the contemporary problem (in the absence of even the minimal conditions of such a worldwide-federation) of Stateless people. Moreover, it is merely a right to visit or a "right of resort" (*Besuchsrecht*). It is not "the right of a guest" (*Gastrecht*) who might expect to be especially favourably treated and entertained by their host. And Kant does not even consider issues around a right to residence. On the other hand, he does introduce (and was perhaps the first formally to do so) what is called the principle of "non-refoulement", a key principle of refugee law which only became enshrined in international treaties in 1951, stating that the stranger "can indeed be turned away" (for example, if the person is not behaving in "a peaceable manner") but only if one can be (within reason) confident that "this can be done without causing his death" (Kant, pp. 105–6).

The institution of a cosmopolitan right is thus, first and foremost, a framework of law for regulating (i.e. making conditional) what Kant calls the right to "universal hospitality", a topic that has been at the forefront of humanitarian interest in recent years. For Kant this right is essentially limited to the right of visitors not to be treated with hostility anywhere in the Federation, and hence a right to make your presence known openly (for example, to do business or to speak) for the time of your stay. This remains a right yet to come for many human beings across the globe. Some States today are more welcoming than others – and some hardly at all. Citizens of some States are also more welcome to visit welcoming States than others – and again some hardly at all.

Nothing in Kant's scheme prevents nation-states having more generous agreements than those he outlines as a universal minimum: his concern is with what should, minimally, be universal. But the fact that his cosmopolitan right is so minimal does raise interesting questions about how far, if at all, it is incumbent on a nation-state to strive for something more ambitious. At the limit, would an "ideal host" (in theory if not in practice) be the one who grants universal unconditional hospitality to anyone or everyone and for any time and for any purpose? Few have investigated this question as insistently as Derrida, but I won't go into his long and patient analyses here. However, it is clear that he thinks that the idea of the "hospitality" of a "host" makes no sense at all "without sovereignty of oneself over one's home", and that this "finite" power of sovereignty "can only be exercised", can only be the sovereign power that it is, "by filtering, choosing, and thus by excluding and doing violence", and hence that "a certain injustice… begins right away, from the very threshold of the right to hospitality" (OfH, p. 55). This is not an argument for abolishing such powers, since that would abolish hospitality too, and that is what we want to cultivate. In short, the call for unconditional hospitality as a State-policy proposal is empty. As should be clear, Kant regards optimising the sovereignty of the "free States" that belong to the Federation as the latter's *raison d'être* – the Federation aims, precisely, to "preserve and secure the *freedom* of each state in itself" (Kant, p. 104). Yes, sovereignty – the power to decide how to live one's interdependence for example – is *limited* by membership of the Federation, but it is not abolished by it. And it belongs to what Derrida calls the "finitude" of sovereignty that hospitality be conditional (selective, excluding). The "injustice" of conditionality begins as soon as there is a (sovereign) host as such, as soon as there is any hospitality at all. It is only what Derrida calls "a pious and irresponsible desire" (CF, p. 23), what Kant might call the excessive rationality of "rational cosmopolitans", to suppose that, when there are and as long as there are nations who understand themselves as such (Kant, p. 105), there might be (un-closeable) "open borders".

The humanitarian ideal of a de-differentiated world, a world without borders and a united humanity with a common heading, is premised on the assumption of the supposedly not-long-for-this-world contingency of the sort of national set-up that is the point of departure and presupposition of Kant's inter-nationalism (Kant, p. 113). Kant has that presupposition hardwired into his conception of human diversity: the human cultural differences that give rise to national communities – specifically linguistic and religious differences – are "nature's" own permanent barriers to any project of the "amalgamation of the separate nations" (Kant, p. 113). But as we have seen, even if one does not accept the theology of this assumption, one can still ask which is more historically plausible: a conception that acknowledges the ongoing potential for "hostile attitudes" between people and peoples (Kant, p. 113), or a conception which thinks that this (everywhere still active) proclivity for violence can be radically overcome. Kant does not only presuppose continuing human differences with political salience, but (like Freud too) rejects the idea that human beings can be entirely rid of "the evil principle" within themselves (Kant, p. 103). Kant thinks the pervasive and ongoing presence of this evil principle is simply undeniable. This means: one can only deny it. I have never seen anything in the world or the history of the world to contradict him. We are not incapable of something better than the worst. But we are not gentle creatures, and even if making war and violence less likely, getting the upper-hand on "the depravity of human nature" (Kant, p. 103) is not the most "rational" end for Man, it is and remains the best one can make of the crooked timber that we are.

What thus always remains a question, and what Kant's analysis at least gives us to think, is how best to cultivate the cultural *ethos* of the home, or – since *ethos* in ancient Greek means, precisely, the abode or dwelling place, the somewhere where you are or reside – how best to cultivate a cultural ethos (simpliciter) as that is expressed or shows itself in the welcome afforded to the newcomer, the new arrival, the stranger; both the newcomer from within (the new arrival that is the child) and from without (the stranger, as we say, "from abroad").

I would like to make one further comment on this before we move on. In *The Other Heading*, Derrida notes that the modern European cultural consciousness in relation to the welcome of foreigners is "divided" between "two concepts of hospitality" (OH, p. 77) which pull us in different directions. Consider these alternatives:

1. "You are welcome here" – and we mean by that that you can join in all of this; you are not excluded from any of this.
2. "You are welcome here" – and we mean by that that you don't have to join in with any of this; you are not required to participate in any of this.

Two traditions, two concepts of hospitality, within the European welcome; calling us to a sort of impossible duty or at least an endlessly wounding trade-off. We find ourselves, as Derrida puts it, with the duty "not only to integrate them but to recognize and accept their alterity" (OH, p. 77). If they really are to be welcome (and not in reality simply excluded from participating) don't you want #1? And if they really are to be welcome (and not in reality simply coerced to assimilate) don't you want #2? I think there are better and worse ways of failing here. But I cannot see any future for a welcome that can attempt to negotiate this *aporia* which does not begin with the expectation that and provision for the newcomer to learn to be able to speak the language of (and so can speak with) the majority, if only to say: "I would prefer not to".

III

For reasons that are unclear to me, but which perhaps have something to do with Hegel and Marx (who seem especially keen to heap scorn on their begetter), Kant's cosmopolitanism tends often to be conceived, as we have seen, as optimistic about the possibility of perpetual peace (which Valéry better located in the skull of Leibnitz), and as an abstract universalism, all based on a wishy-washy appeal to a universal love of Man. But Kant nowhere invokes philanthropic feelings as a helpful motivation to overcome our proclivity to mutual antagonism and violence. In fact, Kant not only conceives "antagonism within society" as the basic "means" of the development of Man's rational capacities, but he conceives international "war" as the "means of attaining [the cosmopolitan] end" (Kant, p. 111). Moreover, he explicitly claims that his concern is exclusively about rightful government, in its national and international dimensions, and "not with philanthropy" (Kant, p. 195).

Nevertheless, a worldwide cosmopolitan (small-s) state, where it is not "since Marx" thought insufficiently radical, can still seem either hopelessly optimistic and utopian, or, equally, drily academic and theoretical. However, while Kant is only concerned with what is possible "in theory" (Kant, p. 92), his account is not affect-free. Not only does he refer to the "feeling" beginning to stir among Europe's nations that prepares the way "for a great political body of the future" (Kant, p. 51), but he also appeals to experiences that he thinks are felt in all of us that attest to or bear witness to "the existence of a tendency within the human race as a whole" that would practically move us in the direction of the kind of cosmopolitan future he anticipates theoretically (Kant, p. 181). What are these experiences? Kant gives examples – or better, predicts that there will already be, for his readers, examples – of two kinds. First, those arising as a result of something bad (of a specific sort) happening outside one's own country. And, second, those arising as a result of something good (of a specific sort) happening outside one's own country.

Kant's example of the first type is akin to Marx's observation, some fifty years later (only fifty years!), that commercial globalisation was creating the conditions for its own transformation:

> The peoples of the earth have thus entered in varying degrees into a universal community, and it has developed to the point where a violation of rights in one part of the world is felt everywhere. The idea of a cosmopolitan right is therefore not fantastic or overstrained. (Kant, p. 108)

Once again, Kant is anxiously keen to head off the threat that his philosophical (hi)story is a deluded fantasy or romance novel. In this example, however, we are not being asked to take a particular representation of our history as authoritative but our own feelings of sympathy towards strangers. If you don't have them, there is nothing he can do about that – but you do have them, don't you? The cases of the first type that Kant has in view are, rather perfectly, the colonial conquests of other people's lands by "the commercial states" of Europe. That is, they concern the acts of Europeans that have brought about the very globalisation which has allowed us to attest to how fundamentally appalling such violent and humiliating colonial activity really is.

Kant's example of the second type is no less interesting, this time concerning a feeling of sympathy towards strangers that is provoked by a change for the better happening in their part of the world. I am going to abstract Kant's description from the particular case he had before him in his and his reader's time, the better (I hope) to provoke you into considering (finding in yourself) examples of your own in our time:

> The [change] which we have seen taking place in our own times in a nation of gifted people may succeed, or it may fail. It may be [followed by nothing but] misery and atrocities... But I maintain that [this event] has aroused in the hearts and desires of all spectators who are not themselves caught up in it a sympathy [which cannot be coupled with selfish interest and hence] cannot have been caused by anything other than a moral disposition within the human race which is directed towards the cosmopolitan ideal...A phenomenon of this kind which has taken place in human history can never be forgotten...But even if the [changes] behind the occurrence we have described were not to be achieved for the present, if [the hoped for reforms] were ultimately to fail,...our own philosophical prediction still loses none of its force. For the occurrence in question is too momentous, too intimately interwoven with the interests of humanity and too widespread in its influence upon all parts of the world for nations not to be reminded of it when favourable circumstances present themselves. (Kant, pp. 182–5)

Kant is concerned with an aspect of an event that may not even be clearly visible to those who made it happen: "the attitude of onlookers [abroad] as it reveals itself in public while the drama of great political changes is taking place" (Kant, p. 182). The event that Kant is reflecting on here is the French Revolution of 1789. Among the examples I have found most striking in our own times is the election of Barack Obama, a black man, to President of the United States of America in 2008. The Kantian point is exclusively about people who are "spectators" on the event, and not those "caught up in it". Or more precisely the thought is exclusively about a "public" abroad (and Kant stresses the public and hence political character of the feelings) that did not take part in (his example) the revolution or, comparably, did not (my example) take part in the US election.

That the experience belongs to an outsider is fundamental. But the aspect of the event that this experience attests to need not only be visible to outsiders, though, being caught up in it, may lead to its being missed. In his first, and more or less immediate response to Obama's election, President Bush, conceding defeat, referred to "the history that was made yesterday", "an inspiring moment" showing something "to the watching world" about "the American story". While the election of a black man to the Presidency was experienced by Bush as an American event, it is clear that he did not take its significance to be an exclusively American event, but of America as a very visible presence in the whole world, America (as he put it) as "the greatest nation on the face of the earth". I am not assessing the terms of this assessment but simply noting its being alive to the more than American significance of this event in America.

While Bush, in his own way, did not miss it, others "caught up in it" did. Two equally immediate responses by eligible voters from American academia, from Simon Critchley (a British philosopher now resident in the United States) and Judith Butler, are notable here. Both made some kind of acknowledgement similar to Bush's. Butler, for example, described the election to President of a black candidate as "historically significant" (UE). But her eyes are more inward-looking than Bush's on this, asserting that the "indisputable significance of his election has everything to do with overcoming the limits implicitly imposed on African-American achievement" (UE). Critchley too acknowledges the event's significance in an exclusively inward-looking way; as "a symbolically powerful moment in American history", "defined as it is by the stain of slavery and the fact of racism" (WL). Neither was unaware that American events are of more than American significance. But both framed that significance entirely in terms of consequences in American foreign policy. Butler expressing relief, for example, that she would no longer have to experience a "sense of revulsion" resulting from the fact "that George W. has 'represented' the United States to the rest of the world" (UE). On the other hand, when she considers Obama in his "representative function", her gaze again turns inward, and it is explored exclusively in terms of his "appeal to voters" in America (UE). Critchley too takes his bearings from a comparative assessment of the foreign policy implications of an Obama presidency, anticipating "hugely beneficial consequences for how the United States is seen throughout the world" (WL). He also considers the possibility that the Obama victory "might unleash...a sequence of progressive radicalizations inside the US and perhaps outside as well", though he thinks "the reverse" just as likely (WL). But the emphasis here is entirely on the (domestic or international) consequences – the significance of what Butler called "his race" (UE), what Critchley refers to as the "symbolic" significance of the event (WL), is experienced by these two citizens caught up in it at that moment, as America's alone.

Caught up in the benefits and consequences, they missed an international political dimension of it that, for Kant, must be thought of as independent of what, if anything, the "change" brings about at home. Such an event could, Kant insists, bring about nothing but "misery and atrocities". (It wasn't that, certainly not simply that, in Obama's case, but that is not relevant.) Moreover, it is an international dimension that is equally independent of any beneficial consequences for people abroad who are not "caught up in it": it is independent of all self-interest in that sense. No, the event is the election of a person of colour to the highest office in the most powerful State on the planet. As an election, it was, minimally, a national-political event, but as the election of a person of colour, it was a cosmo-political one.

Kant tried to impress on us that we already find feelings that testify to the claim of a cosmopolitan tendency in ourselves. He also stresses the importance of events that positively take a step towards realising a universal cosmopolitan state. His example, the French Revolution of 1789, was a revolution made in the name of the Rights of All ("Man"), and not simply the Rights of the French. The French Revolution thus represents an event that is future-producing in a cosmopolitical sense (it can "never be forgotten"), even if it turns out to have been disastrous.

In our time, we are, I think, beginning to experience another sense of cosmopolitan right too, another right of all, in a sense of "all" going beyond anything Kant had in view – an experience in which an as-yet-unattained perfection of the "pure humanity of Man" is beginning to be expressed in the recognition or acknowledgement of a cosmopolitan "fellow feeling" beyond the human, and towards our most other others: towards animals. This cosmopolitanism has its corresponding testimony in feelings: for example, in revulsion felt in the face of the unprecedented industrial subjection of animals all over the world today, as well as the ever-growing number of extinctions. And it also has its testimony in events. Indeed, the mutation in our time on this theme is perhaps inaugurated by an event of cosmopolitical testimony beyond the human horizon, incredibly also written in 1789, when, in a mere footnote, Jeremy Bentham (in fact speaking explicitly against Kant) turned the world around insisting regarding non-human animals: "The question is not, Can they *reason*? nor, Can they *talk*? but, Can they *suffer*?" (Bentham, p. 236). Here we see a mutation within the horizon of the "cosmopolitical" beyond Kant, even if the Benthamite event left the classic metaphysical heritage of the *zōon logon echon*, the *animal rationale* – the speaking animal, the animal possessing reason – otherwise untouched.

We have already seen another such event, another mutation in the cosmopolitical, in Marx. "Since Marx", it has been impossible altogether to "forget" that there are what Bernard Williams calls "unities" of "ethical experience" with a concern to engage in "principled discussion of public matters" that cross and go beyond the boundaries of "the politics of the nation-state" (IBWD, p. 46–7); the concrete reality of "a 'constituency' of persons" which "need not live contiguously to one another" (IBWD, p. 50). Such political unities can be, at the limit, geopolitical. While "barely deserving the name community", as Derrida puts it (SM, p. 90), this concerns alliances across and beyond any inter-national differentiation but nevertheless linked "in a concrete way" as a result of commercial globalisation, for example, or climate change. People linked together in such a global "constituency" may have "never believed in the socialist-Marxist International, in the dictatorship of the proletariat, in the messiano-eschatological role of the universal union of the proletarians of all lands" (SM, p. 86), but their link still inherits a Marxist inspiration, a spirit of Marx, to engage in a geopolitical space – a space especially of international law as we shall see in the next volume – that is dominated today by powerful States (including what Derrida calls "phantom-states", like the mafia and drug cartels (SM, p. 83)) and multi-national corporations in their deployment of what Williams calls, simply, "international power" (IBWD, p. 47). Here too we see a geopolitical mutation within the horizon of the "cosmopolitical" beyond Kant, even if the Marxist event left the classic metaphysical heritage of the *zōon logon echon*, the *animal rationale* – the *archeo-teleo-eschatological* concept of Man and his history – otherwise largely untouched, and even if the Marxist hope for the transcendence of the nation-state, along with its hope for the transcendence of religion, belongs to a scientific dream of a "universal union" that has passed its sell-by date. As I say, I'll come back to this at the end of the next volume.

Such events do not stop there. In the unravelling of the discourse of Europe's modernity, the unravelling of the onto-theological history of "the world made with men in mind", normative-theoretical undertakings and ethical-political protest movements that mark a growing resistance to it have gathered and multiplied: for example, in the history of the long and slow progress of women's liberation from an almost exclusively private and domestic space into a public and political space hitherto reserved only for men; in the similarly long and slow developments in civil rights for people of colour, as well as gay rights, trans rights, disability rights, and so on – all of these linking the history of the history of the world from a cosmopolitan perspective to an ongoing process of democratisation.

As a general rubric for Europe's modern culture and its promise as it moves into our time, such a process of democratisation will be the central theme of the second volume. It is a development that goes beyond Kant, but it is not altogether alien to a thought that had already tied the movement of world history to the formation of what he called "republican states", nation-states with representative governments, States which grant (promise) the legal equality of all citizens, States that we would now regard as democracies. The interest in political democracy will become an increasingly salient characteristic of philosophical history as we shall see in Marx and Lenin in this volume, and throughout the investigations of the next one. And in this history, Kant's texts too are philosophical events. That is, they themselves call or conjure into existence the movement of a universal history of constitutional government that they describe, striving to make it so that it will have been a cosmopolitical movement and not a merely national political one. And while (paradoxically) European and male in its conceptual formation ("we are all sons of God, brothers"), it is (the paradox of the paradox) not reserved for European men alone, but opens onto a self-surpassing of the philosophical from its "roots" in an androcentric and European milieu, (a self-surpassing) that in fact (already) begins "in Greece". Philosophy and its history – "under its Greek name and in its European memory" (UNESCO, p. 8) – opens the history of Europe to the effective de-centering of its own androcentrism and Eurocentrism, a de-centering of "Man" that is inseparable from the process of democratisation internal to the heading of modern Europe.

Hegel saw this process of democratisation that was in his time just starting to appear on the horizon of European history explode into political life through the French Revolution. He really didn't like it. And, as we shall see in the next chapter, as we continue to track "the *archeo-teleological* program of all European discourse about Europe" (OH, p. 27), he blamed Kant for the ruin of European politics that it threatened.

7

ATTAINED FREEDOM

> *In the minds of men and in the actual world [the Kantian doctrine] has assumed a shape, whose horror is without a parallel, except in the shallowness of the thoughts upon which it was founded.*
>
> – G.W.F Hegel

I

Kant will have foregrounded the generational character of world history, anticipating a "perhaps incalculable series of generations" to take the "germ" of potential in Man to its final realisation in the context of a universal cosmopolitan existence (Kant, p. 43). When Derrida was considering the generation of spirits beyond Marx in Valéry's open-ended procession of ghosts from the skull of Kant ("*et Marx qui genuit…*"), he reflected on the possibility that one such spiritual generation is ("among others") Valéry himself. Perhaps unknown to Derrida, Valéry had, in fact, expressed a certain affinity with Marx. In 1918, writing to his friend André Gide, he related how he had just "re-read *Das Kapital*", adding "I am one of the few who have read it. This big book has remarkable things in it – you have only to find them. It's often short on logic, at times a desert of pedantry; but some of its analyses are marvellous, I mean that his method of getting at things is like the one I sometimes use, and I can frequently translate his language into mine" (cited in Valéry's son's "Preface", HP, p. xvii). We will see something of this translation when we look at Valéry's essay "The Crisis of the Mind" in Chapter 9. But what Derrida picks up on as a quasi-Marxist inheritance in Valéry's thought of spirit (and hence of "Man") is the conceptualisation of spirit's generation of itself in terms of "work" (SM, p. 9): Valéry defining spirit as "a power of transformation" (HP, p. 94) that works by working over itself, changing itself, posing itself to itself (thereby creating for itself, in turn, "a spirit of the spirit" [poorly translated in the English as "mind within mind"] (HP, p. 98)), and thereby transposing itself, "giving birth to" any number of "astonishing creations", "cultural works" (of art, poetry, music, philosophy, and so on (HP, p. 95)) *qui genuit* dot-dot-dot, who-knows-what.

Spirit transforms sprit for Valéry because, above all, "*spirit…works*" (cited, SM, p. 9). In Valéry, as we have seen, this motif opens not only onto "incredible achievements" of cultural composition in "cultural capital" (HP, p. 94), but also a "crisis of spirit itself", decline, and decomposition (HP, p. 109). Our line of ghosts, *Kant qui genuit Hegel, qui genuit Marx, qui genuit…*, generates what or whom? In particular, does this lineage only generate the decline that is visible to the European Hamlet? We should take into account that there is always more than one line being generated. Indeed, when Derrida suggests a line to Valéry (and others) from Marx, he proposes another line of spirits at work: "*Shakespeare qui genuit Marx, qui genuit Valéry* (and a few others)" (SM, p.5). And the "others" here might also include Derrida himself, who was also always following Valéry more closely than is typically recognised, and in *Specters of Marx* explicitly situates his reading of Marx *via* Valéry and *via* Shakespeare's *Hamlet*. There is not only one spirit at work in spirit, and we should not extrapolate the sequence of the European Hamlet as one where we only see spirit spirit dispirited spirit. Nevertheless, as we shall see, the unravelling of the onto-theological understanding of the world and the significance of our lives that makes its way through that line of ghosts into our time (where, among others, it generates Lenin, Stalin, and, the inseparable adversary of Marxism, Hitler, for example) leaves "Man" on the floor, spiritually floored, and leaves us in the ruins of an old worn-out world.

We will come back to the crisis of European spirit in the next part of this volume. But the line of perhaps-still-hopeful ghosts that Valéry names – Kant-Hegel-Marx – is itself nowhere free of thoughts of crises and backward steps, nowhere simply the expression of a confident optimism or a simple affirmation of linear progress.

Except perhaps among themselves. In that Kant-Hegel-Marx line we find only scorn on scorn, each, in turn, claiming more adequately to attain the truth of the end of Man, each outdoing the other in apocalyptic eloquence on the end of History, and on Europe's significance in this context. It's quite a scene, we will follow its generations, from Kant to Hegel to Marx, through to one of Marx's most faithful generations, to Lenin.

Their hope – which will always be something of a cosmopolitan hope (even in Hegel as we shall see) – is not over; the project of philosophical history is not over. Not only will there be twentieth century attempts at its revival in classical form – a *teleo-eschatological* discourse of world history and of Europe's modernity – in Husserl and in Fukuyama, but, as Wiggins insists, our generally increasing resistance to these eighteenth and nineteenth century discourses of emancipation and progress does not mean that we have simply "lost interest" in "emancipation or progress themselves (or a correct conception of spiritual advance)". However, as I have suggested, when we are freed from all teleology we are going to have to re-learn what such a classical interest can mean for us, and I want to work my way to that in the course of these two volumes.

As the quotation from Hegel that heads this chapter indicates, the spiritual developments we are focusing on concern the shape-shifting of "the actual world" just as much as "the minds of men". At the end of the last chapter, I hinted that Kant was positioned by Hegel as the principal intellectual impetus in the politics of the French Revolution, and indeed Hegel will see his predecessor as central to the wider development of political liberalism across Europe. We have also seen how Kant's work played a future-producing role for international institutions such as UNESCO and the EU. Hegel fundamentally opposed the cosmopolitan philosophy behind those developments, and his work "gained ascendency" in a very different direction. Influential, first, among "the Prussian people" (HE, p. 931), it articulated "the doctrine of State as power" which became "the doctrine…of Bismark" in the new Germany – a line of spirit that was "fixed in the very marrow" of Hitler (HE, p. 1196). Hegel's genius was worked and turned over otherwise in Marx's, as we shall see, but to similar ends: the shaping of the world into three totalitarianisms (communist, fascist and Nazi) that confronted the parliamentary democracies in the twentieth century have their roots in "the doctrines of Hegel and Marx" (HE, p. 1207).

But we should not go too far too fast. *Kant qui genuit Hegel*. What happened there, in the generation of Hegel, at least as far as Kant and the development of philosophical history is concerned? The first thing that happens in Hegel's text is both telling and extraordinary: *Kant's name disappears.*

II

In the four-hundred and seventy-seven pages of Hegel's mammoth *Philosophy of History,* Kant's name appears…just *once,* and then only in the analytic table of contents, referring the reader to something on p. 462. On that page, however, Hegel does not refer to Kant's philosophical history but to "the *Kantian* philosophy", and specifically the Kantian conception of political freedom. He does so as marking a significant moment or event within the very kind of philosophical history that Kant himself had announced, and whose contribution to which Hegel totally elides.

The appearance of Kant right there bears some comment because this is not just any moment in history. It is in fact the final moment of the movement of world history that Hegel is relating in his philosophical history: the movement into "our own time" (PH, p. 461). This is not as one might imagine (at the end of a book on the end of history) the final chapter that takes us to "the completion of history" (WH, p. 414). On the contrary, Hegel is explicit that the stage he reaches when we get to "our time" is simply that: "This is the point which consciousness has attained" (PH, p. 476). And as he goes on to say, and as he had explicitly noted at the start of his long journey, when we get to that point "the process of the World's History" remains in a moment in which it is *"still incomplete"* (PH, p. 27): "the final aim of history is not yet made the distinct object of desire and interest" (PH, p. 476). Yes, Hegel says, freedom, and consciousness of freedom, does arrive onto the stage of world history in a new and decisive way with "the *Kantian* philosophy", and certainly does belong to the movement of its ending. But at the "point" that consciousness has attained when Hegel stops, at that distinctively Kantian point, the consciousness of freedom is still – note the word because it is going to be very important – merely "*formal*".

What conception of freedom is merely formal? The one that belongs to "the *Kantian* philosophy". We will verify this in a moment, but in order to read Hegel's philosophical history you have to be clear that every time he refers to a merely "formal freedom", he means, and means in a derogatory way: the conception of freedom he attributes to Kant.

And then Kant, miraculously, reappears *everywhere*.

The name of Kant appears just once and refers us to Kantian philosophy, and that refers us to formal freedom, which is a form of consciousness of a universal individual freedom. This is not exactly what Hegel calls (capital-s) "Subjective freedom" within his own thinking, but (supposedly) an impoverished version of that, a thin version of that, a still somewhat "unconscious" consciousness of Subjective freedom as it will be anticipated in its properly final form – in Hegel's own philosophy. Formal freedom is what we get to at the end of Hegel's philosophical history when he relates it up to "the point which consciousness has attained" in "our time", a time in which the consciousness of freedom which is in play in what has actually happened has yet to make "the final aim of history... the distinct object of desire and interest". It is nearly there. But it is not there yet. The final aim is still only "implicit". The final step to come, what remains to take place in the history of the world as the movement of the coming to consciousness of freedom, what Hegel calls (to be) the final end of history, is the appearance on the stage of world history of a time that would embody the consciousness of freedom "achieved by his [Hegel's] own speculative philosophy": a complete self-awareness of Man as Man "finally attained" (WH, p. 413).

Supposing, as Hegel and Kant suppose, that history is the unfolding of reason in time, then the final stage of history for Hegel will be reached when the desires and interest of our own concrete and particular existence as individuals become the Hegelian Subjective. What this means for Hegel is that they now entirely harmonise with the abstract and universal form of rational existence as such – the Hegelian Objective. The Subjective finally becoming itself in its union with the "Universal Abstract Existence" that is the form of a fully rational human life. Kant, for Hegel, conceives the latter only as a mode of being for individuals in which individual freedom is optimally maximised for all. But this kind of individual freedom is, for Hegel, a merely "formal" freedom: it does not take freedom itself as the object of its desire and interest (it is not a form of freedom "having itself alone as its object" (PH, p. 51)), but only whatever it is that the individual Will contingently wills for itself – be that collecting antiques, reading novels, quoting Schiller's poetry (Hegel's hobbies), or anything else. The time in history we have actually attained (Hegel's time of writing), which is for Hegel, as I am trying to show, the time of *Kant*, has still to make way for a new time to come: a time (which Hegel will want to have been) a time of *Hegel*. In the time of Kant, "right in the skull of Kant", a step has been able to be made in the consciousness of freedom beyond Kant. It could not actually do without Kant (and obviously not only Kant), but it could not simply keep to the Kantian subject: a transition has to be made from the "merely formal" freedom attained in Kant and his time ("our time"), to the complete attainment of the Truth, to what "alone is Truth" (PH, p. 27): the "Union of Universal Abstract Existence generally with the Individual" (PH, p. 27); a final unity of the form of free existence itself (Objective Freedom) and the consciousness of freedom (Subjective Freedom); the realisation of actual freedom, real freedom, that is still to come. So the (hi)story ends, just before "The End":

> This is the point which consciousness has attained, and these are the principle phases of that form in which the principle of Freedom has realized itself; – for the History of the World is nothing but the development of the Idea of Freedom. But Objective Freedom – the laws of *real* Freedom – demands the subjugation of the mere contingent Will, – for this is in its nature *formal*. If the Objective is in itself Rational, human insight and conviction must correspond with the Reason which it embodies, and then we have the other essential element – Subjective Freedom – also realized. (PH, p. 476)

As we shall see, the final chapter of the final part of Hegel's philosophical history is really, if implicitly, all about Kant, and about why we cannot leave things with him even if we cannot entirely do without him.

In the context of a discussion of Valéry's chain of ghosts proceeding from the skull of Kant, Derrida notes that ghosts appear in the movement of spirit (appear somewhere where we are) either with the name, where spirit "assumes a body" (SM, p. 6) or, when the name disappears, with "that which marks the name" (SM, p. 9). Well, when we track back to read the marks of Kant's disappeared name in Hegel's text, we find him "there" from the very beginning, right there in the "infinite antithesis" between Hegel's own conception of "the final aim" of history, which is the realisation of "the Idea of Freedom" in its "free, universal form", and the "contrasted form" which is "formal existence-for-self" or "formal freedom" (PH, p. 27). The latter is not nothing, since the formally free activity involved here is what builds societies that unfold towards "the great ideal aim" in the first place (PH, p. 35). Hegel calls this "*the cunning of reason*" (PH, p. 34), an idea already at work in Kant's idea of the "ruse of nature", where "antagonism in society" functions as "the hidden mechanism of nature's scheme" (Kant, p. 52). Hegel of course, knows ("nothing is more familiar") the Kantian conclusion: that eventually, we will have reached a point where "each must restrict his liberty in relation to the liberty of others; that the State is a condition of such reciprocal restrictions; and that the laws are restrictions" (*Encycl.* 1870, p. 439). But the end in view in the Kantian "ruse" falls short of the Hegelian "cunning", whose final aim realises laws that are conceived and lived as the very opposite of restrictions. A State which embodies fully rational laws and institutions will be one which an inherently rational subjectivity cannot but be at one with.

Nevertheless, at the point we have reached in history where Hegel's story ends, we have not entered fully into any such a condition. On the contrary, the "modern" world has merely become Kantian, and at the end of the book, in the final section of the final chapter, Hegel repeats or recapitulates the "infinite antithesis" in terms of the difference between the "philosophy" which has become "dominant", the one "whose sphere is the Understanding", and whose position is "abstract", and which can attain only a consciousness of freedom in terms of a "formal, individual Will", and his (Hegel's) own attained self-awareness. That dominant philosophy "is in the first instance only abstract Thought, not the concrete comprehension of absolute Truth – intellectual positions between which there is an immeasurable chasm" (PH, p. 465).

It is very tempting to appeal to the phenomenon of what Freud called "the narcissism of minor differences" to explain Hegel's relentless distancing himself from Kant, but I agree with Freud that naming it that way is, in reality, to name it with "a name which does not do much to explain" what is going on in such scenes (CD, p. 114). However, there is clearly, in Hegel's work, an endless effort to make it so that the time beyond the time his (hi)story ends will have been Hegelian and not Kantian; to make a name for himself and to do so in part by making Kant's name, as far as possible, disappear. Hegel's philosophical history is from first to last a polemic against Kant, and as we shall see, it concludes with a trenchant effort to present the politics of merely formal freedom – what Hegel, probably justly (if, from his pen, sneeringly), calls "*Liberalism*" (PH, p. 471) – as a road to disaster, a heading for Europe that (he thinks) we can only hope we will not take, and which his whole enterprise is pitted against.

This liberalism is Kantian representative "republican" government, what today we think of as "democratic" government in a liberal democracy. Today, in other words, we are still in a time of Kant, even if, as Derrida notes, this is a time, our time, in which "electoral democracy" and "political representation", at least "*as we have known them up until now*" are being "dangerously weakened" as the structure of a *res publica* that can function in an effective way as an "identifiable and stabilizable body for public speech" (SM, p. 79). Hegel thought the republican model of what today we call "liberal democracy" is inherently vulnerable to ineffectiveness and instability, and he thought it would not last long at all. In any case, he wants something else altogether; and that requires "the subjugation of the mere contingent Will". Hegel thinks better than to propose closing down the basic expression of formal political freedom (free political speech) in a time where it dominates as the "principle of the modern world" (HPR, § 273). In this Kantian time "everybody wishes to participate in discussions and deliberations" (cited from Hegel's *Philosophy of Law* in OSE, p. 637, fn. 62). Hegel would certainly wish that everybody did not wish such a thing – and doubtless thinks that in the reconciling conditions of the Union of Objective and Subjective Freedom that would obtain when finally the consciousness of Freedom is fully attained in "laws of real Freedom", they would not so wish. However, as things are he concedes that this wish can be given some space; not because it has some (say) intrinsic if limited democratic merit but because "once he has had his say...his subjectivity is gratified and *he will put up with a lot*. In France, freedom of speech has proved far less dangerous than silence imposed by force; with the latter... men have to swallow everything, while if they are permitted to argue, they have an outlet as well as some satisfaction; *and in this way, a thing may be pushed ahead more easily*" (cited from Hegel's *Philosophy of Law* in OSE, p. 637, fn. 62). Incredulous in the face of Hegel's cynicism, Karl Popper suggests that it is really with thoughts like this, and not in Kant, that one should speak of merely "formal" freedom (OSE, p. 637, fn. 62).

Formal freedom is perhaps the main "mark of the name" of Kant as it appears in Hegel's text – and it is a stubbornly insistent mark: Hegel states, at the outset, that "the perpetually recurring misapprehension of freedom" that he will need to oppose in his account of the development of the consciousness of freedom "consists in regarding that term only in its formal, [small-s] subjective sense, abstracted from its essential objects and aims" (PH, p. 43). But there are a number of other almost equally significant moments of this erasure of the name of Kant in Hegel's elaboration of philosophical history. Perhaps the most spectacular is one that I have already had reason to mention: that it is Hegel's English-language translator, Leo Rauch, and not Hegel himself who notes that *the* "outstanding example" of a philosophical "construal of history" before Hegel is Kant's. Hegel, at the outset of his study of "Universal history itself" simply states that he "cannot mention any work that will serve as a compendium" for what he wants to say about philosophical history in his lectures (PH, p. 1). Given that Hegel was at pains to give illustrative examples of authors of the two other "methods" of writing history that he mentions, his silence on the third is deafening.

Meanwhile, he nevertheless reiterates (in his own way) an array of already-in-Kant themes: the Kantian point of departure of such a history in reason; its development and progress in a divinely designed world history that ends in a state (with a capital "S" in Hegel) of rational freedom; the Kantian anxiety about the very idea of such a history (that philosophy, as an *a priori* investigation, is "a process diametrically opposed" to history, and hence that philosophers would likely only produce "inventions of their own" instead of a "record of the past" (PH, p. 11)); the Kantian emphasis on the occasional loss of gains made in history; the Kantian emphasis on antagonism and conflict; and, of course, the Kantian emphasis on Europe, and its centrality to world history. Hegel had his own way of presenting the movement of the history of the world in terms of the Greek-Roman-Christian-Modern golden thread of Europe's history-ending history out of an origin in the East, and he liked to repeat it:

> It may be said of Universal History, that it is the exhibition of Spirit in the process of working out the knowledge of that which it is potentially.

And as the germ bears in itself the whole nature of the tree, and the taste and form of its fruits, so do the first traces of Spirit virtually contain the whole of that History. The Orientals have not attained the knowledge that Spirit – Man *as such* – is free; and because they do not know this, they are not free. They only know that *one is free*. But on this very account, the freedom of that one is only caprice; ferocity – brutal recklessness of passion, or a mildness and tameness of the desires, which is itself only an accident of Nature – mere caprice like the former. – That *one* is therefore only a Despot; not a *free man*. The consciousness of Freedom first arose among the *Greeks*, and therefore they were free; but they, and the *Romans* likewise, knew only that *some* are free – not man as such. Even Plato and Aristotle did not know this. The Greeks, therefore, had slaves; and their whole life and the maintenance of their splendid liberty, was implicated with the institution of slavery: a fact moreover, which made that liberty on the one hand only an accidental, transient and limited growth; on the other hand, constituted it a rigorous thraldom of our common nature – of the Human. The *German* nations, under the influence of Christianity, were the first to attain the consciousness that man, as man, is free: that it is the *freedom* of Spirit which constitutes its essence... The History of the world is none other than the progress of the consciousness of Freedom; a progress whose development according to the necessity of its nature, it is our business to investigate. The general statement given above, of the various grades in the consciousness of Freedom – and which we applied in the first instance to the fact that the Eastern nations knew only that *one* is free; the Greek and Roman world only that *some* are free; while *we* know that all men absolutely (man *as man*) are free – supplies us with the natural division of Universal History, and suggests the mode of its discussion. (PH, pp. 18–20)

The History of the World travels from East to West, for Europe is absolutely the end of History, Asia the beginning...The East knew and to the present day knows only that *One* is Free; the Greek and Roman world, that *some* are free; the German World knows that *All* are free. (PH, pp. 109–110)

This development of "gradations" of consciousness of freedom does, indeed, give Hegel the form of his book and the basic structure of his analysis. In the next section, I will gallop through the four-hundred and seventy-seven pages to observe its gathering storm on "the *Kantian* philosophy" and its "merely formal" consciousness of freedom in its closing pages.

But before I do, there is one more already-in-Kant theme to note: the identification of a concept or conception as, precisely, "merely formal". This is itself "right in the skull of Kant", an almost signature formulation that Kant repeatedly uses to specify a conception that abstracts from any determinate content. Kant, for example, speaks of "a mere show of rationality" in a certain use of "merely formal principles" (CPR, A63/B88); describing a certain concept as "without content and merely formal" (CPR, A131/B170 and A152/B191); speaking also of "a merely formal consciousness" of something (CPR, B207–B208), and so on. This signature formulation of theoretical limitation was turned against Kant by Hegel. It will be appropriated in the Marx begat by Hegel too, and, stunningly, against Hegel. What a chain in the chain of ghosts! It is the voyage of the merely formal, and it won't end there.

III

It is, however, just one of the already-in-Kant themes that gives the impetus to Hegel's *gigantomachia*: the connection of philosophical history, the history of reason unfolding in time, "with a further application of it, well known to us" (since Kant, one might add): "in the form, viz. of the *religious truth*, that the world is not abandoned to chance and external contingent causes, but that a *Providence* controls it" (PH, p. 13). This is a connection which, as we have seen, Kant is both totally committed to and fundamentally "modest" about. This belongs to a famous gesture in Kant, perhaps one of the most famous: namely, that the project of his critical philosophy, the attempt to establish *a priori* the limits of genuine knowledge, is not undertaken simply for its own sake but to clarify and demystify our relation to God: "I have therefore found it necessary to deny *knowledge* in order to make room for *faith*" (CPR, Bxxx). In one of his early essays, "Faith and Knowledge" (1802–3), Hegel had already set himself against the idea that the highest possible subject-matter of concern for Man, the content of religious doctrine, might be, as Kant was insisting, "the point where philosophy terminates in faith" (HFK, p. 67). Indeed, it is in that early essay that Hegel first got ahead of Nietzsche's madman and expresses the feeling that with the domination of this new philosophy "God himself is dead" (HFK, p. 190). Deland Anderson summarises (DG, p. 37):

> In the article on faith and knowledge…[Hegel] associates God's death with the critical philosophy of Kant [which] removed God to the hinterlands of thought, disclaiming any genuine knowledge of the divine being… Hegel saw this as a great failure of thinking. The critical philosophy had blocked the path to knowledge; it lacked the essential subject of philosophy, namely, a necessary being. Thus it led us to feel an infinite grief, a loss of what is highest: the death of God himself.

It is perhaps an understatement to regard it as, for Hegel, simply a great failure of thinking; as if it were a merely intellectual affair. Hegel's philosophy is perhaps better understood as bearing witness to this death and attempting to reconcile our time to it. And thence, to work towards not just correcting Kant's theoretical failure, but in doing so to displace the Kantian philosophy from its hold on our time, to usher in a new time in which this limit not just to philosophy but to our culture, in general, is overcome. Were that to come about, a profound spiritual stabilisation of human life would come to pass in which everyone would finally be reconciled to the "religious truth" that "the real the world" as it is – a world which hitherto has been nothing but "a slaughter-bench" (PH, p. 22) – actually is and always has been how it ought to be (PH, p. 38). We may have not been able to get to that thought without Kant – but we cannot get to it with him. So it is here that Hegel takes his leave of Kant in the most decisive way.

We have already seen that Hegel's aim is to "prove" and not just "presuppose" the theodical truth of history. But his ambitions here are far greater than that, seeking to overcome a Kantian limitation that had become a commonplace dogma:

> In noticing the recognition of the plan of Divine Providence generally, I have implicitly touched upon a prominent question of the day; viz. that of the possibility of knowing God: or rather –since public opinion has ceased to allow it to be a matter of question – the doctrine that it is impossible to know God. In direct contravention of what is commanded in Holy Scripture as the highest duty, – that we should not merely love, but *know* God, – the prevalent dogma involves the denial of what is there said; viz that it is the Spirit [*der Geist*] that leads into Truth, knows all things, penetrates even into the deep things of the Godhead. While the Divine Being is thus placed beyond our knowledge, and outside the limit of all human things, we have the convenient license of wandering as far as we list, in the direction of our own fancies. We are freed from the obligation to refer our knowledge to the Divine and True. On the other hand, the vanity and egotism which characterize it find, in this false position, ample justification; and the pious modesty which puts far from it the knowledge of God can well estimate how much furtherance thereby accrues to its own wayward and vain strivings. I have been unwilling to leave out of sight the connection between our thesis – that Reason governs and has governed the World – and the question of the possibility of a knowledge of God, chiefly that I might not lose the opportunity of mentioning the imputation against Philosophy of being shy of noticing religious truths, or of having occasion to be so; in which is insinuated the suspicion that it has anything but a clear conscience in the presence of these truths… God wishes no narrow-hearted souls or empty heads for his children; but those whose spirit is of itself indeed poor, but rich in the knowledge of Him; and who regard this knowledge of God as the only valuable possession. That development of the thinking spirit which has resulted from the revelation of the Divine Being as its original basis must ultimately advance to the intellectual comprehension of what was presented in the first instance, to feeling and imagination. The time must eventually come for understanding that rich product of active Reason, which the History of the World offers to us. (PH, pp. 15–16)

It has been said that Hegel's thought announces a "second Protestant Reformation" to come (Dickey, cited in DP, p. 185). But Hegel takes himself to belong to a time in which it is "Philosophy" and not "Religion" that has become dominant, so one could equally well say his thought announces a "second Enlightenment" to come. It is certainly not his ambition to go back to the "monstrous superstitions" of an enchanted nature "which magic alone could conquer" (PH, p. 459). But a world in which "the Host was simply *dough*, the relics of the Saints mere *bones*,...all miracles *disallowed*"? Kant's thought, for Hegel, wittingly or unwittingly promotes a public consciousness that "can be indifferent to religion" (PH, p. 464), indeed metaphysically speaking it even "maintains an adverse position to religion" (PH, p. 463). And this is a situation that philosophy should, on behalf of everyone, work a way through and beyond.

The spiritual journey, the philosophical history of spirit, begins, for Hegel, as we have seen, in the East, and the first part of the book, "Part I. The Oriental World", starts us there, although only with the interest of witnessing a "transition to the Greek world", among whom, for the first time, "we feel ourselves at home" (PH, p. xxxii). Then we enter the golden thread proper, and the book covers "Part II. The Greek World"; "Part III. The Roman World"; "Part IV. The German World" – with the final Chapter of the final Section ("The Modern Time") of that final Part taking us to the one reference to a Kant whose entry has, as I have indicated, been thoroughly prepared for already. Stepping through the one-some-all of the continuity/transformation of Spirit in history, the final "gradation" is arrived at with the Lutheran reformation, the essence of which, Hegel argues, is the understanding that "Man is destined to be free" (PH, p. xxxix), an understanding that then makes a "slow" introduction into European "political life" (ibid.).

In the Sibree translation, the final chapter of the final part, Chapter Three of Part IV, is entitled "*Eclaircissement* and Revolution", announcing a distinctively French involvement in this passage of history. In fact, Hegel's German title is "*Die Aufklärung und Revolution*", which rather more faithfully articulates the interplay between German thought and French politics that he focusses on, and in which the reference to Kant will announce Kant's pivotal position in both. That Germano-French but, as we shall see, fundamentally Kantian event, "the French Revolution" is at the centre of Hegel's attention in his narration of "the last stage of history, our own time" (PH, p. 461). The book closes with an assessment of how far Kant's merely formal consciousness of freedom has affected Europe's political life more widely, and Hegel's implicit call for a further development which would introduce in turn the radically different, and historically final, understanding of human freedom that he has himself attained. Looking out over Europe from his attained rampart, Hegel can even see its nascent but imperfect realisation – not in post-revolutionary France, and not at all in England either, but...in the Germanic world, and thus brings to the stage of world history the spectre of a new political life of real freedom, first, in a Germanic world to come. To get to that, to beget it, he needs to get past Kant and his merely formal freedom. Hegel's final chapter in the final part of his philosophical history takes a detour through France and the dead end it had reached in the aftermath of its revolution to do what he can to make it so that it will have been the dead end of

Kant too. Chapter Three of Part IV refers only once to Kant – but it is really all about (getting beyond) Kant.

IV

One way in which this movement beyond Kant takes place in Hegel's text is in its presentation of the developments before Kant's entry: Hegel's discussion of the (as we might say) pre-Kantian opening of Europe's modernity is already strikingly Kantian. We are told that the history of Protestantism and Catholicism "left nothing remaining" for thought to contemplate about our own spirit apart from "the form of Universality" – the form of Thought itself, as the "Abstraction of Spirit" (PH, p. 457), abstracted, first of all, from all genuinely spiritual (religious) content, and "moves within the limits of its own sphere". The focus, then, is on "an utter and absolute Freedom for the pure Ego". Nothing encountered for that Ego in its immediate presence is "alien", and the idea of the "unity of thought and its object" is implicitly present too, or again "the Objects of Thoughts are no longer an absolutely distinct form of existence". Hegel describes this as the "ne plus ultra of Inwardness": anything radically "outside" the sphere of the pure "I" is absolutely "other" and "alien". God, the highest subject matter for thought "remained an ultramundane affair" (PH, p. 457), and all mundane affairs are comprehended in terms of "Laws of Nature" which are "recognised as the only bond connecting phenomena with phenomena", but in a world in which Man is fundamentally "at home" (HP, p. 459). Morality too is no longer referred to as "the command of God" but "as having their foundation in the Will of man" (PH, p. 459).

The "intellectual consciousness" Hegel is elucidating here is represented as that belonging to Descartes (PH, p. 458). And so perhaps it is. But this is a Descartes who seems everywhere to be simply Kant *avant la lettre*, Kant spectrally appearing here already even before his name appears. So when Hegel says this thought passes "from France into Germany", and "created a new world of ideas" there (PH, p. 460), one can only feel that what was presented as so far untouched by German thought has already been painted in German, and distinctively Kantian, colours. Even the first Germanic appearances of it "in the first instance", again before Kant's name arrives on the scene, have Kant's fingerprints all over them: "The principle of thought" at the heart of this Franco-Germanic *Eclaircissement/Aufklärung*, is that all authority based on "religious belief and positive ideas of Right" would be replaced "by the verdict passed by Spirit itself on the character of that which is to be believed or obeyed" (HP, p. 460), adding further that, that which is "just and moral", which must be distinguished from anything based on mere "inclination", "belongs to the essential independent, intrinsically universal Will", the Will of "Man", "nay it is even that by which Man becomes Man" (PH, p. 462). Hegel does not leave it there, supplementing his already rich description with his own diagnostic assessment of this development: "In fact, in this form it is nothing more than formal Will": not a "pure Will" which takes itself as "its own object", but a merely "abstract" and "individual" Will (PH, p. 462). If, as Hegel suggests, finally, this principle of formal freedom, the freedom of an atomistic, abstract, and individual Will, "obtained speculative recognition in Germany, in the *Kantian* philosophy" (PH, p. 462, see also, p. 465), it would seem that this is because he (Hegel) had already inscribed it in the pre-Kantian world.

Since Kant, it is, indeed, almost impossible to read Descartes and (as we say) pre-Kantian German philosophy without seeing in it something of Kant. So Hegel's portrait of the Franco-Germanic set-up before Kant's arrival is not absurd. But it streamlines differences with a purpose. Funnelling everything Franco-Germanic into his frame of the emergence of Kant as the champion of a merely formal conception of freedom prepares for a dramatic denouement concerning the political life of Europe after Kant's arrival. On the other side of the Kantian event that "obtained speculative recognition" of the (already rather Kantian) spiritual history of post-Reformation Europe, Hegel identifies a profound fork in the Franco-Germanic road, with quite different developments unfolding in, on the one hand, the Germanic world (later to add a related situation in England), and on the other hand, in France in relation to the Kantian view of freedom. Hegel introduces this divergence by claiming that "among the Germans this [Kantian] view assumed no other form than that of tranquil theory; but the French wished to give it practical effect" (PH, p. 462).

In view here was a differential situation facing, on the one hand, an already Reformed Germanic world, which had begun to restrict the Church's authority in secular relations, and, on the other hand, a France still stuck with the "dead weight" of Catholic power, and its "pernicious institutions" inappropriately involved in secular law. In addition, France still had a King and his "Divine Right". France needed to make the new "theoretical" development in the consciousness of freedom "practical" in a way the Germanic world did not (PH, p. 464). The French Revolution thus received its "first impulse" from Kant's "abstract thought" of universal individual freedom.

Kant is thus presented, strikingly but perhaps correctly, as the progenitor of the French Revolution with the principle of Kantian formal (universal, individual) freedom being "asserted against existing Right" (PH, p. 465), an eventuality made possible by the complete mess existing Right was in at the time in France: "a confused mass of privileges altogether contravening Thought and Reason" (PH, p. 465), simply "one mass of injustice" (PH, p. 466). Despite the fact, then, that Kant's philosophy falls a chasm short of the "concrete comprehension of absolute Truth" belonging to (Hegel's) fully self-conscious consciousness of freedom, it "asserted its authority" and was put to effective service against the old Catholic framework which "could offer no resistance" (PH, p. 466). Going beyond even Kant's assessment of its significance, Hegel observed that "all thinking beings shared the jubilation of this epoch" (presumably Burke was not among thinking beings), and then perhaps thinking specifically of Kant, added that "emotions of a lofty character stirred men's minds at that time" (PH, p. 466). You can feel the Hegelian "but" coming. In fact, there are at least fifteen scattered "buts" planted along Hegel's subsequent review of "the course which the revolution took in France" (PH, p. 467). From a first note of foreboding about a governing stability that could not be achieved in France ("*But* the agency which gives the laws practical effect is the *Government* generally" (PH, p. 467)), to Hegel's final interruptive intervention into the "perpetually recurring misapprehension" of his time, the merely formal consciousness of freedom ("*But* Objective Freedom – the laws of real freedom – demand the subjugation of the mere contingent Will, – for that is in its nature formal" (PH, p. 476)), Hegel attempts to wrest away the hold on his time of "the *Kantian* philosophy". Napoleon, who "knew how to rule" was able, for some time, to "settle the internal affairs of France", and he did so by *sending off* "the abstract-principle men" (PH, p. 470). Settling his grievance, Hegel does his best to be a Napoleon of philosophy, and to *send off* Kant.

We can summarise most of the "buts" with Hegel's claim that by "asserting this formal side of Freedom – this abstraction – no political organization [can] be firmly established" (PH, p. 472). This is an interesting way to deliver the blow of the Hegelian grievance: taking a stand not simply on the theoretical shortcomings of a "perpetually recurring misapprehension" of freedom, but also on the impossibility of its practical implementation. Not only is it unable to deliver the freedom it claims optimally to maximise, it cannot even deliver on what Bernard Williams has called "the 'first' political question": namely, the possibility of "securing order, protection, safety, trust and the conditions of co-operation" within a State (IBWD, p. 3). Williams stresses that this is "first" in the sense that, if you cannot "solve" it, you cannot deliver on anything else at all. He adds, however, that solving it is not a merely theoretical achievement but necessarily an ongoing but always "first" practical requirement: it needs to be answered, "*all the time*" (IBWD, p. 3). A putative political set-up that cannot actually be set up in a way that can deliver even a relatively "identifiable and stabilizable" agency of government (constantly) fails at the "first" political hurdle.

Hegel calls the putative political set-up that belongs to the politics of liberty of the French Revolution by the name it calls itself (to be): "*Liberalism*" (PH, p. 471). And his claim is that the liberty tradition of political Liberalism cannot actually set itself up in any lasting way, cannot solve the "first" political question, and hence cannot be the set-up it claims to be, cannot found itself as a politics of freedom. Kant had celebrated the event of the French Revolution, as a cosmopolitical event, and independently of its (if any) consequences. But if the consequences are internally related to the Kantian conception of freedom that gives the "first impulse" to and "agitates the minds" of those caught up in it, a Kantian cannot remain so indifferent: Kant's political conception of liberty is itself on trial. His thought is caught up in it too. Its failure is his.

And the fault of "Liberalism"? For structural reasons inseparable from its commitment to formal freedom it cannot, according to Hegel, provide for the kind of stable government that can deliver the formal freedoms it promises. Liberalism is that form of political organisation "which insists" that "all government should emanate from [the] express power [of individual wills] and have their express sanction" (PH, pp. 471–2). Hegel has some fun looking at the way "advocates of liberty" in France constantly wind up denying its real attainment by constantly throwing out their governments. This kind of republican government, resting on the sovereignty of the people and hence the "consent of the citizens" (citizens construed as "anyone who has a right to vote", as Kant stressed (Kant, p. 77)), is not a governing principle but a no-governing principle. Zhou Enlai, a Chinese Communist leader during the twentieth century, on being asked about the significance of the French Revolution is famously (disputedly) reported as having replied "It is too soon to say". Hegel did not think we had to wait. "Agitation and unrest is perpetuated" by the democratic spirit of political Liberalism. And yet, this internal fault did not stop it from being diffused "to almost all modern states" in Europe, "particularly all the Romanic nations", but it didn't work anywhere it was tried.

In England…it was not tried. Hegel acknowledges the presence of a liberty tradition in England, but its parliament was so corrupt ("this also they call freedom") that it remained largely unaffected by the democratic upheavals in France. As a result "it provides for the possibility of a government" (PH, p. 475). The Germanic world, though of course "traversed by the victorious French" for a period, "delivered [itself] from this yoke" (PH, p. 475), and with its newly formed sovereign States replacing "the fiction of an Empire" the Germanic world was forging a national identity in opposition to the French one. While proudly noting that "offices of State are open to every citizen" this was not an invitation to perpetual upheaval, since "talent and adaptation" were the "necessary conditions" of office-holding, and not popular consent. As a result the "settled organization of the State" in the German sovereign States, as in England (though for less reprehensible reasons), meant that stable, lasting government was possible, and in part for the same reason: government is run by "*statesmen*": a body of men with "knowledge, experience and facility" in affairs of the State (PH, p. 475 (for England), p. 476 (for the Germanic world)).

But settled government by statesmen only solves the "first" political question. It doesn't make it Right (rather than Wrong). And the addition of a subjective side among the people in the State (an "acquiescence" and "cordial observance" of the laws in what Hegel calls "Disposition", which is basically patriotism) is not sufficient to make it so either. Government and some degree of Disposition are certainly necessary to the "stability of the State" (PH, p. 469), and both in England and in the Germanic world, unlike France, at least something of this "first" political question had been solved. But "intrinsic Right" requires something else too, something that only the Germanic world was beginning to deliver on: "Laws of Rationality", which Hegel calls laws of "Objective or Real Freedom" (PH, p. 467). In what is already a very rapid assault on the republican State form, Hegel drops in his three essential "elements and powers of the State" – Government, Disposition, Laws – fully formed and out of the blue, simply referring his reader to his lectures on the Philosophy of Right. Human beings, that is to say, "Man", could not but resonate to such laws, they "must correspond with the Reason [such laws] embody" (PH, p. 476), and hence these laws, the laws of real and not merely formal freedom, would also realise "Subjective Freedom" too.

Reflecting on the closing pages of Hegel's text, Stephen Houlgate suggests Hegel to suppose that "three modern states – France, England and Germany – more or less imperfectly realize [this] idea of [real] freedom"; they are each in their own way "*free enough* to be seen as essentially free, rational states" (WH, p. 414). But there is basically no stable government in France and only a corrupt stable government in England. The Germanic world alone, with "the Reason incorporated" into its "code of Rights", shows promise for Hegel (PH, p. 475–6). But it too can advance towards real freedom only if it can successfully keep at bay everything politically French – i.e. Kantian – only if it can resist the temptations of "merely formal" freedom, and thus successfully "subjugate…the mere contingent Will" of individuals. German success, were it ever to transpire – and Hegel's wager is that his own attained consciousness of freedom belongs to the conditions which will make it so that it must happen (making that success too a philosophical event) – would not only be a German event, though it would certainly be that, and not just a European event either, though it would be that too, but as the realisation of the freedom of Man as Man, an event of inter-national, world-historical significance: the exemplary possibility of the emancipation of theomorphic rational subjectivity. Hegel's "nationalism" too is a cosmo-nationalism, tied to an intrinsically universal and cosmopolitan horizon, to the promise of a properly State-differentiated globality in conditions of mutual recognition of a genuinely free humanity to come.

Marx was not impressed.

8
REAL HAPPINESS

Hegel, who inverts everything...

– Karl Marx

I

Hegel had wanted his philosophical history to help his reader, and his time, to arrive at what he calls "the concrete comprehension of absolute Truth" (PH, p. 465). This non-formal, non-abstract self-consciousness would amount to an understanding of the world and the significance of our lives (an understanding of the meaning of "Man") in a manner whose "general form" is "Religion", and thus has as its highest subject-matter, God (PH, p. 464). For Hegel, a "merely formal" consciousness of human freedom is and can remain entirely indifferent, even hostile, to religion. His own work, by contrast, is (Hegel believes) to be understood as simultaneously completing both Luther's "concrete" attainment of "Spiritual Freedom and Reconciliation" – establishing the position in religion "that Man's eternal destiny must be wrought out *in himself*, not...a work performed *for him*" (PH, p. 460) – and the Enlightenment demand that "what truth is to become vital in him" is not be "taken for granted as something already given, something revealed by religion" but "must be capable of actual investigation... and inward demonstration" (PH, p. 460). The task of "establishing man's eternal destiny" begun by Luther through the Reformation would be concretely completed in a wholly Enlightened, that is to say, essentially non-dogmatic, way, reconciling Man to the world as God's creation and, we should add, to the death of God in the "real world". Philosophy should thus lead on its own to the "insight" that "the real world is as it ought to be" (PH, p. 38). From a place where one bears witness to God's death in (the history of) the world, one finds one's way, in the sway of that self-sacrifice, to a consciousness that "the truly good – the universal divine reason – is not a mere abstraction, but a vital principle capable of realising itself" (PH, p. 38). This Good, this Reason, in its most concrete form, is God. And "God governs the world; the actual working of his government – the carrying out of his plan – is the History of the World" (PH, p. 38).

In the simple "inner focus" of the religiously informed life of "a shepherd or a peasant" this fundamentally reconciled consciousness has, in a certain way, already been attained (PH, p. 38); there is already something "present" there that is "quite shut out from the noisy din of the World's History" (PH, p. 39) – but its "basis" remains "still obscure and unknown to them" (PH, p. 39). And for many if not most people – all in the same condition of still imperfect self-consciousness – reconciliation is utterly inconceivable; and "they contrast unfavourably things as they *are*, with their idea of things as they *ought* to be" (PH, p. 36). Some may do so only in relation to their own private lives, but others, especially in modern times, in relation to "Reason, Justice, Liberty" – and who thus adopt a position "not merely of discontent, but of open revolt against the actual condition of the world" (PH, p. 36).

However, while the "subjective will" that adopts this kind of position "is that which sets men in activity" (PH, p.41), what is produced or actualised in and through this activity, what "obtains objectivity" through it (if it is not a merely private desire for one's own "prosperity" but is concerned with ideas of what is right and just), belongs internally to the ongoing elaboration of a concern with a social whole; with a fundamentally communalised existence. The activity thus has its "substantial life" in the developing life of what Hegel calls a State. It is the history of that "Whole", the unfolding of its development in time, that is the real "subject" of philosophical history: its development constitutes the history of "the Divine Idea as it exists on earth", making its way towards realisation, and hence towards the realisation of a complete self-consciousness of freedom in a spiritual, rational State governed by real laws of freedom (PH, p. 41).

Here again the "modern" Kantian "solution" of political liberalism, regarding the State as a means of achieving "universal limitation" in a way that might secure a "space of liberty for each", is represented as falling a chasm short of the true realisation of freedom. In our time, "the fundamental but abstractly (and therefore imperfectly) entertained conception of Freedom, has resulted in the Republic being very generally regarded – in theory – as the only just and true political constitution" (PH, p. 47). For Hegel, as we have seen, this "rooted prejudice" (PH, p. 5) needs to be overcome. In its place, Hegel projects the ideal of a State that embodies "real laws of Freedom", laws which "must" (could not but) receive subjective confirmation by rational beings, and hence of a State that forms and forges an ideal unity of the objectively rational and the subjectively rational will. The realisation of these conditions has not yet been achieved; the practical realisation of Hegel's philosophically attained consciousness of freedom is on its way, but remains to come. Nevertheless, real, though uneven, progress towards such practical realisation is a cause for hope, and has, Hegel argues, advanced farthest in those States in Europe which have been, practically speaking, least affected by Kantian liberal modernity: that is to say in the States of the Germanic world. Were it finally to be attained, Man would not become God, but our grieving spirit would be finally reconciled with the world as it is, and the State would attain a condition of ideally immutable stability: when Reason pervades the whole of life – in the existence of the fully rational State, not the perfectly republican State – Man *is* with God.

Before turning from Hegel's effort at overturning Kant to Marx's effort at overturning Hegel in turn, I want to say one more thing about Hegel's final word on the final end of Man in or with God. This time not from the final "The End" of his *Philosophy of History*, but from the final words, which are in fact not entirely Hegel's own words, of his *Phenomenology of Spirit* (§808), a text which will have wanted to lead to this attainment of complete self-understanding in another way:

> The goal, which is Absolute Knowledge or Spirit knowing itself as Spirit, finds its pathway in the recollection of spiritual forms [*Geister*] as they are in themselves and as they accomplish the organization of their spiritual kingdom. Their conservation, looked at from the side of their free existence appearing in the form of contingency, is History; looked at from the side of their intellectually comprehended organization, it is the Science of the ways in which knowledge appears. Both together, or History (intellectually) comprehended [*begriffen*], form at once the recollection and the Golgotha of Absolute Spirit, the reality, the truth, the certainty of its throne, without which it were lifeless, solitary, and alone; only – *from the chalice of this realm of spirits/foams forth for* Him *his own infinitude* [*Aus dem Kelche dieses Geisterreiches Schäumt* ihm *seine Unendlichkeit*].

The final line…drifts into poetry – raising the question of whether philosophy can, finally, reach its end by itself (see HLW, p. 146). In fact, Hegel's ending words borrow from and slightly change the final lines of the final stanza of Schiller's poem "*Die Freundschaft*" ("Friendship"):

> *Freundlos war der grosse Weltenmeister,*
> *Fühlte Mangel – darum schuf er Geister,*
> *Sel'ge Spiegel seiner Seligkeit!*
> *Fand das höchste Wesen schon kein gleiches,*
> *Aus dem Kelche des ganzen Seelenreiches*
> *Schäumt* ihm *– die Unendlichkeit.*

> Friendless was the great world-master
> Felt a lack – and so created spirits,
> Blessed mirrors of his own blessedness
> But the highest being still could find no equal.
> From the chalice of the whole realm of souls
> Foams up to *him* – infinitude.

Compare the two last lines:

HEGEL: *Aus dem Kelche dieses Geisterreiches/Schäumt* ihm *seine Unendlichkeit*
SCHILLER: *Aus dem Kelche des ganzen Seelenreiches/Schäumt* ihm *– die Unendlichkeit.*

Hegel re-writes Schiller. It is his own poetry now. And in Hegel's poetic finishing, what takes place in Man with the attained "recollection and Golgotha of Absolute Spirit" – that is to say from the place (somewhere where we may yet be) that belongs to an attained reconciliation with the death of God – is God attaining His own infinitude. In Man's grief-reconciled attaining to himself, God is given to himself.

Schiller is both more definite and more radically hesitant. What foams forth to Him (but I like the verticality of the English translation "foams *up* to him") is, certainly, the whole realm of souls. It is the movement of transcendence: Man reaching up, raising himself from horizontality, *towards* God. Indeed, as we have seen in a previous chapter, for the onto-theological tradition this "transcending-towards" is what Man *is*. Man is this reaching beyond, foaming *up* towards God. In his solitariness, God creates souls that would be in his own image, "a blessed mirror of his blessedness". But in this mirror, he could find no equal. And yet from the chalice of the whole realm of souls, the souls reach beyond themselves towards Him. Then Schiller writes a long dash: a silent mark of separation, a caesura. And on the other side of that separation, that infinite separation maintained in the "movement towards", it gives/there is (*es gibt*) God "pure and simple" as "the *transcendens*" (to quote Heidegger, on Being (BT, p. 62)).

For Hegel, it would seem that both Man and God find themselves in Man's attaining "the concrete comprehension of absolute truth", in a final reconciling negation of their separation (the dash has gone). Hegel's thought here is that finite spirit finds itself only by recognising itself in God, just as God, for Hegel, thereby sees Himself in the mirror of his creation. Wiggins had said that we are, in our time, more resistant to "mystical and metaphysical" conceptions of the world and the significance of our lives than Europeans of the eighteenth and nineteenth centuries knew how to be. I had begun by treating philosophical history as belonging entirely to the "metaphysical" side of this pair, even when it was "philosophical and religious". However, the Hegelian view is perhaps more "mystical" than it sometimes appears (see HSR, pp. 141–2).

If, as I have suggested, the mystical refers to an experience of Oneness or Unity with the Whole or the One, it also entails a loss of identification confined to or with "the individual", and that is something anyone might feel moved to experiment with. But one might worry about the fate of the individual in Hegel's thinking of the Whole that is the State. This worry might be most sharply felt in the context of Hegel's view of religion itself in the State. This is just one example where one might feel this, but this is obviously not one example among others in a history that aims to come to terms with its religious truth. What one finds, in this case, is that it is the church that matters not the religious individual. Robert Perkins summarises as follows:

> The church is the "Kingdom of the Spirit". It is in this kingdom that the individual has absolute and unqualified worth, and yet it is here that *community* becomes the form of the Christian life. The crux of the considerable tension between the radical worth of the individual and the more radical significance of the community is love. Love is the mediating power between particular and exclusive subjectivity and the church. The emphasis which Hegel placed upon the community in *The Philosophy of Right* is repeated with reference to the church. The same ambiguities of the individual and the State are repeated here. There is no place for the individual considered simply as such. Perhaps nowhere is it more plain than here that Kierkegaard made an authentic criticism of Hegel's philosophy when he says that the *individual* is the decisive Christian category [not the church]. (HSR, p. 136)

The fate of the individual, of our understanding of what it is to be an individual human being, has been central to the philosophical debates that have continued between "liberalism" and "communitarianism" in contemporary political philosophy since Kant and Hegel, and is obviously key to Hegel's critique of Kant, whose political theory he (Hegel) took to have its "basis" in "the principle of isolated individuality – the absolute validity of the subjective will" (PH, p. 50). (Bernard Williams seems to me right when he argues that this conception of the individual "is *not* the foundation of the liberal state" (IBWD, p. 8), but the reader can follow that for themselves.) In his battle with Kant, it is not surprising that his most difficult task is to convince his readers that a radical "limitation of self-will" is not a "fettering of Freedom [but] the indispensable proviso of emancipation" (PH, p. 43). For Kant, such limitation is, of course, both of those things (both freedom-fettering and freedom-emancipating, one through the other), but this is not the kind of "subjugation of the mere contingent Will" that Hegel has to defend. Concretely, as we have seen, Hegel's effort is carried out forcefully but, in its fifteen-carriage train of "buts", rather quickly at the end of the *Philosophy of History*, when he sketches the three necessary conditions for the kind of stable State that is required for rational rights to be conferred on anyone in the first place. In this regard, it is worth recalling that to pursue this cause in such haste, Hegel has to introduce these three elements without independent argument: as we have seen, they are drawn into the text as a summary of an "examination in detail" that Hegel devoted to them in a different work, in fact, the very one Perkins refers to in the quotation above: in the *Philosophy of Right* (see PH, p. 467). This is a significant text for us. For it is with his engagement with Hegel's thought as elaborated in that text that Marx will make his way beyond Hegel.

As we shall see, Marx's revolt against Hegel shares Hegel's antipathy towards Kantianism and its (supposedly) thinned-out conception of the individual. Marx wants to jump over that too. He also shares Hegel's (related) view that the development of political liberalism stops short of the conditions that will really allow for the full self-realisation (and hence freedom) of Man. However, for Marx, the shift required to achieve that is not a shift away from the "formal universality" of the republican form of government to what he (Marx) thinks of (justly I think) as the "mystical universality" of the Hegelian State form, but a shift to the "real universality" of actual democracy. Once more, the generation of spirit will pivot on a dispute about religion. As we shall see, however, the development of philosophical history will be effected by the same critical key or club: namely, that the fundamental defect of the conception to be overcome is that it is *"merely formal"*. I will turn next to Marx's critique of Hegel, and the entrance of a thought of democracy as central to the movement of world history – with Europe, once again, at the head of the pack.

II

With the exception of its Introduction, which was published in 1844, four years before the *Communist Manifesto*, Marx's *Critique of Hegel's Philosophy of Right* is not a text prepared for publication. It comprises a comment-by-comment commentary on just the third (and final) section of the third (and final) part of Hegel's text, the section on "The State", and of that it covers only the preamble and first subsection "Internal Polity", which runs from §§257–320 of Hegel's text. Some of Marx's commentary has been lost, and it finishes abruptly with a comment on §313. It is a pity that Marx did not get to continue a little further – or if he did that we have lost it – because the second subsection is on "International Law" (which we will look at when we consider the prospects for the European Union in the next volume) and the third and final subsection is on "World History", where Hegel runs rapidly through "the four world-historic worlds...(1) the Oriental, (2) the Greek, (3) the Roman, and (4) the Germanic" (HPR, §354), which, in turn, frame the text of the *Philosophy of History*, into which something of the *Philosophy of Right* was dropped in. Hegel's first comment on the last of the four worlds once more sets the scene of his own work in terms of what, in the *Phenomenology of Spirit*, he called "the recollection and the Golgotha of Absolute Spirit"; foregrounding the Germanic world as a world steeped in "the infinite grief for the Crucified God", and announcing that the reconciliation of the divine and human, of objective truth and freedom, is "entrusted to the Germans to *complete*" (HPR, §258). That is to say, entrusted to Hegel to complete.

The text by Marx that we have does not get to that, but from what he says in the published Introduction to the unpublished *Critique* one can be sure that he would have had at best an ambivalent sympathy for Hegel's "infinite grief". The turn from a universal history that is "philosophical and religious" to one that is "philosophical and scientific" is not only "without God", not just non-religious, but is essentially anti-religious, "irreligious":

> For Germany, the criticism of religion has been essentially completed, and the criticism of religion is the prerequisite of all criticism.
>
> The profane existence of error is compromised as soon as its heavenly *oratio pro aris et focis* ["speech for the altars and hearths"] has been refuted. Man, who has found only the reflection of himself in the fantastic reality of heaven, where he sought a superman, will no longer feel disposed to find the mere appearance of himself, the non-man [*Unmensch*], where he seeks and must seek his true reality.
>
> The foundation of irreligious criticism is: Man makes religion, religion does not make man.
>
> Religion is, indeed, the self-consciousness and self-esteem of man who has either not yet won through to himself, or has already lost himself again. But, *man* is no abstract being squatting outside the world. Man is *the world of man* — state, society. This state and this society produce religion, which is an *inverted* consciousness of the world, because they are an inverted world. Religion is the general theory of this world, its encyclopaedic compendium, its logic in popular form, its spiritual *point d'honneur*, its enthusiasm, its moral sanction, its solemn complement, and its universal basis of consolation and justification. It is the fantastic realization of the human essence since the human essence has not acquired any true reality. The struggle against religion is, therefore, indirectly the struggle against that world whose spiritual aroma is religion.
>
> Religious suffering is, at one and the same time, the expression of real suffering and a protest against real suffering. Religion is the sigh of the oppressed creature, the heart of a heartless world, and the soul of soulless conditions. It is the opium of the people.
>
> The abolition of religion as the *illusory* happiness of the people is the demand for their *real* happiness. To call on them to give up their illusions about their condition is to call on them to give up a condition that requires illusions. The criticism of religion is, therefore, in embryo, the criticism of that vale of tears of which religion is the halo.
>
> Criticism has plucked the imaginary flowers on the chain not in order that man shall continue to bear that chain without fantasy or consolation, but so that he shall throw off the chain and pluck the living flower. The criticism of religion disillusions man, so that he will think, act, and fashion his reality like a man who has discarded his illusions and regained his senses, so that he will move around himself as his own true Sun. Religion is only the illusory Sun which revolves around man as long as he does not revolve around himself.
>
> It is, therefore, the task of history, once the other-world of truth has vanished, to establish the truth of this world. It is the immediate task of

philosophy, which is in the service of history, to unmask self-estrangement in its unholy forms once the holy form of human self-estrangement has been unmasked. Thus, the criticism of Heaven turns into the criticism of Earth… (CHPR, p. 3)

Marx's thundering rhetoric anticipates the basic "dialectical" movement of his comments on Hegel in the *Critique*: it has everything back to front, and it needs to be "reversed" (CHPR, p. 14). Marx is famous for expressing his relation to Hegel in this way, stating in the opening of *Capital* (Volume 1, p. 25) that "with [Hegel] dialectics is standing on its head. It must be turned right side up again, if you would discover the rational kernel within the mystical shell". Or again:

> My dialectic method is not only different from the Hegelian, but is its direct opposite. To Hegel,…the process of thinking which, under the name of "the Idea", he even transforms into an independent subject, is the *demiurgos* [creator] of the real world, and the real world is only the external, phenomenal form of "the Idea". With me, on the contrary, the ideal is nothing else than the material world reflected by the human mind and translated into forms of thought. (Marx, Afterword to the Second German Edition of Volume I of *Capital*.)

Nowhere is Hegel more mystifying for Marx than in his conception of history. And as Marx insists it will be *via* history, *via* a very philosophical history as we shall see, that we can "establish the truth of this world". Indeed, the surviving critical commentary begins with an interpretation of Hegel's approach to history that tries to bring out "an obvious mystification" in it (CHPR, p. 19). History, for Hegel, is always a "two-fold history": one "esoteric" (largely unknown to anyone) and one "exoteric" (likely to be understood by anyone). The first is the development of the Idea; the second, the circumstance and choices of "real people". Marx emphasises that for Hegel what should be described as "real", the "real development", "proceeds on the esoteric side". Defending Hegel against Marx's seeing something problematic here, Stephen Houlgate shows in compelling detail that Hegel does "not…downplay the importance of human agency in history" (WH, p. 98). This is absolutely true, but I don't think Marx would disagree. Marx recognises Hegel's stress on the "empirical actuality" of human agency, and its rationality. The issue is not the significance of human agency but that agency's significance. And here, Marx thinks, Hegel presents the "real" significance of that agency as lying beyond the rationality of its own reason; not in its own reason but the Idea in its necessary development "glimmering in them" (CHPR, p. 15). This, for Marx, is the fundamental mysticism of Hegel's conception of history as "the inner self-development of the Idea" (CHPR, p. 16). Instead of drawing, or attempting to draw, a conception of history "out of what is objective" in an empirical-theoretical and scientific way, Hegel bases his history on "a ready-made thought which has its origin in the abstract sphere of logic" (CHPR, p. 19).

This is, of course, the basic objection to philosophical history as both Kant and Hegel pursue it, indeed it is the objection that provokes their own anxiety that only a work of fiction can result from an "*a priori*" approach to history. Marx thinks that when a conception of the "end [*telos*] of the State" is so fundamentally divorced from the real existence and empirical actuality of political agents – real human beings – and their own reason with its properly "exoteric" intelligibility, when this is not acknowledged to be the dimension in which "the real development proceeds", then our approach "is an obvious mystification" (CHPR, p. 19).

With the esoteric/exoteric distinction in view, and with Hegel wanting to dignify "esoteric" history with the title "real" and "concrete", Marx concludes the first phase of his reading. In doing so, he introduces (or re-introduces) into the discussion the concept of the "formal" that structures Hegel's assault on Kant's conception of freedom: "The concrete content, the actual determination, appears to be formal, and the wholly abstract formal determination appears to be the concrete content" (CHPR, p. 21). The concept of the formal, and especially the "merely formal", will once again be central to the battle, central to Marx's effort to stand the Hegelian logic on its head. And when you stand Hegel's logic on its head, you are back on your feet.

Back on your feet – but not back to Kant. Marx's "real human beings", the real subjects of history, are (supposedly) individuals of a completely ordinary sort; some of them have "beards", for example (CHPR, p. 25). But for Marx, just as for Hegel, the Kantian individual is an individual abstractly conceived, conceived, that is to say, in isolation and not in society. Marx's "real human beings" are social beings through and through (including their beards, for those with beards), realising themselves in society; and for that part of humanity which has come historically to organise itself socially in a State, as part of a *demos*, each as among the "all" that is "the people". Again, Marx reverses Hegel: "As though the people [*das Volk*] were not the real State. The State is an abstraction, the people alone is the concrete". Marx finds "a great confusion" prevailing in Hegel when he "ascribes living qualities to the abstraction" without hesitation, but "only hesitantly to real people" (CHPR, p. 30).

The concept of the *demos* will tie the general form of every State, every such communalised form of human existence, to the concept of *democracy*, as that mode of human self-organisation that belongs to the "self-determination of the people" (CHPR, p. 32). So when Marx begins to speak about "the people" and "the sovereignty of the people" in a specifically "modern" State, his language shifts away from and displaces Hegel's Kantian specification: it is not to be understood as "a republican form of government" but (always) some kind of "a democratic form". All States are, formally speaking, democracies since all states are historically self-organised, self-determined, modes of existence for human beings in society. "*Democracy is human existence*" (CHPR, p. 31), says Marx, and different forms of the State are particular modifications of this universal form. In a monarchy, for example, "we have the people of the constitution", but where the democratic form is itself a democracy we have "the constitution of the people".

In the latter, however, the constitution has been returned to "its real ground", the "actual people", to "actual man" – "its own work" becomes its own work (CHPR, p. 31). In an actual and not only formal democracy we thus find "the first true unity of the universal and the particular" in human social existence (CHPR, p. 31).

For Hegel, the State as an organised "body" is a specialised whole (administration, bureaucracy, executive, legislature, and so on) which leaves out of a genuinely political existence the vast majority of society as merely "civil society". In an actual democracy, the political State as a particular "differentiated" from the whole disappears: it is both in form and in concrete reality "self-determination of the people". All States have this structure as their "truth", and thus all are "false" to the extent that they are not actual democracies. The Republican form is just such a "false" form (CHPR, p. 32). It is a profoundly teleological conception: democracy as the general form of all human political society realises itself in history, the end [*telos*] of democracy as a political form (a form of State) is the end [*terminus*] of the State form as a differentiated power within society. That is, because democracy is essentially the form of the State in general, the end [*telos*] of democracy is the end [*terminus*] of democracy as a differentiated State form. (At issue here is a particularly clear case of what Geoffrey Bennington has identified as a characteristic of all teleological conceptions of politics, "for which the end of politics is the end of politics" (*Scatter 1*, p. 243).) Ultimately, in fact, the State form of a democracy will itself "wither away" altogether in a communist society, with no need for a State apparatus at all. As Engels put it, the end of the history of class antagonism is a condition in which "the government of persons is replaced by the administration of things" (cited SR, p. 13). In a formulation of Lenin's that I will come back to, history will then have delivered "the final word" on democracy. Moreover, the universalisation of this achievement to the whole of humanity – the internationalisation of the end of democracy as the end of politics – is at the same time the de-differentiation of States, one from another. The withering away of the political State announces the possibility of the withering away of the nation and its "mystique" in the "religion" of the people, and hence announces, as we have seen, a (politically) de-differentiated humanity to come as the final goal of human self-development.

It is, however, once more, from Germany, from a specifically German heading, that this communist future will be led. Indeed, in Marx's first words of the Critique, it is "for Germany", that this future, which is the "near future" for other "modern nations" in Europe, is most sharply immediate: it is "for Germany" to raise itself "to the height of humanity" – and by that example to lead the way for all other nations, first in Europe (CHPR, p. 7).

Marx describes his criticism of Hegel as getting him (Marx) involved with a representation and defence of a German *status quo* that needs not to be refuted but destroyed. He is relentlessly aggressive here: he is involved "in a hand-to-hand fight, and in such a fight the point is not whether the opponent is a noble, equal, interesting opponent, the point is to strike him" (CHPR, p. 5). Let's watch this fight over the meaning of history, and Europe's centrality to that history, and see Marx's generation from Hegel in the turnabouts of the "merely formal" that proceed and process from the skull of Kant.

III

Hegel's history, for Marx, is a "biography" (CHPR, p. 38). But within the schema of an esoteric history, this appears now as the biography of "an abstract Idea" and no longer the activity of socially real humanity: it is the activity "of something other than Man", even if, exoterically, the activity of human beings remains necessary (CHPR, p. 38). With this set-up "the impression of something mystical" is created, and the critical-scientific spirit of Marx finds this intolerable, once again insisting that "the true method is turned upside down" (CHPR, p. 39). However, turning Hegel on his head will still require something to take the position of the interest of "universal Reason". For Marx, this is "the proletariat": a class of society whose "particular" interest can, he argues, become "universal", and in a true democracy can simply be "really universal" (CHPR, p. 47). The proletariat comprises propertyless persons, people whose only "their own", and all they "have", is their own labour-power – which they must sell in return for wages, in order, simply, to live. This class is given no part to play in and hence has no particular interest in the differentiated State/society system of Germany and only suffers from it, and hence "cannot emancipate itself without emancipating itself from all other spheres of society and thereby emancipating all other spheres of society" (CHPR, p. 10). Their interest coincides with their only "title": human interest (CHPR, p. 10). Within any State/Society system, this interest is already formally everyone's interest, and in conditions of actual democracy, the satisfaction of private interests would be replaced by the satisfaction of that universal interest, the only real interest.

When the proletariat act in their interest, they act with the interest of the whole. Marx contrasts this with the formally parallel group in Hegel's system: those who (in Hegel's view) "forego the satisfaction of private ends" by acting only in the interest of "the whole": the disinterested dedication to the State offered by "the civil servants" (CHPR, p. 47). Entry into the civil service is the one "democratic" moment that Hegel is unequivocally in favour of: the "chance" is open, in principle, as we have noted, to every citizen (though not everyone in society qualifies as a citizen). In terms of the movement towards genuine democracy, the "chance" to become part of this "pseudo-universal" class is effectively, as Marx puts it, "desertion" to the enemy (CHPR, p. 47). In this formal parallel between these two groups, we are heading towards Marx's generation of a new charge of the "merely formal" beyond Hegel's charge against Kant.

Marx begins this phase of his commentary with the observation that while Hegel shows "great respect" for the universal *Staatgeist* embodied in the disinterested work of state officers and employees, and their concern for public affairs, he shows no interest or respect for the "public consciousness" (roughly what today we call "public opinion") that belongs to "the Many" in civil society, which he (Hegel) identifies only as "an empirical universal". Marx is not simply going to reverse this opposition, but wants to note that Hegel delimits the concept of *"those concerned with public affairs"* in such a way as to exclude from the content of that concept the very public whose affairs they concern. In the modern German state, a concern with "public affairs" is anything but a public affair. The concept of "public affairs" is thus, in Hegel, "purely formal", whereas the public affairs it concerns is, Marx reminds us, the people's "substantial existence" – an existence which is thus excluded by the existing State/society set-up from having as its business the very thing that most immediately concerns it: itself. "The form which is supposed [by Hegel] to be the *actual* form of the content doesn't have the actual content for its content" (CHPR, p. 57). Hence, Marx concludes, wielding against Hegel the Kantian weapon that Hegel had wielded against Kant, in the Hegelian analysis and defence of the German State the conception of the "true actuality of public affairs" is *"merely formal"* (CHPR, p. 58).

Against this set-up, Marx calls for the concern with public affairs to become a properly public affair since they really "actually" are public affairs. Once again, the call is for the realisation of a "true" democracy: a democratic form ("the self-determination of the people") that takes its own content ("the self-determination of the people") as its content. If we call those who have a concern for public affairs distinctively "political citizens", we can see that the State set-up Hegel defends generally reserves that title for a specialised citizenry, and the "communal being" [*das Kommunistiche Wesen*] within which real individuals "exist" is separated from, indeed "alienated" from political existence (CHPR, p. 70). And yet, as beings for whom a communal or social being is the basic mode of their being – we are political animals after all (this is still in the tradition of Aristotle) – Hegel's denial to the "Many" of a properly political citizenship shows up yet another merely formal character of his account of existence in the State: "political existence" itself, existence in the *polis*.

It is not that the apparatus of the German State had no connection to civil society. The election of one of the Estates, the Chamber of Deputies, was a representative body of sorts, elected by propertied citizens. This is also what was politically "modern" in the German constitution, a constitution which had, as Hegel had happily pointed out, remained largely untouched by Kantian modernity. In the *Philosophy of History*, he had claimed that a polity based on "merely formal" freedom was structurally unstable and couldn't last. The *Philosophy of Right* makes a similar claim, and does so in terms that challenge Marx's argument over public affairs:

> To hold that every single person should share in deliberating and deciding on political matters of general concern on the ground that all individuals are members of the State, that its concerns are their concerns, and that it is their right that what is done should be done with their knowledge and

> volition, is tantamount to a proposal to put the democratic element without any rational form into the organism of the State, although it is only in virtue of the possession of such a form that the State is an organism at all. This idea comes readily to mind because it does not go beyond the abstraction of "being a member of the State" and it is superficial thinking which clings to abstractions. (cited, CHPR, p. 96)

In the ongoing battle over what is "abstract" and "formal" and what is "real" and "concrete", Marx's response changes their places at breakneck speed to great effect:

> Hegel calls being a member of the State an abstraction, although according to the idea, [and therefore] the intention of his own doctrinal development, it is the highest and most concrete social determination of the legal person, of the member of the State. To stop at the abstraction of "being a member of the State" and to conceive of individuals in terms of this abstraction does not therefore seem to be just superficial thinking which clings to abstractions. That the abstraction of "being a member of the State" is really an abstraction is not, however, the fault of this thinking but of Hegel's line of argument and actual modern conditions, which presuppose the separation of actual life from political life and make the political quality an abstraction of actual participation in the State. (CHPR, p. 96)

Marx's basic point is surely a good one: it is only because citizens of the State are not all equally "political citizens" that Hegel can call citizenship an abstraction. That is to say, Hegel's response belongs with and only makes sense in terms of a State form that effectively separates the actual life of civil society from political life.

As we have seen Hegel is hostile to the State becoming politically "modern". Or rather he rejects what he calls the merely formal conception of freedom that is affirmed in the modern-state idea that "every single person should share in deliberating and deciding on political matters of general concern". In Hegel's view, that basically Kantian idea falls a chasm short of a properly rational State. Marx is not averse to the idea that a truly or actually democratic State should be thought of as a rational State, but he does not think democracy deprives a polity of any rational form, indeed he thinks that it is its realest form and nothing could be more rational. However, that does not mean he subscribes to a (supposedly) Kantian – which is to say individualist – conception of being a member of the State. Marx now jumps over Kant at the same time as he jumps over Hegel:

> In a really rational State one could [indeed, with Hegel] answer, "Not every single person should share in deliberating and deciding on political matters of general concern", because the individuals share in deliberating

and deciding on matters of general concern as the "all", that is to say, within and as members of the society. Not all individually, but the individuals as all. (CHPR, p. 96)

For Marx, "the self-determination of the people" has its historical reality in the State organisation of its life, and simply is "the matter of general concern"; it is the place for deliberating and deciding on matters of public concern. For this reason, being a member of a democratic State, having a properly political existence, is in the interest of all. When such an existence is fully realised, or realised to the utmost, "the people" will, finally, be objectively free, existing in a State in which self-determination of the people is nothing other than self-determination by the people.

It is a question about freedom for all, a form of freedom that, against Hegel, Marx will also call [small "s"] "subjective" in a non-formal sense: "[small 's'] subjective freedom appears in Hegel as formal freedom precisely because Hegel has not presented objective freedom as the actualization, the activity of subjective freedom". "Actual subjective freedom…takes on a formal meaning" for Hegel because he takes the real and objective content of freedom in terms of his "mystical" determination of it, as "knowing what the absolute Will, Reason, Wills" (CHPR, p. 57). For Marx, the "actual content of freedom" is free self-realisation of all in the *polis*. It is the end [*telos*] of democracy. In the *Critique*, he explicitly holds back from developing this idea beyond the context of reforming the German State so as to catch up with the political modernity that (as Hegel supposed too) German philosophy had, *via* Kant, stimulated elsewhere in Europe ("Germans *thought* what other nations *did*" (CHPR, p. 7)). So in the *Critique*, Marx limits himself to a call for universal suffrage and the transformation of Germany to the "official level" of Europe's modern nations, and to do everything one could to make interest representation from civil society in the State something resembling a representation of its interests.

This was 1843. Four years later the *Communist Manifesto* declared that properly constituted Communist Parties have only one interest: "they have no interest separate and apart from those of the proletariat as a whole", and their aim was to achieve "political power by the proletariat" (CM, p. 17). That interest did not in the least contradict the ambition for the reforms called for in the *Critique*. Indeed, in both texts, electoral reform was clearly seen as a first step only in a very quick two-step. The first step was to become a modern State: "If I negate the situation in Germany in 1843, then according to the French calendar I have barely reached 1789, much less the vital centre of our present age…The struggle against the German political present is the struggle against the past of the modern nations" (CHPR, pp. 4–5). But Marx did not think there was a future for Germany in which it would simply become contemporary with modern nations. In a way, rather uncannily like Hegel, Marx was convinced that the German State apparatus could not long survive in a republican form, especially in conditions of universal suffrage. Germany's anachronistic not-yet-modern State set-up was not beyond reform but attaining the first reform, "the merely political revolution", would require an emancipatory act by the proletariat so widespread – an act through which it would "attain general domination" (CHPR, p. 9) – that having once got there it could not stop there. "In Germany, no form of bondage can be broken without breaking all forms of bondage. Germany... cannot make a revolution unless it is a thorough one" (CHPR, p.11). For Marx, then, the task required simply to achieve "the extension and greatest possible universalisation of voting" in Germany (CHPR, p. 99) that would, perforce, lead immediately to a mould-breaking shift from the existing order, smashing the edifice of the old differentiated State order in producing a new and properly democratic and de-differentiating proletarian State. The first step, the becoming modern of the German State, could not, in Germany, be attained and still "leave the pillars of the house standing": a new proletarian democratic State, radically de-differentiating State and society, comes into being (CHPR, p. 9). As I suggested at the end of the last section, Marx seems to have had no doubt that a change that would take Germany "to the *official level* of modern nations" would immediately drive it on further "to the *height of humanity*", the German nation thereby giving the example "which will be the near future of those [modern] nations" too (CHPR, p. 7), and the more distant future of all. In the classic style of European philosophical history, Marx affirms his Communist promise with the philosophical prediction or prophesy that "the emancipation of the German is the emancipation of Man" (CHPR, p. 11). The German philosophical event that had given birth to Europe's political modernity, the liberal Kantian one, would be followed by a new German philosophical event – not Hegelian but self-consciously Marxist, an event that would beget a communist future first for Europe, and then for the whole world.

It didn't happen in Germany. It happened in Russia. In the next chapter we will follow it there, following the line of begetting that takes us to the generation of Lenin. At that point we will also stumble across another ghost in Valéry's chain: Valéry himself appearing on the wider European scene, there where, in the ruins of old Europe, the discourse of Europe's modernity would become a discourse of modern Europe's crisis.

9
COMPLETE DEMOCRACY

> *Our Revolution, which was haunted by the Museum of Antiquities, is now in turn haunting the first impulses of the revolution in Russia*
>
> – Paul Valéry

I

Marx reiterated his Germanic two-step in the *Communist Manifesto*, placing Germany squarely at the forefront of the universal human development towards the end [*telos*] of democracy:

> The Communists turn their attention chiefly to Germany, because that country is on the eve of a bourgeois revolution that is bound to be carried out under more advanced conditions of European civilization, and with a much more developed proletariat, than that of England was in the seventeenth, and France in the eighteenth century, and because the bourgeois revolution in Germany will be but the prelude to an immediately following proletarian revolution. (CM, p. 39)

To the surprise of many, perhaps not least themselves, it was not the German Communists who managed to lead the only successful Marxist coup ("so far") against "the powers of old Europe", but the Russian Bolsheviks. Already a potential candidate when Valéry was composing his European Hamlet in 1919, one possible interpolation into the chain of ghosts had already arrived on the scene when he composed it ...*and Marx qui genuit Lenin*. I want to open this chapter by looking at Lenin's discussion of democracy and democratic freedom in his book *State and Revolution*, composed in August and September 1917, right on the actual eve of the October coup. And I will join the battle over the merely formal.

The parenthetical "so far" I feel I had to concede a moment ago touches on one of the great difficulties of writing about Marx and Marxism "since Marx": the Marxist event is not over, it is still "haunting Europe", still sending its "*Marx qui genuit…*" back, in the form of an at least seemingly inevitable return of an always possible "next time". One cannot argue with that, but one can try to come to terms with it, and as Derrida suggests in *Specters of Marx*, learn to "filter" its inheritance in a responsible way (SM, p. 54). We encountered the fundamental distinction of the Marxist event earlier: it effected a changeover for philosophical history from a form that was "philosophical and religious" to one that was "philosophical and scientific", binding philosophy in that movement to a newly internationalised geopolitics of freedom within an increasingly (politically) de-differentiated human horizon, as well as proposing and projecting new concepts of the withering away of the State, the nation, and religion in an age of market globalisation. We remain in this event, somewhere where we are. Derrida summarises some of the immense difficulties of this situation:

> Whatever one may think of this event [viz. the appearance in history of Marx's "philosophical and scientific" text], of the sometimes terrifying failure of that which was thus begun, of the techno-economic or ecological disasters, and the totalitarian perversions to which it gave rise (perversions that some have been saying for a long time are precisely not perversions, that is, they are not pathological and accidental corruptions but the necessary deployment of an essential logic present at the birth, of an originary disadjustment – let us say, for our part, in a too elliptical fashion and without contradicting this hypothesis, they are the effect of an ontological treatment of the spectrality of the ghost), whatever one may think also of the trauma in human memory that may follow, this unique attempt took place. A messianic promise, even if it was not fulfilled, at least in the form in which it was uttered, even if it rushed headlong toward an ontological content, will have imprinted an inaugural and unique mark in history. And whether we like it or not, whatever consciousness we have of it, we cannot not be its heirs. (SM, p. 91)

The totalitarian perversions that ensued in the twentieth century are, many have said, "precisely not perversions". And Derrida does not contradict this hypothesis. Indeed, against those who still yearn for a specifically Marxist revolutionary event that might (once again) "this time" or (failing that) "next time" succeed rather than lead to yet another terrifying failure, he affirms it. He speaks about it here "elliptically" in terms of an "ontological treatment of the spectrality of the ghost". In the next volume, I will be going into this idea in greater detail in relation to all three forms of twentieth century totalitarianism (communism, fascism and Nazism). I will begin this chapter with a more limited ambition: to see this "ontological treatment" at work in Lenin's discourse on democracy and the end of democracy. In doing so I aim to show how a certain ghostly spectrality that belongs to the concept of democracy – not its abstract form but an essential openness to unknown futures internal to its "real content" – gets closed down by a Marxist desire for what I will call a final word on the end of democracy, and hence a final word on the proper end of the history of Man.

Lenin's text is bristling with unrelenting and pugilistic antagonism against his political rivals, both on the side of "petty-bourgeois democrats" who shy away from Marx's revolutionary message, contenting themselves with ideas of a bourgeois-democratic republic, and on the side of "anarchists" who resist Marx's recognition of the need for political centralism and severe revolutionary discipline, and who think one can get beyond the politics of the State without first seizing it and mobilising State power. He wants to "restore Marxism by purging it of distortions" (SR, p. 68), and he does this quite brilliantly, if chillingly.

Most of the discussion in *State and Revolution* concerns a point related to the German two-step, or its logical development into a three-step: the first two being the condition of possibility for a step into an altogether new world "a future communism" (in which the anarchist hope for the disappearance of the State is finally realised); this third step now projected, presupposing a preliminary and "forthcoming" seizure of State power by the proletariat (SR, p. 88) which is the one-thing-after-another two-step. It all starts (whether by election or not) with the accession of the proletariat to political power, a first step which is notionally separable from but is immediately followed by a second step that consists in "smashing", "shattering" and "abolishing" the existing political State. This is the beginning of a period in which the "special machine" of a State apparatus – which is nothing more than an instrument of violence "for the suppression of one class by another" (SR, p. 94) – is nevertheless maintained in order to impose, for a time, perhaps a long time, a "despotic" working-class State (SR, p. 67). The sole purpose of this "*dictatorship of the proletariat*" is to maximise the capacity of the new ruling class to suppress resistance from, and finally totally to destroy, the old ruling class. This will be the "advent" of a new order of society in which the "minority" will be suppressed by the "majority" in a State-like way (SR, p. 86).

As Marx had noted in the *Communist Manifesto*, this is a totally unfamiliar and, for some, no doubt troubling reversal of the usual form of emancipation, which had hitherto all been about "movements of minorities" (CM, p. 14). But in this case, there is a decisive difference: the new despotic State order is, Lenin insists, in the form of a "truly democratic" State (SR, p. 82), and the minority to be suppressed are just those who have hitherto done everything in their power to protect their wealth and privilege, and who have always been willing to use a State apparatus to do so, across the board subjecting the "immense majority" to conditions of immiseration, humiliation and suffering.

Like the "armed workers" he invokes as the instrument of violence in this new State power, Lenin is totally unsentimental about this need for a period of despotic State power. He is also extremely clear-eyed about the claims being made by Engels about this passing on to a third step: the transition to communism as involving the "withering away of the State". The State that withers is not the old State order (that disappears almost immediately, is abolished almost immediately, albeit in two steps, through the accession to power of the proletariat), but the new "truly democratic" one. As I noted earlier, Lenin clarifies the logic of this conception by construing it as the teleological development of democracy: democracy for Lenin has a *telos* which is also its *terminus*. As we saw in the last chapter, the end of democracy [*telos*] is the end of democracy [*terminus*]. Discussing conditions after the seizure of power by the proletariat, Lenin comments:

> We all know that the political form of the "State" at that time is the most complete democracy. But it never enters the head of any of the opportunists who shamelessly distort Marxism that Engels is consequently speaking here of democracy "ceasing itself," or "withering away". This seems very strange at first sight; but it is "incomprehensible" only to those who have not pondered over the fact that *democracy is also a State* and that, consequently, democracy will also disappear when the State disappears. Revolution alone can "abolish" the bourgeois State. The State in general, i.e. the most complete democracy, can only "wither away". (SR, p. 15, emphasis mine)

The battle for democracy thus transitions towards its final end (in both senses) in the third-step attainment of a fully communist society in which the people take over for themselves all the old State functions. In the preceding phase of a genuinely democratic State, however, the basic trajectory towards this third step is the ongoing de-differentiation of State and society, and hence "the more complete the democracy, the nearer the moment approaches when it becomes unnecessary" (SR, p. 107). The end of democracy is thus the beginning of real freedom "for a new generation" in the wake of what will finally be "the world proletarian revolution" (SR, p. 37). *Marx qui genuit…*:

> Only in communist society…when there are no classes…*only* then "the State…ceases to exist", and it "*becomes possible to speak of freedom*". Only then will a truly complete democracy become possible and be realized – a democracy without any exceptions whatsoever. And only then will democracy begin to wither away, owing to the simple fact that…people will gradually become accustomed to observing the elementary rules of social intercourse that have been known for centuries. (SR, p. 93)

On this conception, a "*fully* consistent democracy", "democracy *to the utmost*", a "*truly* democratic" society (SR, p. 82) can produce a mode of equality among human beings that is always and only merely "formal", and must be overstepped or must overstep itself into a communist society with "real equality" (SR, p. 104). For Marx, democracy is, as we have seen, the form of the State in general, a truly democratic State is one where the content of that form is taken as its content, which signifies, as Lenin puts it, "the formal recognition of the equality of all citizens" (SR, p. 105). But taken to its "utmost" this calls for a society in which that merely formal recognition is actually realised: "from each according to his ability, to each according to his needs" – and the attainment of this third and final step is communism.

There is a movement of thought within Marxism with respect to democracy that is not incorporated into this analysis, neither in Lenin nor, I believe, in Marx: it is "present from birth". One of the initial specifications that Marx gives for a democratic polity is the way in which "individuals share in deliberating and deciding on matters of general concern as the 'all', that is to say, within and as members of the society". But "matters of general concern" surely and irreducibly includes what we mean by "democracy", the concept of "democracy" itself. Lenin is convinced that Marxism provides what might be called (to use the form of words Lenin uses in another context (SR, p. 78)) "the last word" on democracy, and so can specify what an ideally democratic polity – a "fully consistent democracy", "democracy *to the utmost*", a "truly democratic" society – must be like. His establishing here-and-now a teleological "end of democracy" to come is also a terminal end from here-and-now on to all discussion and deliberation on what democracy is. But what if democracy itself, in its concrete concept, demands that it can and hence must (this transition from possibility to necessity is internal here) itself only be thought democratically – as essentially open to ongoing discussion and deliberation? What if democracy is therefore the name of a "regime" in which calling into question its own historical concept *belongs* to its concept, and hence remains in question, remains to be thought, and is not given in any given here-and-now (even as a "forthcoming" reality)? As we shall see in detail in the next volume, in view here is what Stanley Cavell has called "a perfectionism that happily consents to democracy", perfectionism "democratized" in a form of endless self-criticism itself "called for by the democratic aspiration" (CHU, p. 1). In contrast to this essentially "open-ended" conception of democratic perfectionism (CHU, p. 4), Lenin's writings on democracy and the freedom that is its end, conceives democracy without taking its own concept as part of its essential content. In short, the Marxist conception of democracy is *merely formal*.

By assuming to think "the end of democracy" Marxism gives "concrete" content to a concept whose own proper content essentially resists any such "final" determination. Against this closing down of the spectral openness internal to democracy in its concrete concept we should affirm instead that what is "proper" to the concept of democracy is that it does not have a finally adequate "full" or "true" or "proper" content; it (can and must) give itself as remaining to be thought, and hence, as Derrida will put it, at every time, including every future time, it remains to come. This is a perfectionism unthought in the classic

140 The history of the world

tradition of thinking Man and his teleology, and its ramifications for us will be profound.

Tragically, rather than opening onto the freedom it promises, Marxism leaves everyone, to borrow Lenin's words once again "with nowhere to go" (SR, p. 197). In 1919, Valéry wondered about a European "who is doing God knows what under a Russian name" (HP, p. 30). We might have anticipated what was coming:

> When all have learned to administer and actually do independently administer social production...the escape from this popular accounting and control will inevitably become so incredibly difficult, such a rare exception, and will probably be accompanied by such swift and severe punishment (for the armed workers are practical men and not sentimental intellectuals, and they will scarcely allow anyone to trifle with them) that the necessity of observing the simple, fundamental rules of human intercourse will very soon become a habit. (SR, pp. 107–8)

What a miserable habit. Be operational, comrade, or *disappear...*

II

Disappearance. We have already seen the European Hamlet "watching millions of ghosts". The millions, many nameless, who had died in the First World War are invoked there even as Valéry is about to transpose this into an intellectual scene of "the death of truths" (HP, p. 29). Writing in 1992, and reflecting on Marx's "Marxist" successors, Derrida adds to this appalling parade of death, by that time after a second World War too, reminding those who might try to forget it, "the response of 'Marxist' successors" to Marx's text, the response especially concerning its "political consequences": that is "wherever they have drawn, practically, concretely, in a terribly effective massive and immediate fashion, its political consequences (at the cost of millions and millions of supplementary ghosts who will keep on protesting in us)" (SM, p. 30). While there are no agreed figures or even categories by which to collect figures for victims of Soviet terrors, man-made famines, and so on – and no agreement among historians and historical demographers about how to go about the task of counting them – there is no doubt that human beings paid with their lives in frighteningly large numbers for the "political consequences" of the Marxist idea of democracy under Lenin, and not just under Stalin. Beyond those who died during two world wars of European origin, there are, indeed, "millions and millions of supplementary ghosts who will keep on protesting in us".

The revolution in Russia belonged to the general process of democratisation that unfolded in Europe after the revolution in France. European imperial and monarchical power was waning, and the Great War only accelerated the process of stripping the world of its royalty (to amend a phrase of Simone Weil's). We will now begin to work our way into the dramatic mutation of the European self-understanding that unfolds in this time; the unravelling of the old discourse of Europe's modernity and its promise, and its transition into a discourse of modern Europe's crisis. We have taken our direction thus far from Valéry's European Hamlet and the chain of ghosts emerging from the skull of Kant. Forged on the anvil of the "merely formal", this chain sees philosophical history – the Europe-centred (hi)story of the world as the history of the emancipation of Man – become increasingly intertwined with the thought and advance of political democracy. Stepping further into the twentieth century, I will first track the mutation in Europe's self-understanding – the development of an increasingly de-centred perspective on itself – as it is attested by Valéry himself. I will do so by attending to a little literary mystery in Valéry's own work: a self-citation of the European Hamlet in 1932 in which one sentence in that passage silently... disappears.

And it is not just any sentence. It is the very sentence that has guided us: "And this one was *Kant...and Kant begat Hegel, and Hegel begat Marx, and Marx begat...*"

III

Disappearance. Derrida cited Valéry's text of the European Hamlet at the start of his investigation of the spirits (plural) of Marx in *Specters of Marx*. But he was stopped in his tracks by the fact that when Valéry recited the text himself some thirteen years later, in an essay originally delivered as a public lecture, "Politics of Spirit" ("*La politque de l'esprit*"), he (Valéry) did not cite all of it, but "omits from it only *one* sentence, *just one*, without even signalling the omission by an ellipsis: the one that names Marx, in the very skull of Kant" (SM, p. 5).

Derrida is strangely single-minded about this omission: "The name of Marx has disappeared" (SM, p. 5). Indeed, it has. But it wasn't just Marx's name. It was, as he had just noted, a sentence-worth of names, the sentence that had Kant and Hegel in it as well as Marx, and which "finished" (in the original) with an ellipsis. The original ellipsis was not an omission but an open inclusion, and who knows what names it might include. But Derrida is quite right. This is a sentence that Valéry omits, and omits without admitting omission, in his recitation of himself in 1932. What is going on here?

I have noted Derrida's remarking that ghosts appear in the movement of spirit (appear "somewhere where we are") either with the name, where spirit "assumes a body" (SM, p. 6) or, when the name disappears, with "that which marks the name" (SM, p. 9). I followed this spirit guidance in reading the disappearance of the name of Kant in Hegel's text. With the omission in Valéry's self-citation, a single-minded Derrida gets on the hunt of where Marx's name might have been inscribed elsewhere in Valéry's text. He found something, and not too far away (though perhaps a little further than he acknowledges), specifying the line "*Marx qui genuit Valéry*" with the appearance in a text by Valéry ("*Lettre sur la sociéte des espirits*") that commented on his (Valéry's) own concept of "the transformative power of spirit" with the supplementary specification which we have already noted: that *"spirit…works"* (cited, SM, p. 9).

But it was not only Marx's name that had disappeared. Derrida says that "the name of the one who disappeared must have gotten inscribed someplace else" (SM, p. 5). It is that "someplace else", for the whole name-list and its open inclusion that I want to track down here.

Let's ask then, since it isn't just the name of Marx that went missing, what made *that* sentence ("*Enter Ghost[s] and Hamlet*"), with all those names, no longer work for Valéry in the later text ("*Exeunt ghost[s] and Marx*" (SM, p. 5)).

First of all, one may well wonder about the work done by more than just that one sentence in the self-citation in the later essay: for the whole self-citation of the European Hamlet, with its one-sentence omission if one can say that, is completely omitted in the English edition of Valéry's *Collected Works*, marked more or less silently by the editor with an across-the-page ellipsis or "line of dots" (HP, p. 104). It's as if the editor thought it did no work at all. In fact, as we shall see, the English text's omitting it all makes it even clearer why Valéry might have omitted just that one sentence when he included the European Hamlet in his new text. We will then be well on our way towards specifying the "someplace else" where Valery's omission of names in 1932 are all inscribed. (We will also see how the editor tried, nevertheless, in a certain way, to put something of his own omission back again.) And with that, well on our way to seeing a new mutation in the European self-understanding.

The European Hamlet had seen how Leonardo's flying man had begotten great swans that scattered bombs rather than snow on the streets of towns; how Leibnitz's dream of universal peace lay in shatters in war; and how *Kant qui genuit Hegel, et Hegel qui genuit Marx, et Marx qui genuit…* All of these are wonders of Europe's intellectual spirit, and all have begotten…disasters. I have interpolated one such disaster, *Marx qui genuit Lenin*, which was already on the horizon for Valéry in 1919. We will see shortly that this is not all that he had in mind.

Derrida had a sharp eye seeing the line of great German spirits omitted from the self-citation. But actually, and Derrida didn't notice this at all, that was not the only moment of omission in the later text. The European Hamlet belongs to the closing paragraphs of the 1919 essay "The Crisis of Spirit" that Valéry recites and Derrida recalls and the English editor omits from "Politics of Spirit". But that self-citation was in fact the second of two such self-citations in the later text – both of which were removed by the editor of the English text. Valéry's original text hosts another interpolation, this time from the opening paragraphs of the "The Crisis of Spirit". And in that first self-citation, Valery makes four further silent omissions, three of which also contain names.

Counting them in the order they occur in the text (but not taking them in order for a moment), the fourth omission is a little two-line quote from a text by Aurelius Prudentius Clemens, a fourth century Roman Christian poet, on the survival of a hope when all seems hopeless, cited by Valéry in 1919. It is in Latin, and as such is likely to be utterly obscure for most people. One can well understand that for the 1932 text, which as I say was composed for a public lecture, it was felt unsuitable. I won't say more about this omission, although more could be said. It is the first three that are the real puzzle.

The first is the omission of "Elam", the name of an ancient state-like region to the west of Mesopotamia, that was the first in a list of three "beautiful vague names" – "Elam, Ninevah, Babylon" – that belong to worlds that have fallen into "the abyss of history", the abyss into which "we...now know" our own world too can fall (it is "deep enough to hold us all"). The second omission, from the same paragraph, removes two sentences that contain a list of names from our own world, which one day too, Valéry says, "would be beautiful names": "France, England, Russia", and he then adds that "*Lusitania,* too, is a beautiful name", which also goes in 1932 (HP, p. 23). (The *Lusitania* referred to here is a British ocean liner that was sunk by a German U-boat in 1915, resulting in the death of 1,198 passengers and crew.) If the first two are not already puzzling enough, the third omission is the most striking for us since it clearly anticipates the line of begetting that will singularly disappear in the second self-citation from the European Hamlet. With this third omission from the first self-citation, two whole paragraphs of the original text are removed, paragraphs in which Valéry "cite[s] but one example" of our bearing witness to the "extraordinary phenomena" of what he calls "a paradox suddenly become fact". Here is what goes missing from the 1919 text in the third omission from the first self-citation in 1932:

> I shall cite but one example: the great virtues of the German peoples have *begotten* more evils than idleness ever bred vices. With our own eyes, we have seen conscientious labor, the most solid learning, the most serious discipline and application adapted to appalling ends.
>
> So many horrors could not have been possible without so many virtues. Doubtless, much science was needed to kill so many, to waste so much property, annihilate so many cities in so short a time; but *moral qualities* in like number were also needed. Are Knowledge and Duty, then, suspect? (HP, p. 24, first emphasis mine)

The line of ghosts proceeding from the skull of Kant is not in itself a line of decline. They belong together as a chain of what "would be beautiful names". But like the other beautiful names in the European Hamlet – Leonardo and Leibniz – they do not exclude begetting evils. And in 1919, at the close of the Great War, what Valéry seems most clearly, if not exclusively, to have in mind was political horrors of German origin. In 1933, in a different essay, Valéry made the point again, although without the exclusively German example:

> Nothing is more remarkable than to see that ideas, separated from the intellect that conceived them, isolated from the complex conditions of their

> birth, from the delicate analyses and the hundreds of tests and comparisons that preceded them, can become *political agents…signals…weapons… stimulants* – that products of reflection may be used purely for their value as provocation. How many examples there have been in the past hundred and fifty years! Fichte, Hegel, Marx, Gobineau, Nietzsche, even Darwin, have been put to use, turned into crude slogans. (HP, p. 275)

Derrida would sometimes recall Marx saying "I am not a Marxist" (Derrida did so, however, in order, like Marx, to say the words in his own name, and hence as far as possible also without Marx), but we should not suppose that the "products of reflection" Valéry recalls here are not themselves *"stimulants"*, or that the *"political agents"* that deploy them deploy *"weapons"* that are simply absent from the "conditions of their birth". Valéry's sense of the extraordinary phenomenon of a remarkable "paradox" – that great virtues are needed in the carrying out of political horrors – should not obscure the general provocation to political agency (whether for good or ill) that belongs internally to the philosophical (and indeed scientific) productions he lists here. Adding a few years to Valéry's list from the last one hundred and fifty years that he looks back on, we could add Kant's name to the list (as Hegel would approve if he did not want to omit that name himself) so that all of our three names would be there, along with some others. But all three disappeared from the second self-citation, the imminence of their arrival anticipated in the paragraphs of the "paradox" of begetting omitted from the first self-citation. And perhaps that explains their omission. Perhaps they were removed because they were no longer doing their work.

Actually, I don't think that is all that's going on here. If we look at the omissions we can see a disappearance (still not the only one) more pointed than the one Derrida picked out: with the third omission from the first self-citation and the single omission from the second, it looks like Valéry has gone to some lengths to make a paradoxical "*Germany qui genuit…*" disappear. And he did this at a time (1932) when that paradox was appearing so distressingly, once again, on Europe's horizon. In 1939, when Hitler had already "proceeded against the weakest states on his frontiers" (HP, p. 469), Valéry had a new and more extreme example of the German example in full view: "What a strange people is that great people! They have produced admirable and universal works of spirit, and yet they deliver themselves up to a persecutor of spirit" (HP, p. 468; translation modified). In 1932 something of that imminence was certainly already in plain view, and the reminder of the paradox that had become fact would not have been out of place at all. Indeed, in that context, one might think the German example could hardly be omitted, especially in a text on the politics of spirit which, in its opening line states that the speaker proposes "to evoke for you the disorder in which we live" (HP, p. 89). It is very puzzling.

Beyond that puzzle (which I will try to sort out in a moment), I think the singular omission in the second self-citation will bear a supplementary interpretation that will be, for us, most telling. However, I want now to note that while the disappearance of Germany in 1932 is striking and odd, the fact that Valéry omitted what it seems *prima facie* so appropriate to include, should make us wonder afresh what is going on. And it sends us back to the first and second omission in the first self-citation, which might now take on a new significance. For with the omission of the "beautiful names" of "Elam", "France, England, Russia" (and even "Lusitania" if registered as the name of an old State-like region on the Iberian peninsula), Valéry has removed the names of any States whatsoever. He has wiped his text clean of States. His new text in 1932 has no such beautiful names at all. You'd think he meant it. I think he did.

IV

In 1932, Valéry wants to address his audience, and uses the first-person plural, to "evoke for you" something about "us" and "the disorder in which we live". The text is at first less personal, however, with reflections about "man" in general, and the orders and disorders of "the world of man" in general (HP, p. 91), and how things are "different with man" compared to the world of "an animal" (HP, p. 97). As Derrida notes, the definition and difference of man outlined here will prepare for a discussion on a theme that should by now be familiar: namely, that "*all politics imply a certain idea of man*" (HP, p. 103, italics in original). However, it is not just "man" that concerns Valéry but, explicitly and above all, the "we" that is "*modern man*" (HP, p. 93, emphasis in original). And note: not modern man here or there, in this or that State, but modern man, he says and stresses, in "*all States*" (HP, p. 108, emphasis in original). Unfortunately for the English reader, the puzzle of the complete omission (by Valéry) of all state-name particularity is compounded by the English edition's complete omission (by the editor) of the two self-citations themselves, for in doing so it also strips from Valéry's text the only sentences in the 1932 text in which Valéry named any "someplace else" whatsoever. The English editor's omissions removed from the scene the last surviving name: "Europe".

From the first self-citation, which is introduced in 1932 with a stress on the fact that his questions about "modern man" are not new but were already his concerns in 1919, we find four explicit references to Europe in the French text. From the second self-citation (the European Hamlet), we find two further references to Europe in the French text, and the introduction of that self-citation (obviously also omitted in the English edition) introduced one more too. So, in all, seven references to Europe, and none to any States.

Stripped of its self-citations the English version of the French text is strikingly bare. With all State names omitted by Valéry himself, the only references to a place (apart from a few scattered city names) which would gather the text as a discourse on (some)place get omitted too. All that is left is just man, the animal, and modern man. But what the citations set on the stage so vividly and expressly, what is presented in these two self-citing centre-pieces of Valéry's whole talk, is precisely the "someplace else" that is the somewhere

where we moderns are: Europe. That is where those State names got re-inscribed. Retaining the State names would shatter the scene into something constantly comparative (it's not so bad here, it's worse here, that place is just strange, it's really bad here, etc). Without fear or favour to any particular State, even Germany in 1932, it is all about the fate of the spirit of modern European man as such and in any State in what Valéry calls a "phase", a "*critical phase*" of "our civilization", and its "*age*" (HP, p. 93, emphasis in original).

In removing all the references to State names in the self-citation, and so, along with all the others, removing Germany and the evils the great virtues of its people have begotten, the skull of Kant and its begetting onto an open question of its further begetting no longer does its work for Valéry either. It doesn't work now that the earlier reference has gone. So it had to go too.

Perhaps. However, as I have indicated, there is room for a supplementary interpretation of the omission of the Kant-Hegel-Marx sentence, a further and I think more critical reason for supposing its not working. And this is related to what comes to the fore when it is just a question of the "*critical phase*" of modern European man (in any State), which is the theme of Valéry's European theme. It is, he says, a question of "*one* remarkable feature" of "the modern world". It will be here that Valéry broaches a new perspective on Europe's modernity, a perspective that is perhaps not conceivable without Kant-Hegel-Marx but which is not so visible with them: the "strange contrast" and "curious split" between "man" as understood in the lexicon of *modern politics* ("the *citizen*, the *voter*, the *candidate*, the *taxpayer*, the *common man*"), and "man", as understood in the lexicon of *modern science* ("contemporary biology, psychology, or even psychiatry") (HP, p. 92). In the times of science, a time after Darwin, a time after Freud, and perhaps, let me add, also a time after Marx, *our whole self-understanding is changed*. As early as 1906 the young Valéry, writing in a letter to André Lebey, noted – and I would stress, noted with Marx but also beyond Marx – that with the arrival of Darwin, "the whole of history is changed. I mean all thinking about history" (HP, p. 6). He means thinking about the meaning of history. As we have seen, Marx had been delighted that the idea of a teleology of nature had been dealt a death-blow by Darwin. But he accommodated the blow, and maintained the idea of a teleological sense of world history nonetheless. Valéry is not so sanguine, and sees in the transition into an age in which, as Edmund Husserl would put it around the same time, "the total worldview of modern man...let itself be determined by the positive sciences" (CES, p. 6), a situation in which we modern Europeans were struggling to see any teleological meaning in world history at all.

However, one crucial area of our life had yet to be swamped by positive science: our politics. Our time, Valéry suggests, is one in which there has emerged what he calls a profound "antinomy" between "political reality" and "scientific truth" (HP, p. 104). This was not always so, says Valéry. There was a time when this "gap" did not exist. And this is because the understanding of "Man" that belongs to the "science" side of this contrast had not always been the product of *positive science* – not the upshot of "objective research, founded on *verifiable* evidence (which is the exact meaning of the word 'scientific')". Rather it was "the conception of man...formulated by the *philosophy* of the time" (HP, p. 104). We are, of course, travelling along the road of this very changeover. In the earlier time, the lexicon of *European science* about Man was primarily the lexicon of *European philosophy* about Man, where Man is conceived as theomorphic rational animality. And in that earlier time, the lexicon of European politics aligned with that: the same conception of Man belonged to both. But, says Valéry, not today, no longer today. And it is then, exactly then, that Valéry quotes himself, and cites the European Hamlet *sans* the generation of the ghosts Kant-Hegel-Marx and the open ellipsis of what might be generated in turn by Marx.

Leonardo and Leibniz – they comfortably belong to that older time. And the European Hamlet sees the decline into positivist techno-scientific modernity, its killing machines and wars, that befalls their work into our time. But that other skull – the skull of Kant – that belongs to a line of generations in time that does not just represent that former time. On the contrary, with its chain of ghosts, it represents a line that is caught up in the general movement *between* these times, between, say, the time of the Renaissance and our own time: the Kant-Hegel-Marx chain itself belonging to the movement towards an increasing domination of our self-understanding by positive science. These generations represent something of what goes on between the times that interest Valéry.

We have called attention to a shift within the history of philosophical history from texts that were "philosophical and religious" to ones that were "philosophical and scientific". The status of the philosophical had always implied some idea of itself as a science (which gets called "metaphysics"). However, in the shift we see in Marx, the irreligious character of Marxist criticism is inseparable from its commitment to grounding its claims not in abstract ideas, still less in Providence, but in the empirical study of real human beings in society.

Of course, this shift is not only in Marx or since Marx. Moreover, beyond Marx, even the philosophical (teleological) part of the project of philosophical history is overwhelmed by what Valéry calls "the growth of a positivist mentality" (HP, 106), and belongs to an upheaval in the European self-understanding that had been gathering pace, at least, since Darwin. Nevertheless, with Kant-to-Marx we are concerned with "what went on between the generations", as Derrida (with something else in mind) put it (SM, p. 5). A "between" in the movement in European spirit between "a certain idea of man...and a conception of the world" which had belonged to philosophical science in the past, and the idea of man and a conception of the world that belongs to (philosophy-displacing) positive science today (HP, p. 106). But, and this is Valéry's main point, "the idea of man implied in political notions" has not followed a related development. And so the idea of "man" in modern politics and the idea of "man" in modern science are now profoundly misaligned: "there is already an abyss between them" (HP, p. 103).

It is important to see that Valéry does not recommend closing that abyss by pushing our (old) conception of Man in politics towards the conception of Man we now have from positive science. Not at all. The situation is far more distressing, almost pure distress, because that gap-closing effort would only make things worse, far, far worse:

> Let us give an example: if we tried to apply, in the realm of politics, the ideas about man which we find in the current doctrines of science, life would probably become unbearable for most of us. There would be a general revolt of feeling in the face of such strict application of perfectly rational data. For it would end, in fact, by classifying each individual, invading his personal life, sometimes killing or mutilating certain degenerate or inferior types… (HP, p. 103)

Michel Foucault's celebrated elaboration of a conception of modern "biopolitics" witnesses the world of this gap-closing. And, indeed, Foucault picked up a word that had been incubating since the 1920s. The German physician, Hans Reiter – an enthusiastic supporter of and participant in enforced racial sterilisation, who undertook experiments on typhus inoculation at the Buchenwald concentration camp during the Second World War, and who edited a book on "racial hygiene" – used the word biopolitics (affirmatively) in the 1930s. An American biologist, Robert Kuttner – an enthusiastic supporter of eugenics and co-founder of the "Institute of Biopolitics" in the 1950s – used it in relation to what he called "scientific racism". Biopolitics would belong for Valéry, to a disaster of realignment between modern science and modern politics. When he wrote the original lecture in 1932 Valéry thought his projection was "exaggerated" (HP, p. 104). Only four years later, he added a footnote to his essay when it was prepared for publication in 1936: "A recent piece of legislation in a certain foreign country has fulfilled this prediction by prescribing several such strictly rational methods" (HP, p. 103).

Sticking to what appears to be his intention – of omitting all names of States – Valéry does not name the "foreign country" in question. But there, wherever it was, modern science was becoming part of modern political reality. He was probably thinking, once more, of Germany. For example, the "Law for the Prevention of Genetically Diseased Offspring" came into force under the National Socialist regime in 1934. As we shall see in a moment, the editor of the English edition is confident that it was Germany that Valéry had in mind, but eugenics laws were not in fact confined to Germany at that time. It could have been one of quite a number of "foreign countries".

Biopolitics is one form of distressing realignment. But it was not the only one on the horizon. The Bolsheviks in the Soviet Union also wanted scientifically to re-fashion "Man" through the "application of perfectly rational data", although in their case it was principally on the basis of a social science rather than a biological science. That being said, eugenics did not simply disappear in the pre-War Soviet

Union either, although its association with Nazism later made it as (officially) unwelcome there as it increasingly became elsewhere. Nevertheless, a general scientific spirit was part of the fabric of Marxism, as it was already in Marx. Both Engels and Lenin went out of their way to present Marx's work as "Scientific Socialism", stressing, for example, that the questions Marx posed concerning the transformation of the State in communist society "can only be answered scientifically" (Engels), Lenin adding that the answer given by Marxism had indeed been developed "by using firmly established scientific data" (SR, pp. 89–90). Non-Marxist views, by contrast, were condemned by Lenin as being "scientifically wrong" (SR, p. 84). We have also seen how Lenin expected (on the basis of similarly firmly established scientific data, no doubt, since this was science and not "utopian speculation") that the new communist society of the future would see the arrival of a "new generation" of human beings for whom the proper ways of being human will have become a "habit". In America, a similar positive-scientific spirit would urge us to find our needs, even at the highest level, serviced by a single convenience store with a gas station.

Science – or at least an idea of science – is central to the language of "spiritual" progress in the politics of the nineteenth and twentieth centuries – so much so that we no longer call it spiritual progress but scientific progress, or just progress.

All of this provides a supplementary reason why the sentence with our line of ghosts might need to disappear. The work of the second self-citation (the citation of the European Hamlet) was to illustrate a changeover from a time in which the understanding of the world and the significance of our lives proposed by science and the idea of Man belonging to politics were more or less aligned. The line of ghosts proceeding from the skull of Kant does not represent that aligned (let's say) Renaissance condition, but belongs to the movement of increasing misalignment. Valéry wanted to represent the generations (the time before, and the time now), not what went on between the generations. The sentence did not really work anymore. It had to go.

V

Jackson Matthews, the editor of the English edition of Valéry's *Collected Works*, could not resist responding to Valéry's omitting to name the "foreign country" that realised his prediction, adding a footnote to Valéry's footnote which asserts that "there is little doubt" that he is referring to Germany (HP, p. 583). Intriguingly, he then adds a sort of footnote to his own footnote to a footnote, sending the reader to another footnote of his own, a footnote where Matthews identifies two books that Valéry "must have had in mind" but omitted to mention when he wrote (in 1937) of "two books…by two different theorists of the nineteenth century" to illustrate a point. Valéry's point there is importantly related to our discussion. He was insisting in that essay that "reflective thought… endows action with the means…of becoming real" (HP, p. 367). And he writes (without naming them) of "Two States, two very great and powerful States, owing their ideas to these two books" (HP, p. 368). The two books, the editor insists, must be Marx's *Das Kapital* (1867) ("of course") and Arthur de Gobineau's race-theoretical *Essai sur l'inégalité des races humaines* (1854) (HP, p. 600). This footnote then chases us further round the houses, referring to another essay in the volume (from 1926) in which Valéry comments explicitly on "the attention Gobineau's work [had] aroused in Germany" (HP, p. 536), and then finally to another essay in the volume (from 1937) in which Valéry names the two books by name himself (HP, p. 551). The editor who had omitted the self-citations which had omitted the German philosophical/scientific production-line that had made its way into Russian politics, restores the name of Marx that Valéry had to omit, adding to it the name of the (more implicitly omitted, if one can say that) French philosophical/scientific production that had made its way into the German politics that Valéry didn't name either.

Valéry's text retained the names of cities, regions and landmarks of both place and history, but in his representation of the "disorder in which we live" in the original text, the "somewhere where we are" is marked exclusively supra-nationally, in the name, only, of Europe. He spoke, one might say, to the universality of a new modern condition for all European humanity, in whatever State. (And, one might add, he remained rigorously faithful to his sense of his own French particularity in doing so: "specializing in the sense of the universal".) And in this new modern condition, something fundamental has changed. Europe can no longer conceive itself through a discourse of its own exemplarity: this is now a discourse of modern Europe's excessive modern disorder and not, or no longer, a discourse of Europe's exemplary modernity, no longer a philosophical history of the emancipation and progress of "Man" with Europe at the front.

It is, in other words, a universal European history of the crisis of the old culture of universal history, the crisis of the particular culture which had seen itself heading off towards a universal future of freedom for all humanity, the crisis of the kind of Eurocentric discourse on Europe elaborated so confidently in the variations of philosophical history that we have seen in Kant, Hegel and Marx. Modern Europe, for Valéry, was still caught up with a global trajectory; commodifying its scientific and technological attainments and distributing them to the whole of humanity as "articles...that can be imitated and produced almost anywhere" (HP, p. 35). The history of the world was still inseparable from Europe's modernity spreading out with "the most intense power of radiation", and on a truly global scale (HP, p. 31). However, "the modern world with all its power, its prodigious technological capital, its thorough discipline in scientific and practical methods" (HP, p. 92), was not forging anything like a political heading towards a final "end of Man". On the contrary, our current situation has completely changed. We now no longer know where we are going at all: we have lost our heading. "*We are backing into the future*", says Valéry, and "*headed I know not where*" (HP, p. 113, emphasis in original).

The discourse of Europe's modernity had become a discourse of modern Europe's crisis:

> Will Europe become *what it is in reality* – that is, a little promontory on the continent of Asia?
> Or will it remain *what it seems* – that is, the elect portion of the terrestrial globe, the pearl of the sphere, the brain of a vast body? (HP, p. 31, emphasis in original)

Europe's greatness had always been a kind of "appearance", a constructed seeming not a natural reality. Europe had made itself by evoking itself, *calling itself to appear* as an "advanced point of exemplarity" for global humanity (OH, p. 24). This pearly appearance belongs to an idea of Man and his teleology that was dissolving in the times of science – and the projects of political freedom that were inspired by the likes of Kant (in a teleology of nature), Hegel (in a teleology of spirit), and Marx (in a teleology of the democratic state) are, for us, increasingly unbelievable. And yet, we seem to have nothing to replace them with that does not make it so much worse. Europe's old spirit, dispirited and shattered, the history of its spiritual heading in ruins, its current statesmen begetting little more than "the fury of a scientifically waged war" (HP, p. 331). And then the generation of Lenin *qui genuit* Stalin was joined, in a profoundly anti-Marxist recoil, by another man, "simply a man", prepared to "set fire to Europe" once again (HP, p. 468) – joined by Adolf Hitler.

Valéry's conclusion to "Politics of Spirit" presents attempts to realign Europe's politics to its science as anything but a "solution", still less a "final solution" to our contemporary disorders. Rational technological-scientific politics takes various forms: in the form of revolutionary international socialism (we imagine it provides the "clear solution" to our troubles, but…"we know that this is not true" (HP, p. 112)); or of reactionary national socialism and fascism (which robs a people of its "free self-determination" and "degrades their spirits" (HP, pp. 468–9)); or, even of the not so hopeless hopes of "those happy people" in America who have no history ("or next to none") to destroy (HP, p. 227). These are all attempts experimentally "to fashion a new man" (HP, p. 136), but all of them produce only cultures of mass conformity and uniformity – of the single office, the *Vaterland*, or the convenience store; all-in-all effecting what Valéry in a very Nietzschean spirit calls the "levelling" of human life down "towards the lowest type" (HP, p. 111), all associated with "modern ideas" in science and society, all part of the spirit of "progress" in our time.

Europe in transition: the great historical wealth of a European culture of more than one culture – Valéry too will specify the historical line of the Greek-Roman-Christian-Modern golden thread as "absolutely European" (HP, p. 322) – is unravelling, degrading, de-valuing. And what is to become of Europe now? The European Hamlet made just one prediction about Europe's future: we would witness "the miracle of an animal society, the perfect and ultimate anthill" (HP, p. 30).

Valéry describes the scene of Europe's modernity as entry into "an era permeated by the sciences" (HP, p. 46). In "Politics of Spirit", he stresses that this is not a merely intellectual affair nor is the scientific spirit a neutral one. It is a phase marked everywhere by its "positivism", meaning a restriction of intellectual interest to empirical methods and verifiable results. "The growth of the positivist mentality", says Valéry, "is undermining the ancient foundations of society" (HP, p. 106). Where "science" in its history had been characterised by a concern with, precisely, everything, modern positive science had fragmented into particular special sciences with no integrative interest in the whole, still less with "all higher values of spirit" (HP, p. 109).

Valéry appropriates Nietzsche's famous formulation for this situation: we are undergoing "a transvaluation of all values" (HP, p. 189), and "everything is affected by it" (HP, p. 109). The word that rings through Valéry's writings on Europe is, however, crisis: a crisis of its "confidence", but more generally in its "values", its "fundamental conceptions" and, especially, its "spirit" (HP, p. 109). The closing passages of "Politics of Spirit" emphasise the point he had made about a time since Darwin: all thinking about history has changed. Formerly, we had successfully, if fictively, imported "conclusions into history" (HP, p. 112). Europe had given itself a golden-thread history with a meaning, a direction, a trajectory, a heading, and not just for itself but for all humanity. And hence Europeans had lived too with some kind of "prediction or presentiment of the future" that made sense to them as universal (HP, p. 113). The teleological discourse of world history, the discourse that belonged to Kant, Hegel, and Marx, all with their centre of gravity in developments which took place first in Europe but which open out onto a final end of history for the whole of humanity, the great discourse of Europe's modernity was dying. Valéry concludes that his "subject", the only one he can keep to (following in Flaubert's steps against stupidity), is "the impossibility of concluding" (HP, p. 112). We do not know, we no longer believe we know, where we are heading.

And yet Valéry doesn't give up on Europe and its promise; he keeps to what he still finds compelling in the old subject: "the will to lucid understanding and precision of mind, a sense of greatness and risk, a sense of the extraordinary adventure on which mankind has set out" (HP, p. 113). At least since Nietzsche, our newly disoriented condition has, for some, been felt a cause for hope rather than despair. Isn't the idea of the human adventure "headed I know not where" as exhilarating as it is challenging? Cavell's thought of perfectionism "democratized" and Derrida's account of democracy conceived as always "to come", introduced earlier in this chapter, suggests that we are learning to internalise the new self-understanding in a more promising political way too. We will explore this thought of democracy and perfectionism freed from all teleology in greater detail in the second volume as we get closer to our own time. However, in the first half of the twentieth century, the paralysing challenge was far more likely to be felt than the hopeful chance, the question of an adventure without a determinate heading heard entirely rhetorically: "If history has nothing more to teach us than that all the shapes of the spiritual world…form and dissolve themselves like fleeting waves…can we console ourselves with that?" (CES, pp. 6–7).

From a text which also frames the discourse of Europe's modernity as a discourse of modern Europe's crisis, this is Edmund Husserl's opening question from his unfinished book on "the crisis of European sciences" from 1936. Husserl, very classically, conceived the promise of Europe's modernity as inseparable from a teleological sense of world history; and for him, the loss of that sense could only accelerate the sickness he saw Europe succumbing to. Unfortunately, it is far more complicated than that: Husserl will participate in that sickness in the very effort to overcome it. Let's follow the Europe crisis there.

PART IV
A sense of an ending

10

EUROPE IN CRISIS

All politics imply a certain idea of man

– Paul Valéry

I

None of the thinkers of the history of Man that we have been exploring supposed its unfolding would be free off crises. In fact, they all stressed their recurrent likelihood. Nevertheless, no providential history, no "theodicy" of rational animality, no history that is a philosophical history of reason, no teleological discourse on the proper end of Man and History, no history which is the history of the emancipation, progress and de-alienation of Man as self-realising subjectivity, can regard such eventualities as other than a "holding back" or "holding up" of progressive developments, developments which they themselves "finally force" into being (Kant, p. 49). As David Carr puts it in a discussion of Hegel's philosophical history, every failure is "only an apparent failure, the crisis only an apparent crisis, whose purpose is to prepare for the necessary fulfilment, which is to come" (CES, p. xxxv).

In Marx's writing, too, "crisis" is a structurally recurrent feature of world history. And despite his anti-religious, scientific programme, the archeo-teleological conception of world history as a movement of the emancipation and progress of Man centred on Europe is, if anything, even more confidently affirmed in his work. His end-times apocalyptic tone, positively bursts through the *Communist Manifesto*, a text which is written in the accelerating and hyperbolic rhythm of the "ever more and more" of the movement towards a climactic end – of ever-intensifying, ever-growing, ever-rising, ever-expanding, ever more destructive, ever more precarious, each time more threatening developments and crises, as we move, rapidly and apparently inexorably, towards the "decisive hour" (CM, p. 13), towards *the last crisis*. (The Greek word *krinein*, we should note again, means both crisis and decision or judgement.) For Marx, each epochal social order in the golden thread has a characteristic form of economy and productive activity (a form of work) – but its stabilisation within a given social order also effectively limits it and hinders its working and development. As the incompatibility between the social order and its productive capacities grows, crises threaten to overwhelm it, and finally do. Marx supposes we saw this in the transition from feudal to bourgeois society. And with the "more massive and more colossal productive forces" (CM, p. 7) unleashed by the "constant revolutionizing of production", the "immense development" and "extension", of "the giant, Modern Industry" (CM, p. 4), we are, Marx says, seeing it again:

> It is enough to mention the commercial crises that by their periodical return put on its trial, each time more threateningly, the existence of the entire bourgeois society… And how does the bourgeoisie get over these crises? On the one hand, by enforced destruction of a mass of productive forces [i.e. war SG]; and on the other, by the conquest of new markets, and by the more thorough exploitation of the old ones [i.e. globalisation and intensification SG]. That is to say, paving the way for more extensive and more destructive crises, and by diminishing the means whereby crises are prevented. (CM, pp. 8–9)

Just as feudalism gave birth to a bourgeois class that would overthrow it, so too bourgeois society has conjured up and "has called into existence" a new class that will turn against the bourgeoisie: the proletarian class. This, as we have seen, fundamentally universal class "holds the future in its hands" (CM, p. 13), and promises to become a new ruling class, presently threatening the "conditions of existence" of the old ruling class by its own "ever-expanding union" and the organisation of a proletarian "political party" (CM, p. 12). Standing face to face with each other, these "two great classes" maintain an increasingly intense struggle to rule. Marx imagines – and attempts to make it so that there will have been – a time to come "when the class struggle nears the decisive hour" (CM, p. 13). Having already reached in Germany the "eve" of a revolution that would (he supposed) rapidly become trans-European and finally completely international and global in its reach, Marx anticipated ("scientifically") the "inevitable" fall from power of the old ruling class and the final "victory of the proletariat" (CM, p. 16). The decisive hour seemed to Marx to be drawing ever closer, and his writing is rocket-fuelled by the sense that the present condition in Germany and Europe simply cannot last much longer.

The great characteristic of the sense of a "European crisis" in the eighteenth and nineteenth century was: its sense of an ending. However, as we have begun to see in Valéry, in the course of the twentieth century the sense of a "European crisis" began to take a new turn – a crisis of the very discourse which had given European humanity its "modern" self-understanding. "More and more" the archeo-teleological frame of the history of the world with Europe at its head was unravelling, falling apart, becoming increasingly unbelievable, increasingly incredible, worn-out and exhausted. Kant had attested already to the anxiety that "only a *novel* could result" from the premises of philosophical history (Kant, pp. 51–2). This original anxiety was looking "ever more and more" like a factual description. Indeed, when the very idea of an archeo-teleological conception of world history is itself in crisis we have a radically different order of trouble: a crisis of crisis, as it were. As the basic form of all European discourse about Europe, a crisis for this conception is not just a crisis in Europe but for Europe, the idea of Europe itself in crisis. In view here is a completely new sense of an ending. In this section, we will witness its looming threat, and the extent of the *"phase"* of the "extraordinary shudder" that "ran through the marrow of Europe" (HP, pp. 24–5) after the Great War.

II

The idea of Man which had organised the modern European self-understanding and produced the idea of Europe as a missionary culture was waning as Europe's cultural default. Both European science and European history were conspiring against it. And, as a result, Europe in the twentieth century found itself increasingly adrift, without a heading, "backing into the future". For some Europeans (for a few) the horizon was opening, and a new chance sought of working in creative solitude, freed from the deluge of immediate responses flowing daily from the media and politicians, and beyond the old grid of what makesmost sense to us. "Perhaps in seeking that freedom we may create it", said Valéry (HP, p. 36; cp. OH, p. 104). For many others, life in modern society was encouraging *embourgeoisement*, and finding satisfaction in materialism and private interests. At the start of the nineteenth century, Hegel had already identified an "aim of existence" which did not seem to go beyond individual hopes for "prosperity" [*Gutgehen*], increases in material wealth and the satisfaction of immediate entertainments and pleasures. This only increased in the second half of the nineteenth century, with European science and technology seeming to deliver ever more and more impressive and wonderful results and commercial applications, dampening the "Litany of Lamentations" that arise when only "the wicked prosper" (PH, p. 36). Where prosperity was seen as a shallow ambition, or in any case, not widely shared or simply not delivered, others, Hegel noted, took pride in expressing moral discontent, lamenting with a more "lofty bearing" the actual condition of the world. Hegel thought that "at no time so much as our own" were so many and varied complaints and demands for reform being made, "passions and interests essentially subjective, but under the mask of higher sanctions" (PH, pp. 36–7). In 1820, Hegel had supposed that philosophical history could answer both the personal and the moral laments, proving that "Universal Reason *does* realize itself" (PH, p. 37). It will always be easy, he thought, to "give oneself airs" and to discover "a deficiency in Providence", and call for changes and reforms in the light of one's own "ideals", but philosophical history can lead us to the insight that "the real world is as it ought to be" (PH, pp. 38), reconciling us to the "religious truth" that the course of world history, the destiny of reason, follows "the plan of Divine Providence" (PH, pp. 13–15).

A little over a hundred years later, in 1932, in a post-War Europe whose elect appearance as "the pearl of the sphere" was giving way to its provincial reality as "a little promontory on the continent of Asia" (HP, p. 31), Valéry writes of the "impossibility of representing the present world on a single plan and a single scale" and concludes that "it is useless…to conjecture what will be the sequel to our state of general bewilderment" (HP, p. 93). The "great novelty" of our time is not the imminence of a new world to come (HP, p. 89), but that we are lost and all at sea, and far from expecting an imminent end to this condition. Indeed, there are no signs of its ending at all: no end in sight, no end of crises, and hence also no end of "*boundless hopes*" (this time, next time), "*immense disappointments*" (another betrayal, another failure) and "*sinister expectations*" (nothing good will come of this) (HP, p. 94, emphasis in original). The Europe-crisis of the twentieth century is the very opposite of the nineteenth: not a strong sense of the present condition as capable of making philosophical-historical (teleological) sense – and hence, of all crises as only apparent crises – but a strong sense that any such sense of the present condition is lacking.

As Edmund Husserl will put it, this is not only a radical cultural crisis for Europe, but in view of Europe's cultural rootedness in Greek philosophy, an inseparably philosophical one: we have lost "faith in the meaning of history" (CES, p. 13) – and this means, above all, that we have lost faith in the fundamental metanarrative of philosophical history, lost faith in the old meaning of "Man" as a "rational being" on his way to his proper end (CES, p. 14).

Born in 1859 to a fairly scrupulously assimilated Jewish family, Husserl was a proud German, and regarded his own work in philosophy as a contribution to German culture, and hence also to world culture – universalism had always been, for him, the great lesson of German thought. In 1886 he was baptised in the Lutheran Church in Vienna. He is best known today as the inaugurator of "phenomenology" as a philosophical method and movement, although he is generally less widely known or read today than some of those who pursued philosophy in the name of phenomenology after him: Heidegger, Sartre, and Merleau-Ponty all came to eclipse (and challenge) the founding thoughts of what Husserl had hoped would be a new "rigorous science" that would rescue metaphysics from Kantian scepticism and Hegelian obscurity. In his own time, however, Husserl had become, by the late nineteen-twenties, "an international figure of great renown, and also something of an elder statesman of German philosophy" (IP, p. 86).

However, neither his baptism nor his social status could prevent him from being caught up in the rise of National Socialism. In 1935, his teaching licence and his German citizenship were both revoked. He was personally affected, but it would be quite wrong to say that his response was narrowly personal. He saw the developments in Germany within a much wider and much longer cultural development, part of a very long run dissolution of the European culture he so cherished: the slow dissolution of the culture of philosophy and science that had forged Europe in the first place. As Husserl saw it in the mid-1930s, Europeans were not only turning away from religious teachings and authorities (a development so concerning to Hegel and so welcomed by Marx), but, despite extraordinary scientific and technical developments, were increasingly sceptical about the idea that philosophy and science belong to (still less contribute to) a development which is "destined to create a genuine and contented humanity that is master of its fate" (CES, p, 290). Who today, Husserl asks, still believes that reason and science are allied to such grand ambitions of social and moral progress? Hardly anyone.

But Husserl himself was still a believer. He retained his faith in Europe and its modern promise – and wanted to do what he could to revive the European spirit that had become so "sick" in his time, hoping to renew Europe's spirit, and to renew it "as the pledge of a great and distant future for Man" (CES, p. 299); renewing Europe's promise, and along with that, inside that, its "mission for humanity" (CES, p. 299). As we shall see in this chapter, in a time when "the philosophical-historical idea (or the teleological sense) of European humanity" (CES, p. 269) – the old discourse of Europe's modernity – had seemed utterly overwhelmed by the course of both European science and European history, Husserl attempted to identify "the source of Man's now unbearable lack of clarity about his own existence" (CES, p. 297), and to forge "a rebirth of Europe" (CES, p. 299) through the reactivation of the original and in a certain way "immortal" source of both Europe's promise and its contemporary distress: the source that gave birth to historical Europe itself in "the first breakthrough to what is essential to humanity" (CES, p. 15) in "the spirit of philosophy" (CES, p. 299). Not only were his hopes in this regard to prove unfulfilled, his own work, as we shall see in the next chapter, his own universalism, was as freighted by Eurocentrism and racism as the German nationalism he unswervingly pitted himself against.

III

Husserl's writings from the 1930s, on the "the crisis of European humanity", are written in the shadow of an already up-and-running concern about the state of European life in his time as a state of crisis. But what is this up-and-running talk about a "European crisis" all about? Husserl certainly agrees that there is one, and takes up this question in order to provide "a new elucidation" of this "frequently treated theme" (CES, p. 269), taking up in his own way "the general lament about the crisis of our culture" that marked his time (CES, p. 5).

What was "the general lament"? What had been so widely said on that now recurrent theme that provides the background to Husserl's contribution to it? In fact, on that question, Husserl has very little to say. We are told that "it is said", that "Europe itself is in crisis" (CES, p. 270). But while his own sense of the crisis is, as we shall see, crystal clear, it is clearly his own. Piecing together a fair picture of the scene as he saw and heard it expressed by others entails working from just a few references in his texts, and is bound to be somewhat speculative. But a picture does emerge. I will attempt to reconstruct it here.

We can begin with his first reference to something "heard so often these days". That reference concerns the most puzzling aspect of his discussion of the "radical life-crisis of European humanity": namely, his wanting to relate it to what he calls "the crisis of the sciences". This is an immediately paradoxical set-up. For while the former is the sort of thing almost anyone might have had something to say about in the 1930s (and did), the latter hardly makes sense at all, and he admits it:

> A crisis of our sciences as such: can we seriously speak of it? Is not this talk, heard so often these days, an exaggeration?...This may be true of philosophy, which in our time threatens to succumb to scepticism, irrationalism, and mysticism...But how could we speak straightforwardly and quite seriously of a crisis of the sciences in general?...Thus we concede in advance some justification to the first inner protest against the title of these lectures. (CES, pp. 3–5)

So, if he did not think the positive sciences were anything other than "rigorous and highly successful" disciplines which "we can never cease to admire", why did he entitle the lectures that he gave in Prague in 1935, and which formed that basis of his work on the Europe-crisis theme, "The Crisis of European Sciences and Psychology" (CES, pp. 3–4)? The addition or special singling out of psychology, and the identification of "its own peculiar 'crisis'" (CES, p. 5), will be an important part of Husserl's own elucidation of the crisis of the sciences. But a connection between, on the one hand, "a crisis of our sciences as such" ("heard so often these days") and, on the other hand, (the "frequently treated theme" and "general lament" concerning) a crisis of European culture as such, of "Europe itself", seems already to be in the air. What is the perceived connection here?

Readers might understandably pick up on Husserl's reference to an increasingly unscientific character of philosophy (perhaps especially among his own students), and even more understandably the rise of the Nazis, as key background considerations. Both are significant, most obviously to Husserl himself. But even if we focus on these themes, we have to note that Husserl explicitly contrasts the situation in the sciences with that of philosophy, and it is not immediately obvious why the rise of Nazism would motivate talk of a crisis in European sciences either. Let's read on. Husserl soon returns to what he has heard, and how he heard it. It is worth attending to:

> We make our beginning with a change which set in at the turn of the past century in the general evaluation of the sciences. It concerns not the scientific character of the sciences but rather what they, or what science in

general, had meant and could mean for human existence. The exclusiveness with which the total world view of modern man, in the second half of the nineteenth century, let itself be determined by the positive sciences and be blinded by the "prosperity" [in English in the original SG] they produced, meant an indifferent turning-away from the questions which are decisive for a genuine humanity. Merely fact-minded sciences make merely fact-minded people. The change in public evaluation was unavoidable, especially after the war, and we know that it has gradually become a feeling of hostility among the younger generation. In our vital need – so we are told – this science has nothing to say to us. (CES, p. 6)

That Husserl turns to the English word "prosperity" is a clear marker of the general cultural condition he saw holding sway before the First World War: a turn towards commercial materialism, and a life in which "the whole of man's existence" is more and more informed by "merely private or otherwise limited cultural goals" (CES, p. 17). This was a shallow materialism that was, as I have indicated, (as one might say) super-sized by new scientific and technological advances developed for commercial ends. Examples from the second half of the nineteenth century include: the typewriter, tungsten steel, traffic lights, the telephone, the internal combustion engine, electric light-bulbs, photographic film, the dishwasher, the gramophone, the zip, nylon and rayon, tin cans, the fountain-pen, and – reminding us that what is in view here is an American commercial spirit or sprite achieving global prominence – Coca Cola.

Significantly, this commercialisation of the general culture, far from being an anxiety about Nazism, was in fact a standard anxiety for Nazism too. Indeed, Hitler saw his national task as providing a buffer against developments where "individual countries increasingly assumed the appearance of commercial undertakings", developments which "seemed bound eventually to transform the world into a mammoth department store" (MK, p. 138). Hitler did not decry "the enormous scientific and technical achievements of Europe" and of "European sciences" (MK, p. 241), but the idea, widely associated with the English-speaking world, that achieving economic prosperity was the main business of the State, and that the State "was, above all, an economic institution and should be constituted in accordance with economic interests" (MK, p. 131), seemed to him a fatal weakening of European and especially German cultural life. Hitler wanted completely to reject this view of the State ("nothing whatsoever to do with…economic development" (MK, p. 131)), emphasising that "the triumphant progress of technical science in Germany and the marvellous development of German industries and commerce led us to forget that a powerful State had been the necessary pre-requisite of that success" (MK, p. 131).

In order to see what is at stake in Husserl's discussion of the background discussion of the Europe-crisis – and the "vital need" he wanted to respond to in his own way – it is (unfortunately) worth tracking Hitler's concerns in *Mein Kampf* regarding the condition of the State and of a "general culture" which had become increasingly (as Husserl put it) "blinded by the 'prosperity'" that the European sciences had helped so much to produce.

For Hitler, the real and first purpose of the State was to secure "the conservation of a folk-community" and to help it fulfil its own ends (MK, 316). Material prosperity may "redound to the benefit of the individual citizen", and the State should "keep the national economic system in smooth working order" (MK, p. 488) as "one of the many auxiliary means which are necessary for the attainment of those [folk-community] aims" (MK, p. 131). But business is not the business of the State, and "a State has never arisen from commercial causes for the purpose of peacefully serving commercial ends" (MK, p. 133). Yet, in the latter part of the nineteenth century, especially under the sway of "the growing influence of America in the commercial markets of the world" (MK, p. 500), personal and egoistic "prosperity" was becoming increasingly the main (as Hegel put it) "aim of existence", and "in proportion to the extent that commerce assumed definite control of the State, money became more and more of a God whom all had to serve and bow down to" (MK, p. 198).

Hitler conceded that material prosperity may have delivered a certain "happiness" for a time, but the idea that it would deliver international peace ("that absurd notion of conquering the world by peaceful commercial means" (MK, p. 127)) let alone genuine national flourishing was a profound (and, he thought, largely Anglo-Saxon) falsehood. Hitler called for a "general culture" that, through a renewed cultural *Bildung*, shifted away from "what is real and practical" ("this 'commercialization' of the German nation" MK, p. 199) and "towards ideals":

> It is a characteristic of our materialistic epoch that our scientific education shows a growing emphasis on what is real and practical: such subjects, for instance, as applied mathematics, physics, chemistry, etc. Of course they are necessary in an age that is dominated by industrial technology and chemistry, and where everyday life shows at least the external manifestations of these. But it is a perilous thing to base the general culture of a nation on the knowledge of these subjects. On the contrary, that general culture ought always to be directed towards ideals. It ought to be founded on the humanist disciplines and should aim at giving only the ground work of further specialized instruction in the various practical sciences. Otherwise we should sacrifice those forces that are more important for the preservation of the nation than any technical knowledge. In the historical department the study of ancient history should not be omitted. Roman history, along general lines, is and will remain the best teacher, not only for our own time but also for the future. And the ideal of Hellenic culture should be preserved for us in all its marvellous beauty....A civilization is fighting for its existence. It is a civilization that is the product of thousands of years of historical development, and the Greek as well as the German forms part of it.

A clear-cut division must be made between general culture and the special branches. Today the latter threaten more and more to devote themselves exclusively to the service of Mammon. To counterbalance this tendency, general culture should be preserved, at least in its ideal forms. The principle should be repeatedly emphasized, that industrial and technical progress, trade and commerce, can flourish only so long as a folk community exists whose general system of thought is inspired by ideals, since that is the preliminary condition for a flourishing development of the enterprises I have spoken of. That condition is not created by a spirit of materialist egotism but by a spirit of self-denial and the joy of giving one's self in the service of others." (MK, p. 348)

And again:

It is just at those junctures when the idealistic attitude threatens to disappear that we notice a weakening of this force which is a necessary constituent in the founding and maintenance of the community and is thereby a necessary condition of civilization. As soon as the spirit of egotism begins to prevail among a people then the bonds of the social order break and man, by seeking his own personal happiness, veritably tumbles out of heaven and falls into hell. (MK, p. 249)

The sense of peril regarding the fate of the golden thread of Europe's Greek-Roman-Christian-Germanic/Modern civilisation arising from the materialistic techno-scientific commercialisation of general culture is, I think, exactly the sort of thing that Husserl has in view in the "general lament" concerning the Europe-crisis. It is, as Valéry, said too, "a general crisis of values" (HP, p. 109), which, at its heart, is a crisis concerning the European understanding of the meaning of human life, the meaning of Man.

It is at this point that a genuine sense of a connected "crisis of European sciences" might appear. In the face of a generally perceived evacuation from life of higher "ideals", Husserl sees, and would not be alone in seeing, a veritable "flood of naïve and excessive suggestions for reform" making their way (CES, p. 270) – among those suggestions, indeed surely first and foremost among them, the responses to the life-crisis that proceeds from the "ideals" promoted by Hitlerian National Socialism. I cut a sentence from the preceding quotation from *Mein Kampf* that tells us something about them. When urging a return to and revival of Europe's classical past he adds: "The differences between the various peoples [Greek-Roman-German] should not prevent us from recognizing the community of race which unites them on a higher plane. The conflict of our times is one that is being waged around great objectives".

Presupposing a natural-scientific validation for a racism and racist white-supremacism that Nazism always lacked, always called for, and would never attain, the Hitlerian response to commercialisation promised a cure for Europe's life-crisis, offering a discourse of "higher" ideals for the German people based on the (presumed to be) natural, and, he explicitly asserted, providentially pre-programmed superiority of "the white race" (MK, p. 507). Finding "the architype of what we understand by MAN" (MK, p. 241) in the European "community of race" (MK, p. 348) would rescue Europe, and first of all Germany, from the threatened meaninglessness of materialistic existence, and lead Europe back to its former world-historical leadership.

On the other hand, anyone repelled by the rise of Nazism, anyone witness, "in our unhappy times, to the most portentous upheavals" (CES, p. 6) that this rise was bringing with it, would with considerable justice want to turn to our best minds, to those whose work belongs to Europe's greatest intellectual achievements – the most "rigorous and highly successful" disciplines which "we can never cease to admire" – to hear what this science, European science, has to say on the "burning questions" concerning the meaning of our human existence.

And this is where troubles massively intensify: "in our vital need – so we are told – this science has nothing to say to us" (CES, p. 6).

That is the crisis of the European sciences. Science, this great achievement of modern European humanity, promised progress, prosperity and peace. But the progress and prosperity were existentially shallow and the peace short-lived. Into the space left vacant by the loss of confidence in the increasingly materialistic cultural heading of techno-scientific and commercial Europe, calls for changes and reforms multiplied, and grew ever more "excessive". Revolutionary international socialists and revolutionary national socialists found a growing following for their "ideals". In Germany, Hitler's party had even assumed political power. And where else might the public look to for such ideals? If "the European nations are sick" surely the sciences – and especially "the humanistic sciences" – should "perform the service" of providing "a medicine for nations and supra-national communities" (CES, p. 270). What, today, many would ask, do our "richly developed" sciences that deal with human life tell us in our hour of vital need? "What does science have to say about reason and unreason", and about the human not just as a biological organism but as a "free, self-determining being... free in his capacities for rationally shaping himself and his surrounding world"? What, in short, do they have to say about "Man" and "Man's spiritual existence" that might help guide us towards a properly human path of life (CES, p. 6)? Nothing. Nothing at all. And so the field was open – to fanatics.

IV

The questions that European science ("science" in the broad sense of *Gewissenshaft*) seemed to Husserl incapable of providing answers to – the "burning questions" of the time concerning the meaning of human existence, what it means to be a human being, the meaning of "Man", the whole enigmatic puzzle of coming to terms with who we are – may seem hopelessly vague and obscure. But rational, scientific inquiry had opened up the complexities of the natural world to our understanding. Is it really too much to "demand universal reflections and answers based on rational insight" to the complex questions of our own existence too? Husserl noted that pre-scientific humanity had developed a "lore of the nature cure" to attend to the human body in its times of crisis. Scientific medicine was not just an extension of "native experience and tradition" but was developed on the basis of theoretical insights accruing from the "fundamental sciences of nature" (CES, p. 269). But in the "life-crisis" now facing Europe ("Europe itself is sick") we still seem only to have "something like nature doctors" to turn to (CES, p. 270).

"Life" here (a "life-crisis") does not, Husserl stresses – immediately distancing himself from any biologism – have a "physiological sense" (CES, p. 270), rather it "concerns Man as a free, self-determining being" (CES, p. 6). And so we ask again: "What does science have to say about reason and about us men as subjects of this freedom?" (CES, p. 6). Nothing, again, nothing:

> The mere science of bodies clearly has nothing to say; it abstracts from everything subjective. As for the humanistic sciences, on the other hand, all the special and general disciplines which deal with man's spiritual existence,…their rigorous scientific character requires, we are told, that the scholar carefully excludes all evaluative positions… Scientific, objective truth is exclusively a matter of establishing how the world, the physical as well as the spiritual world, is in fact. But can the world, and human existence in it, truthfully have a meaning if the sciences recognise as true only what is objectively established in this fashion, and if history has nothing more to teach us than that all the shapes of the spiritual world, all the conditions of life, ideals norms upon which Man relies, form and dissolve themselves like fleeting waves?… Can we console ourselves with that? Can we live in this world, where historical occurrence is nothing but an unending concatenation of illusory progress and bitter disappointment? (CES, p. 6)

This is a wonderfully rich passage, beautifully summarising a sense of the predicament of modern Europe as its greatest achievement, the European sciences, close themselves off from any contribution to the unfolding of European spiritual life. Husserl's description for this condition is fairly straightforward: science, in his time, cleaves to a *positivistic* self-conception. Valéry had seen the same development as fundamental to the crisis condition of Europe's general culture too: "the growth of a positivist mentality" (HP, 106) which produces a "crisis in the sciences" having given up on "their ancient ideal of explaining the universe as a unified whole" (HP, p. 109).

This description is, however, merely descriptive. It specifies the restricted character of the ambitions of science. But Husserl, like Valéry, wants to see this restricted (positivistic) character of science as the expression of its self-conception being also a "residual" one. The positivist conception is what remains as the idea of science when it has "dropped" from the scope of its proper interest any interest in attaining an understanding that is "all encompassing" (CES, p. 8); limiting itself to "the world understood as the universe of mere facts" (CES, p. 9).

To understand this, we should note what, precisely, has been dropped. Husserl summarises them as *"problems of reason"* (CES, p. 9). There are standard topics in the theory of knowledge (rational justification), ethics (moral reasoning), the philosophy of action (practical reasoning) here, but Husserl's stress is that in all of these areas, and in relation to other more "metaphysical" questions (God, immortality, freedom), we are ultimately concerned with questions that concern "Man" as "a rational being" and hence also with questions "of the 'meaning' or reason in history" (CES, p. 9). They all engage with the meaning of our own being understood as rational subjectivity, and its developmental history. And this seems to have been expelled from the domain of rigorous science, which now maintains an interest in Man as a subjective being only in psychology, although it does so there only beginning with objective corporeity which is assumed to be the causal ground or foundation of "psychic life" (CES, p. 271).

There is widespread agreement on the basic trajectory. It is all about the ongoing movement of scientific specialisation that characterises the history of European science out of its Greek beginnings. But to see why Husserl is convinced that "the whole way of thinking" that manifests itself in this development rests on "prejudices", and in fact has a significant share in "the responsibility for the European sickness" (CES, p. 272), we need to run through some of his clarification of that history in the *Crisis* text.

In Husserl's telling of it, the story begins with the emergence in ancient Greece of individuals and small groups who called themselves philosophers. Husserl presents this as the birth of a new culture characterised by "a *new sort of attitude* of individuals to their surrounding world" (CES, p. 276), and its "consequence", he continues "is the breakthrough of a completely new sort of spiritual structure, rapidly growing into a systematically self-enclosed cultural form; the Greeks called it *philosophy*" (CES, 276):

> Correctly translated, in the original sense, that means nothing other than universal science, science of the universe, of the all-encompassing unity of all that is. Soon the interest in the All…begins to particularize itself according to the general forms and regions of being, and thus philosophy, the one science, branches out into many particular sciences. (CES, p. 276)

This is the first step only, *en route* towards a positivist conception: "specifically human questions were not…banned from the realm of science" (CES, p. 7). Perhaps paradoxically, the next and most fateful step "determining the whole meaning of the *modern* period" (CES, p. 197) comes at the time in this history of specialisation when the attempt is made again to retrieve the ancient idea of a universal science, and of seeing all of the special sciences as "branches of the One philosophy": the time of the Renaissance (CES, p. 8). But this distinctively modern step came with a crucial change. The idea of an all-encompassing universality of interest is replaced with the idea of a method with universal validity. This was in no way intended to limit the scope of scientific interest, but definitively to solve "all conceivable problems…problems of fact and of reason" (CES, p. 9). But this conviction, Husserl argues "could not survive for long": the method – "mathematical natural science" – was only ever going to bring "unquestionable success" in the positive sciences of corporeal nature (CES, p. 10). Rapidly, the One philosophical science bifurcates into "metaphysics", which comes to be understood as concerned with "specifically philosophical questions" – viz. the problems of reason – and the "positive sciences" which dealt with "nature" understood as "corporeal nature" or "the objective world" (CES, p. 272). Philosophy had once been understood as "the queen of the sciences", establishing the unity of and providing the epistemological foundations for all knowledge; in our time this inspiring ambition is replaced by "a growing feeling of failure" (CES, p. 11). This feeling was motivated not only by the external impression of a "monstrous" contrast between the developments in the two fields (metaphysics and science), but also by internal developments in philosophy, "extending from Hume and Kant to our own time", which came to regard "the repeated failures of metaphysics" as failures in principle, and thus joins with the general protest over the "deeply rooted assumptions" of the old ideal of philosophy, and a rising "scepticism about the possibility of metaphysics" (CES, pp. 11–12).

The ideal of a universal philosophy opens the "modern age" and "the primal establishment of modern European humanity itself – humanity which seeks to renew itself radically, as against the medieval and ancient age, precisely through its new philosophy" (CES, p. 11). However, instead of giving rise to lasting lines of development "this ideal suffers inner dissolution" (CES, p. 12). For Husserl, this is what has led to the crisis of the European sciences as we have set it out here. The sciences continue to flourish in their own now-limited, residual domain; and metaphysics, the queen of sciences, collapses within the development of its own internal, philosophical critique. In this condition, in the face of "humanity struggling to understand itself", Husserl calls for a *new* sense of a "renaissance of ancient philosophy" and to "initiate a new age", with "a new beginning" that can overcome "the sceptical deluge" that is threatening to undermine the aspiration of seeking the true meaning of being "everywhere" (CES, p. 13).

The reference to Hume and Kant as drivers of the historical "inner dissolution" of the Renaissance ideal is in some ways understandable: both insist that genuine knowledge is restricted to the domain of possible experience. But these figures are profoundly ambiguous for Husserl: for both also opened up a "turn" in the history of philosophy towards what he calls "*a completely new way* of assessing the objectivity of the world…and correlatively that of the objective sciences" (CES, p. 90). Indeed, for Husserl, they inaugurate a turn in philosophy which is "on the way" to overcoming the positivistic "decapitation" of philosophy that they also contribute to (CES, p. 9). There was a positive Humean contribution here, as we shall see, but the great step is, for Husserl, fundamentally Kantian:

> [Kant's] is a philosophy which, in opposition to prescientific and scientific objectivism, goes back to knowing subjectivity as the primal locus of all objective formations of sense and ontic [i.e. worldly SG] validities, undertakes to understand the existing world as a structure of sense and validity, and in this way seeks to set in motion an essentially new type of scientific attitude and a new type of philosophy. In fact, if we do not count the negativistic, sceptical philosophy of a Hume, the Kantian system is the first attempt, and one carried out with impressive scientific seriousness, at a truly transcendental philosophy meant to be a rigorous science in a sense of scientific rigor which has only now been discovered and which is the only genuine sense. (CES, p. 99)

Reading Hume, not unproblematically, as thinking in the wake of Berkeley's transformational construal of the "data" of human sensibility – shifting from a Cartesian conception of "pictures of the world" towards an idealist construction of *"the world of bodies itself"* – Husserl conceives the positive contribution of Hume's philosophy as lying in Hume's affirmation that the mind (with its "impressions" and "ideas", and laws of "association") "engendered the whole world, *the world itself*, not merely something like a picture" (CES, p. 89). Kant then adds to this the thought that "if common experience really is to be of *objects of nature*" of the kind that is explored by the positive sciences, then the "data" of the Humean "world" must be constructed *a priori* by the mind not in merely psychological terms but in the very terms that genuinely belong to "the practice of the pure mathematical sciences" and of "all natural scientific thinking" (CES, p. 94). Kant, following on from and reacting against Hume thus "outlines a great, systematically constructed, and *in a new way* still scientific philosophy in which the Cartesian turn to conscious subjectivity works itself out in the form of a transcendental subjectivism" (CES, p. 95).

For Husserl then, the philosophical (internal) critique of metaphysics both undermines the Renaissance goal of grounding science on foundations that are rational and objectively real, and is "on the way" to a renewed restoration of its ideal sense, a sense that his (Husserl's) own work aims to complete in a *"final turn"* in and beyond the subjectivism of "modern" (Cartesian) philosophy (CES, p. 100). Following Hume and Kant, this will be a turn to the "deeply concealed subjective ground" of all structures of objectivity, the originary source of the sense of the objective world, including the sense of its being, and indeed the self-concealing source of the "misguided rationalism" (CES, p. 290) that is internal to the modern understanding of "objective-scientific method" itself

(CES, p. 100). This turn will be at once a turn towards a future of "radical self-responsibility" for Man, and a re-turn back to the "genuine sense" of philosophy established in its originating Greek commencement, as the thought of the unity of "*reason*" (Greek "*nous*" [νοῦς]) and "*everything that is*" or "*being*" (Greek "*on*" [ὄν]) or "*ousia*" [οὐσία]) (CES, p. 11).

For Husserl, there is an inherent teleology in the history of philosophy (CES, p. 98); a "latent orientation toward reason" that unfolds in its development (CES, p. 15), in which reason "seeks to come to itself" (CES, p. 97). The "naïve objectivism" of modern European science is a sort of necessary, or at least understandable, detour in this process. We are, in the natural attitude of everyday life where we unreflectively inhabit the sense-making "framework of meaning" that characterises what Husserl calls the "life-world" (CES, p. 284), directed towards objects in the "surrounding world" (CES, p. 294), and object-oriented science merely follows this natural objective orientation (CES, p. 297). But this objectivism has led, with equal inevitability, to the crisis of European humanity. For far from "psychic" life arising causally from corporeal nature, from "true nature in the sense of natural science", on the contrary, that sense of nature (of "objectivity as self-sufficiency") "is a product of the spirit that investigates nature", and that spirit can only be apprehended and understood in terms of the historical "life" (in the non-physiological sense) of the community it belongs to and its historical surrounding world: in terms of the "spiritual shape" of the "life world" that the investigators of nature inhabit.

For Husserl, this is none other than "spiritual shape" of Europe itself, the "life-world" of European humanity, and the "supranationality of a completely new sort" that comes into being there (CES, p. 289). It now faces a "life-crisis" – a crisis of meaningfulness – and the "crisis of the sciences" is its deepest expression. Nevertheless, for Husserl just as much as for Kant, Hegel and Marx, this crisis, which is essentially a crisis of rational subjectivity in its self-development, is not conceived as a real crisis, not a life/death moment for European rationalism but only a crisis concerning the "*apparent* failure of rationalism" (CES, p. 299) due to the rise of the "absurd naturalism", the "naïve objectivism" that the natural attitude seems to speak for (CES, p. 297). It is a "mistake", but an "understandable one"; not one that threatens the discourse of Europe's modernity as such, not one that would render the project of philosophical history a fantasy or fiction. Nevertheless, the situation is one of "distress" (CES, p. 294), and in a time of "burning need" (CES, 296) Husserl will have wanted to do everything: to explain how we have got here; to lead us back, "*before all decisions*" (CES, p. 17) – which is to say, especially, before all political decisions aimed at "curing" the present crisis – to a sense of the subjective source of all sense; and to take Europe back on to its promising path towards radical self-responsibility for the meaning of Man.

Husserl never finished his Europe-crisis book. It was not that the War intervened; he simply never finished it. Wanting to find a new way to articulate a discourse of reason "coming to terms with itself" (CES, p. 298), a new path towards the realisation of a self-responsible rational humanity from the grounds of European philosophy, and "speaking according to [his] best lights" (CES, p. 18), the lights gave out. And in 1939, the "portentous upheavals" Husserl was witnessing in 1935 finally exploded into the second terrible World War of European origin of the twentieth century. Modern Europe, and its promise, would never be the same again.

11

DISPIRITING EUROPE

Of Spirit, what the devil!

— Jacques Derrida

*

[The following text was left at the top of the manuscript for this chapter, with no further sign that there was a settled location or clear continuation for it, either in this volume or as part of the second volume. We leave it here as indicative of its aim.]

It would be so much easier if there were just good Europeans and bad Europeans.

Husserl concluded the "Vienna Lecture" – in words recalling many of Valéry's remarks and actually citing Nietzsche – by saying that "Europe's greatest danger is weariness", and that *"we"* "struggle against this greatest of all dangers" as "'good Europeans'" (CES, p. 299). It really would have been so much easier if there were just good Europeans ("we") and bad Europeans ("they").

But ghost stories have to live with cohabitation. And any too-simple effort at distributively sorting out the cohabiting of virtues and vices in Europe's modern self-understanding belongs to a vision of progress that is itself too simple, too modern, too modern European.

Husserl's text on "spiritual Europe" opposed itself to the rising tide of National Socialism. But his text has more than one spirit. It is not everywhere simply in conflict with the dispiriting biologistic racism that was making its way. Indeed, the spirit in Husserl that stands most squarely against that racism seems itself caught up in a racist logic. Nevertheless, we can and should begin to read their co-workings, their co-operations, and at least make a start to form and forge

[The text ends here.]

I

Concluding his introduction to the crisis of the European sciences and the task to "bring latent reason to the understanding of its own possibilities", Husserl returns to the question of the significance of "European humanity":

> [Taking up this task] is the only way to decide whether the *telos* which was inborn in European humanity at the birth of Greek philosophy – that of humanity which seeks to exist, and is only possible, through philosophical reason, moving endlessly from latent to manifest reason and forever seeking its own norms through this, its truth and genuine human nature – whether this *telos*, then, is merely a factual, historical delusion, the accidental acquisition of merely one among many other civilisations and histories, or whether Greek humanity was not rather the first breakthrough to what is essential to humanity as such, its *entelechy*. (CES, p. 16)

The question of the relationship between, on the one hand, philosophy and its history, and, on the other hand, Europe and its history, is posed here in a fundamental way. Is what has been called "philosophy" just one among other pursuits that went on in this place, and concerning which Europe would perhaps be marked but nevertheless marked only as one human heading among others, or is Europe the place that it is only insofar as its heading is inseparable from the teleology of philosophy as the coming to itself of reason?

In the latter case, and "if Man is a rational being (*animal rationale*)", Europe would be divided off from other human cultures in a profoundly original way. Europe would no longer be conceivable as a merely regional site, of one "empirical anthropological type" of humanity, among others, where "Europe" might be set side-by-side with other regional cultures, "China" and "India", for example (CES, p. 16). Instead, there would be an essential relationship between this developing culture, with its "birth" in Greek philosophy, and humanity's essential business of "being in the business" (this is what "its *entelechy*" means here) of becoming properly human as such. Just as much as it does in Kant and Hegel, "Europe" belongs to Husserl's philosophical history in an internal and not just factual historical way. Europe plays, as Derrida puts it, "a major, organizing role in the transcendental teleology of reason", making Husserl's discourse of Europe's modernity, once more, a history of the world in which Europe is assigned a "special mission" for humanity; "*men of universality*", as Valéry puts it, with his (French) "paradox": "to specialize in the sense of the universal" (HP, p. 436).

The deep significance of the crisis of European culture that belongs to the crisis of European science is that it is precisely a crisis of the classic discourse of Europe's modernity, and hence also of the classic European discourse of the history Man. Can we really believe today that Europe's golden-thread history carries it beyond traditional forms of human life towards the proper end of Man? Can we still today persist in thinking that there is something like a "history of the world" that charts the development of Man from an originally primitive condition towards an increasingly "rational civilisation" (CES, p. 14)? "It would seem", as Kant had anxiously worried at the start of this adventure, "that only a *novel* [*Roman*] could result from such premises" (Kant, p. 52). We have been reading this novel – and it is no romance.

Is there any life left in the Greco-Biblical conception of Man, and of Europe's modern promise? Is there another way for philosophical history? Is there anything that survives the worn-out programmes of its Eurocentrism and anti-Eurocentrism? In the second volume, my theme will be an exhausted Europe rather than a crisis-Europe, and I will try to come to terms with the European cultural heritage in a way that goes beyond the old modern understanding of Europe and its history, and of Man and his teleology. Small steps will already have been made in thinking about democracy freed from teleology in this volume, and this theme will emerge again at the end of this chapter too.

Husserl, as we have seen, wants to raise a phoenix from the ashes, and resists the thought that the idea of a universal and infinite *telos* "inborn" in European humanity is an "historical delusion" or fiction. He wants to be able to affirm that the "portentous upheavals" of his time can only be, must only be, an apparent crisis of European rationalism. Keeping to the modern European subject, keeping "faith" with "the possibility of universal knowledge" that had been "the vocation" and the "calling" of philosophers is something that Husserl, as a philosopher "educated by the genuine philosophers of the great past", "cannot let go" (CES, p. 17); and hence, he finds a Europe-responsibility here that he simply cannot duck. For Husserl, the fundamental meaning of "being European" is to belong to the historical culture which originates from, and has been fundamentally determined by, the emergence of a radically new attitude – the theoretical attitude – that appeared for the first time in the history of the world in ancient Greece, of which all Europeans, as such, and first of all "we ourselves, we philosophers of the present", are "the heirs" (CES, pp. 16–17). Philosophers, European philosophers, as such, are "functionaries" not only in the development of a new regional-cultural type, but "functionaries of mankind" (CES, p. 17). Pitting himself against a Eurocentric racist biologism, Husserl will affirm an equally Eurocentric cultural universalism: everyone is entitled to and has a motivation to "Europeanize", the right to the culture of philosophy is a universal right. In this chapter, I will carry this thought back to the theme broached earlier in this book regarding what Derrida called "the paradox of the paradox" of European identity (OH, p. 75): namely that, when Europe cultivates itself most intensely, when it relates itself to itself in terms of its "feeling of being 'men of universality'", it pledges itself to an interest that cannot be and, in principle, should not be reserved for Europeans alone. In Husserl's work, this pledge is run through with a Eurocentrism that is every bit as troubling as its opponent's. However, without recoiling to a naive anti-Eurocentrism, I aim to show that Husserl's universalism can be taken in a different, more pluralist and democratic direction, opening onto a new call for the right to philosophy as a cosmopolitan right, a right that belongs to all.

II

What happened in ancient Greece? Derrida's *Diplôme* dissertation on Husserl identifies a striking puzzle concerning the possibility of this first-time appearance in the history of the world. On the one hand, it seems to be completely beyond the limits of any philosophical history to explain why "at a certain moment, the pure idea of philosophy came and merged itself with the destiny of a people" (PG, p. 156). And yet, the mere historical-empirical existence of these people is supposed to have brought into being an idea with respect to which that historical-empirical existence now appears (for the modern philosophical historian) as never having been merely historical-empirical, as belonging to something other than a natural-empirical causality. It would belong, rather, to a development that this idea of philosophy will (later) show to have been internal to "the very being of transcendental subjectivity" and the teleology that is inseparable from it (PG, p. 157). Here is the puzzle: the appearance of philosophy cannot take place outside the history of the development of rational subjectivity, and yet it cannot be fully explained by that history either. Indeed, it seems to be explicable only in the terms of the very "naturalism" or "historicism" that philosophical history will reveal as insufficient to comprehending the meaning and truth of human history.

Although Derrida does not mention this passage, Husserl does offer some kind of humanly natural explanation of the historical-empirical appearance of philosophy when he refers to the attitude of *"wonder"*, which the Greek philosophers took to be the origin of the attitude of pure *theoria*, the origin of the origin of philosophy (CES, p. 285). This attitude might arise, Husserl suggests, from "a playful looking-about when one's quite immediate vital needs are satisfied or when working hours are over" (CES, p. 285). However, this perhaps necessary but certainly not sufficient condition is really no match for the eruptive Greek event that Husserl wants to identify: "the developmental beginning of a new human epoch" (CES, p. 274), the appearance in history of "a completely new sort of spiritual structure" (CES, p. 276). Husserl's beginning is already something of a fiction, and it runs into a story that rapidly configures Europe as a figure of the exemplary heading of Man as such. This new theoretical beginning, which begins in historical time with just a few disruptive individuals, "a few Greek eccentrics" (CES, p. 289), develops itself into "a new type of communalization" (CES, p. 277), a form of social life powerfully irrigated by a commitment to "a voluntary *epochē* [or suspension] of all natural praxis including the higher level praxis [directed to the general welfare of a community] that serves the natural sphere" (CES, p. 282). With this new attitude, "a new humanity made capable of an absolute self-responsibility" emerges (CES, p. 283). With "the peculiar universality of his critical stance", where no "pregiven opinion" is accepted uncritically (CES, p. 286), philosophers form and forge a culture, the culture of "we, the Europeans", that is neither bound by any local traditions, nor indeed by any form of local humanness, but which inaugurates a new and universally fitting heading for Man, and "a distant future" for all (CES, p. 299).

Against the background of racist National Socialism in power in Germany, everything in Husserl's discussion of Europe and its contemporary crisis can be seen – and was seen by Nazi academics – as devoted to providing a rigorously humanistic-scientific counter-narrative to the "ideals" of race thinking that were beginning to be followed so ruthlessly in his own country. And it is with his uprooting of philosophy from the "soil" of any regional humanity that the most radical (and perhaps still radically disruptive) dimension of Husserl's conception of the idea of Europe makes itself felt, and is where his challenge to the prevailing discourse on race is at its strongest. For this "European tradition" of philosophy is, Husserl insists, essentially not "bound to the soil" of any people or any place (CES, p. 286). Indeed, it precisely delocalises itself from any particular regional-cultural heading in its constantly being-towards a "way to be" for Man "defined as the rational animal" which therefore *can* belong (and normatively should belong) to absolutely anyone: "man is the rational animal, and in this broad sense even the Papuan is a man and not a beast" (CES, p. 290): "the universal critical attitude toward anything and everything pregiven in the tradition is not inhibited in its spread by any national boundaries" nor any regionally-traditional "way to be" (CES, p. 288).

III

"Europe", as Derrida noted in his *Diplôme*, is not understood by Husserl "in a 'worldly' sense that it might acquire from a geographical, political or other specification" (PG, p. 154). "Europe" is not reducible to "empirical Europe". As "born" with a "spiritual meaning from the idea of philosophy" (PG, p. 155) it is linked internally to a teleology which "presid[es] over the very constitution of 'worldly' history", a teleology presiding over the history of empirical humanity as such (PG, p. 154). Born of philosophy, Europe is, equally, born to spread out or enlarge, geophilosophically preconfigured in a geopolitical way as "a colonial and missionary culture" (UNESCO, p. 9).

Born to missionary exemplarity, Europe's spreading out thus also makes it the spectral site of cohabitation of both a humanist universalism and a Europo-ethnocentrism, a cohabitation perhaps nowhere more densely entangled than in the little phrase of Husserl's that we have just cited, and which he repeated again with a minor alteration in the space of a few sentences: "even the Papuan". Two representative passages from Husserl's "Vienna Lecture" introduce the troubling scene:

> How is the spiritual shape of Europe to be characterized? Thus we refer to Europe not as it is understood geographically, as on a map, as if thereby the group of people who live together in this territory would define European humanity. In the spiritual sense the English Dominions, the United State, etc., clearly belong to Europe, whereas the Eskimos or Indians presented

> as curiosities at fairs, or the Gypsies, who constantly wander about Europe, do not. (CES, p. 273)

and

> Reason is a broad title. According to the old familiar definition, man is the rational animal, and in this broad sense even the Papuan is a man and not a beast. He has his ends and he acts reflectively, considering the practical possibilities. The works and methods that grow out of this go to make up a tradition, being understandable again by others in virtue of their rationality. But just as man and even the Papuan represent a new stage of animal nature, i.e. as opposed to the beast, so philosophical reason represents a new stage of human nature and its reason. (CES, p. 290)

"Even the Papuan". It is clearly intended as a gesture of maximal humanist inclusion, and yet, as Dermot Moran notes, it has also been appealed to by others "to accuse Husserl of a certain 'Eurocentrism', even racism" (EP, p. 466). Frankly, I think both accusations are entirely justified. But I do not think that is the end of the story, or even the end of the line for the "philosophical reason" that has tied Europe's history to the history of the world. First, there certainly is "a certain 'Eurocentrism'" in Husserl's philosophical history, massively so. True, it is not exactly the sort of Europo-ethnocentrism that some of his accusers might want to see here: not the exceptionalism or supremacism that ranks different world ethnicities or races according to their relative attainments, achievements or accomplishments, and places Europe and Europeans at the top. Europe is definitely "at the top", or rather "at the head", for Husserl, but we have to remember what "Europe" means, what "European humanity" is, for Husserl. It is not an "anthropological type" among others, with its own "works and methods", its particular customs, local traditions, cultural goals and so on. (And Husserl says absolutely nothing about ethnicity or race. I will come back to this.) On the contrary, the philosophical-scientific character of "spiritual Europe" means that, as Moran puts it, "it is precisely an overcoming of finite particularity (including that of the 'Greek' folk-*Umwelt*)" (EP, 478). With the development of a philosophical culture the "ancient Greeks" are not simply or are already no longer simply culturally-particular "Greeks", and the Europeans are never simply an empirical ethno-cultural group among others either.

But how free of all ethnocentrism is this "spiritual" determination of Europe? On the one hand, "Europeanization" is, for Husserl, an essential possibility for any people, and a possibility for which he sees "a motive" – a rational reason, a reason rooted in our being as rational creatures – for "all other human groups": everyone, "even the Papuan", can in this sense "Europeanize themselves", and have an essential motive to do so (CES, p. 275). "European culture" is, for Husserl, an "ideal" culture of "ideal forms", corresponding to what he calls "universal and infinite tasks"; an ideally human spiritual configuration shaped by the *entelechy* of Man (as rational animality) as such. Thus, insofar as the teleology of universal history "is immanent" in Europe, its only "particularity" is the radical movement beyond finite particularity, and towards the universal and infinite task of attaining a form of communalisation that lives "in the free shaping of its existence" (CES, p. 274), and hence a "development towards an ideal shape of life and being as an eternal pole" (CES, p. 275).

Hitler had suggested that "it will be the task of those who set themselves to the study of a universal history of civilization to investigate history from [the racial] point of view, instead of allowing themselves to be smothered under the mass of external data, as is only too often the case with our present historical science" (MK, 243). Husserl might agree with the last part of this, which points directly towards the crisis of the European sciences as he understands that, but it is precisely with that in view that he would have wanted his universalism completely to oppose the very idea of the racist point of view specified in the first part.

The Nazis knew an enemy when they saw one. Indeed, as Dermot Moran has shown in detail, "Husserl's universalism was specifically singled out for ridicule by quite a number of professional philosophers sympathetic to the National Socialist outlook" (EP, p. 468), with Husserl himself identified as "the Jewish philosopher" (EP, p. 473). And yet, on the other hand, it is not so simple. Only two sentences after Husserl had articulated his Papuan, including a sense of Man *qua* rational animality, he repeats his gesture in a subtly different formulation: "Man and even the Papuan represent a new stage of animal nature" (CES, p 290). Man *and*? Is the Papuan both Man (broadly speaking) and yet not Man or not yet Man (in some other way of speaking)? In his reading of Husserl's "Vienna Lecture" in *Of Spirit* Derrida picks up on this formulation with growing concern and suspicion, already anxious that "this 'spiritual' determination of European humanity" is not as innocent as it may seem (OS, p. 120). What sort of "spirit" is at work in this "spiritual" determination?

Derrida's hackles had already been raised by Husserl's delimitation of "spiritual Europe", highlighting how, in the very sentence in which Husserl includes "the English Dominions and the United States" he then excludes (as the English translation of *Of Spirit* renders Husserl's words) "Eskimoes, Indians, travelling zoos or gypsies permanently wandering all over Europe" from the same space (OS, p. 120). Derrida calls this a "sinister passage" and "a ludicrous kind of... philosophical non-sequitur" (OS, p. 120):

> The retention of the English colonies in "spiritual" Europe would be proof of a ludicrous enough kind – by the comic load weighing down this sinister passage – of a philosophical non-sequitur whose gravity can be measured in two dimensions: (1) It is apparently necessary, therefore, in order to save the English dominions, the power and culture they represent, to make a distinction between, for example, good and bad Indians. This is not very "logical," either in "spiritualist" logic or in "racist" logic. (2) This text was delivered in 1935 in Vienna! (OS, pp. 120–1)

A central line of this interpretation pretty clearly misunderstands what Husserl is saying. Unfortunately, however, things only look worse, not better for Husserl when one reads it right. The good/bad Indian worry seems to arise because, on the one hand, India is among "the English Dominions" that are included within spiritual Europe, and yet other Indians "in" geographical Europe are excluded from it. "This is not very 'logical', either in a 'spiritualist' logic or in a 'racist' logic", Derrida concludes. However, the Indian case can't be what Husserl was (or could have been) thinking about. Here's the problem. Derrida takes Husserl's first gesture to be one that attempts "the retention of *the English colonies* in 'spiritual' Europe" (emphasis mine). But the "English colonies" that Derrida invokes and the "English Dominions" that Husserl refers to are quite different. In 1931 Dominion status (a certain degree of sovereign independence) was given to *some* of the English colonies; namely, those which were conceived by the British colonisers as already heading (themselves) towards full independence. And until 1947, the English Dominions included *only*: Canada, Australia, New Zealand, the Union of South Africa, the Irish Free State, and Newfoundland. India was not conferred this status until 1947, rather meaninglessly, at the time of its attaining for itself actual independence. (We should recall here our pro-Turkish European Bloom: "Geography does not matter. What matters are the cultural and historical associations. Australasia and the Americas are largely European settler colonies, with claims to be 'European' that may even be superior to those of Turkey, which are still strong.") With this in view, Husserl's reference to "the English Dominions and the United States" (as inside), and "Eskimos, Indians, travelling zoos [and] gypsies, wandering all over Europe" (as outside) is, unfortunately, all too logical both in a "spiritualist" logic and in a "racist" logic.

Recall again Husserl's claim: "…we refer to Europe not as it is understood geographically, as on a map, as if thereby the group of people who live together in this territory would define European humanity. In the spiritual sense the English Dominions, the United State, etc., clearly belong to Europe, whereas the Eskimos or Indians presented as curiosities at fairs, or the Gypsies, who constantly wander about Europe, do not" (CES, p. 273). Regarding the first part of the second sentence, we should note that when Husserl picks out the English Dominions and the United States – neither of which are historically understandable apart from a racist logic – he is implicitly attending to a contrast with a more general reference to the English colonies (the British Empire), a contrast that Hitler stressed too when he noted that "glancing casually over the map of the British Empire one is inclined easily to overlook the existence of a whole Anglo-Saxon world" (MK, p. 122). After 1931, the existence of that Anglo-Saxon world was somewhat more visible, and Husserl's identification of "the English Dominions and the United States" as part of Europe "in the spiritual sense" sees it. It does not get better. Regarding the second part of the second sentence, the English translation in *Of Spirit* understates another European racism at work in the very language Husserl uses and the very phenomenon he calls or recalls (without perceptible horror) in a supposedly "spiritual" description of "spiritual Europe". The second sentence runs on "...*nicht aber die Eskimos oder Indianer der jahrmarktsmenagerien oder die Zigeuner, die dauernd in Europa herumvagabundieren*". The first few words of this are better translated, I think, as "...but not the Eskimos or [Red-]Indians of the fairground menageries..." Husserl is speaking here of what today would be called "human zoos". And I think Husserl probably takes two American examples in order to distinguish between "European" and "non-European" Americans, thus re-introducing something of Derrida's otherwise not convincing good/bad Indians contrast in terms of a good/bad American contrast, but now with a clear racial sense, or at the very least a clearly "spiritualist" logic. Husserl could have used other (no less problematic) examples, since Africans, Samoans and Papuans were also regularly "exhibited" as examples of "purely natural" human beings at these foul and humiliating side-shows at European fairs.

It gets still worse with the rest of the second sentence, which runs on "... or [and now a German word often but not always laden with racist connotations, and the very one used by the Nazis, so we might say] the Pikeys, that forever bum around Europe".

Nice. Very spiritual that spiritual Europe. On the other hand, would it have been any better if he had said: "...but not the Inuit or Native Americans exhibited in those appalling fairground side-shows or the Roma, that make their way around Europe"? Would that have made it alright? Would it have helped the example? It certainly would not put the Europe example in a more congenial light. Indeed, it would serve then only to show up something deeply troubling and dark in its spirit, something that Husserl seems altogether untroubled by. At this point, one might begin to wonder whether a "spiritualist" logic and a "racist" logic are really so different anyway.

This is what Derrida has in view in the second dimension for "measuring the gravity" of Husserl's statement on spiritual Europe: "This text was delivered in 1935 in Vienna!". This simple fact does indeed raise a powerful point in view of Husserl's own ambition to be speaking against the "monstrous upheavals" of his time, a time when, for example, the Roma – like the Jews – were already being systematically persecuted by the Nazis (see EP, p. 465). It is an enigmatic, troubling and thought-provoking fact that, although Husserl's text elaborates, as Derrida puts it, "a discourse which in general is not suspected of the worst", "the reference to *spirit*, to the *freedom* of spirit, and to spirit as *European* spirit could and still can ally itself with the politics one would want to oppose to it" (OS, p. 121).

And, of course, one should oppose Husserl's universalism to that racist politics; just as that racist politics would oppose itself to the universalism of "the Jewish philosopher" Husserl. Despite its more than merely condescending formulation, but precisely because it takes *the* example of a humanness which his audience in Vienna in 1935 would have familiarly and unhesitatingly situated as "man closest to animality" (Papua New Guinea was a German protectorate at the time, and the Papuan's were widely discussed in both academic anthropological literature and public media, as well as "exhibited" at *jahrmarktsmenagerien*),

Husserl's genuinely inclusive gesture places the greatest emphasis possible on the fact that the thought of race difference has absolutely nothing to do with the movement of universal history. While not every part of humanity is, for Husserl, at the same stage of history, it is an irreducible feature of "the history of Man", as he understands it, that no one is "thrown…out of Europe"; every human type, "even the Papuan", has access, can and should have access, to the higher stage of humanity that is, for Husserl, "imminent" in "spiritual Europe".

The phrase "thrown…out of Europe" comes from the immediate continuation of Derrida's discussion of Husserl's sinister passage, where Derrida asks (more or less rhetorically) whether Heidegger, who is always "suspected of the worst", would "have thrown the 'non-Aryans' out of Europe, as did he who knew he was himself 'non-Aryan,' i.e. Husserl?" (OS, p. 122). Independently of the Heidegger question (which I will come back to later in this chapter), I find this accusation aimed at Husserl, and especially its re-introduction of a standard racial lexicon (even in quotation marks) that plays no part in Husserl's own analysis, un-called for. For unless one wants completely to forget all history and to subscribe to a completely abstract universalism, Husserl's parting of the human ways (if not the way he parts them) is simply undeniable. Indeed, one risks losing sight of everything if one denies it. The "exhibits" at the human zoos were humiliated by the Europeans who brought them there. But there is no discourse, and certainly none in Heidegger, that could lead us to affirm that those poor souls were, after all, "European" or should have been counted as "European" by virtue of their presence in those dreadful European travelling fairs. Despite the oddness of the second iteration ("Man and even the Papuan"), which I will come back to in the next section, Husserl's decisive category is rationality, which is universal, and his Europe-crisis texts (including the "Vienna Lecture") never invoke racial categories to distinguish different ways of being human. Nevertheless, Derrida is right to want us to see that indulging in self-righteous delight in interminably condemning Heidegger (easy to do) oversimplifies a very complex conceptual nexus to the extent that we can "forget what certain 'victims' wrote and thought", and thought not in the name of race or Germany but in the name of spirit (OS, p. 121). Husserl's universalist and missionary philosophical history is undeniably attended and assisted by a racist and colonial spectre. And this leaves us with a deep, paradoxical and perhaps yet to be understood fact about the spectral character of racism in general: not only can something one can and should call "racism" do without (and has in fact always done without) a foundation in racial (biologistic) science, it does not even depend on a racist (biologistic) logic.

IV

In order to see how these discourses – universalist and racist – can run together in this way, I want to look more closely at Husserl's second iteration of the Papuan inclusion, the strikingly Janus-faced "Man and even the Papuan". This oddly separating formulation – coming hot-on-the-heels of a sibling that might have authorised more naturally something more unifying like "Man, and I mean even the Papuan" – in fact, has an internal justification in Husserl's thinking, and highlights a recurrent and perhaps even irreducible feature of all classic European philosophical history, a feature that will have always summoned something like a "racist" spirit into Europe's spirit, and will have done so even before European race theory actually came on the scene. I will explain this.

Race theories of the sort taken up by Hitler and the Nazis deploy what one might call a vertical hierarchy of more or less fixed racial (and mixed-racial) types. Each and every type, simply as human, can be placed "above the level of mere animal existence" (MK, p. 314); but among humanity, different races are scaled in a movement of ranking "higher and higher above the animal world" (MK, p. 366), with "the Aryan alone" attaining the most "superior type of humanity" (MK, p. 241). Universal history is then the history of the "permanent struggle" for power between races in relations of domination and subjugation, with the domination by the most "superior race" being the "prerequisite condition of all human progress" (MK, p. 240).

As should be clear, this conception fixes in vertical form a horizontal developmental conception which invariably configures the temporal history of Man in European philosophical histories of the world; a history which is always drawn, as Valéry put it, "on a single plan and a single scale". The point is, however, that the horizontal schema, as a transcending movement-in-stages of progress and de-alienation, will always incline towards the vertical. "Man" in European philosophical history is understood as the being whose being unfolds in time from primitive and barbarian animality *up* to fully rational and civilised humanity.

History for modern European philosophical history is the unfolding of the reason in Man in time. No form of humanness is outside this history. But not all forms of humanness are at the same stage of its development. And according to this schema, some human groups, as both Hegel and Husserl explicitly affirmed, have not yet even stepped onto "the stage of history". The teleological movement of "spirit" coming to itself is not evenly distributed over the whole of humanity at once or as a whole. On the contrary, human beings around the globe are at different stages of development, and some have not moved above the first rung of the human ladder, stalled only one rung above "mere animal existence". Here is Hegel on sub-Saharan Africa (what he calls "Africa proper"):

> Africa proper, as far as History goes back, has remained shut up; it is...the land of childhood...enveloped in the dark mantle of Night... The Negro exhibits the natural man in his completely wild and untamed state... At this point we leave Africa, not to mention it again. (PH, pp. 95–103. Hegel stays true to his word.)

If "Africa proper" remains "in the condition of mere nature" for Man, and stands only at the threshold of History, Europe is furthest along the path. And the idea of this exemplary heading is, in one way or another, invariant in all philosophical history of the world, fundamental to the discourse of Europe's modernity. Husserl too distinguishes between pre-scientific cultures that do and pre-scientific cultures that do not have, for themselves, a temporal history or "biography" of their own, and clearly thinks that belonging to the History of Man presupposes some pre-integration into an historically perspectival and teleological self-understanding. Moran cites Husserl's unpublished notes on the French social anthropologist Lucian Lévy-Bruhl, where he (Husserl) affirms the idea that "primitive life...is life lived without history, without the trajectory of a temporality that extends indefinitely in both directions" (EP, p. 491). It is life lived, Husserl suggests, "always in the present; past and future have no teleological sense" (cited, EP, p. 491). Significantly, the Papuans are once more the representative people for Husserl here. Moran cites a text written by Husserl in 1934 where he (Husserl) claims that "a Papuan has in the genuine (pregnant) sense no biography and a Papuan tribe has no life-history, no history of the people" (cited, EP, p. 490). It is this distinction – fundamentally challenged by Freud as a complete distortion, a completely ignorant projection we should remember – that works its way into Husserl's odd formulation "Man and even the Papuan": it introduces into the "broad" sense of Man a distinction between historical and non-historical humanity, where Man in the narrower sense ("Man proper", one might say, aping Hegel) is rational animality already on the move *up*. (Think of that cartoon of human evolution of apes towards an "erect posture" in modern man. Think also of newer versions of this, where the man at the front has turned round and urges everyone in the line to *"go back"*. It's a nice image of the unfolding and unravelling of the archeo-teleological discourse of Man. Other "post-modern" variants of the original are available, and many are instructive.)

Husserl then further distinguishes within historical Man (understood in the narrower sense that excludes the Papuan) between prescientific-but-already-historical cultural types and the philosophical-scientific culture imminent in Europe, where the latter "represents a new stage of human nature" and "the humanity of higher human nature" (CES, pp. 290–1). Unless one undergoes missionary conversion, attaining this "higher" stage presupposes passing through the earlier already-historical stage. However, and this is where philosophical history will want to distinguish itself from every other historical science (even if it really can't), the development beyond that stage, entry to the "higher" stage in principle accessible to all, "requires...a genuine *philosophy*" (CES, p. 291). And, for Husserl, just as much as for all the other thinkers of the golden thread, the beginning of this new epoch of humanity erupted into world history, uniquely and somehow (unfathomably) spontaneously, *sua sponte*, with the "birth" of Europe in ancient Greece – a development whose essential promise thus resides, in one way or another, in its missionary call or pledge for a cosmopolitan right to *"genuine philosophy"* for all.

V

This suggestion takes our discussion back to the integration into UNESCO's charter of a universal and cosmopolitan right to philosophy that I introduced in Chapter 6. As Derrida noted in his UNESCO lecture, the idea of this right (which Derrida does not simply oppose) is historically inseparable from a philosophical discourse of universal history that has been, invariably, a Eurocentric discourse of Europe's modernity giving the law to the world. Let's recall the entry of our chain of ghosts chained to the novel-resembling history of the world that was elaborated in "a great short text" by Kant, and run it on a little further:

> The teleological axis of this [Kantian] discourse [of world history] has become the tradition of European modernity. One encounters it again and again, intact and invariable throughout variations as serious as those that distinguish Hegel, Husserl, Heidegger and Valéry. One encounters it in its practical form, sometimes through denial, in a number of politico-institutional discourses, whether on the European or world scale. This Eurocentric discourse forces us to ask ourselves…whether today our reflection concerning the unlimited extension and the reaffirmation of a right to philosophy should not both *take into account and delimit* the assignation of philosophy to its Greco-European origin or memory. (UNESCO, p. 9, emphasis in original)

As this traditional philosophical history has come increasingly to resemble a novel-like fiction (and too often a horror story at that), there have been growing calls for (at least) a more inclusive conception of this "right to philosophy": not simply a right to *European* philosophy, but to a philosophical culture which welcomes contributions from non-European traditions of philosophy as well. Husserl himself voices this "objection", what he calls "an obvious objection", to the idea that the "revolutionising… of mankind through philosophy" means or can only mean the effective Europeanisation of all humanity:

> Here we encounter an obvious objection: philosophy, the science of the Greeks, is not something peculiar to them which came into the world for the first time with them. After all, they themselves tell of the wise Egyptians, Babylonians, etc., and did in fact learn much from them. Today we have a plethora of works about Indian philosophy, Chinese philosophy, etc., in which these are placed on a plane with Greek philosophy and are taken as merely different historical forms under one and the same idea of culture. (CES, p. 279)

Shouldn't these other works be taken on board? Aren't there other ways for philosophy to be practised, ways other than the Greco-European way? Indeed, might not they rather than this (end of the) line of Dead White European Males help us today better, help us overcome better, the real "crises of humanity" (colonialism, racism, international exploitation, poverty, etc.) that they had such a hand in creating?

We cannot and should not ignore that Husserl completely rejects this "obvious objection", and wants to demonstrate that "it is a mistake…to speak [for example] of Indian and Chinese philosophy" (CES, p. 284). His argument is to distinguish two sorts of higher-level functionaries, one concerned with the "practical" management of the "religious-mythic interests and their tradition in a unified way", what he calls "a priestly caste", in a pre-philosophical culture (CES, p. 284), and the other, the philosopher, who "turns away from all practical interests…and strives for nothing but pure *theōria*" (CES, p. 285). The wisdom of the first has universal significance only for a particular cultural-world-as-a-whole; it concerns *ideally* everything that goes on there, and everything within it, those norms and truths required for ordering "worldy life in the happiest possible way and shield it from disease, from every sort of evil fate, from disaster and death" (CES, p. 284). The second, by contrast, concerns *ideally* the actual world as such (valid beyond the variety of all culturally particular "world-representations") and the truth of everything that is. Thus, whereas the first aims at an essentially practical and tradition-bound totality, and its own ideal task is universal and finite, the second aims at an essentially theoretical and un-bound totality, and its own ideal task is universal and infinite, an ideal pole of an ideal task.

We can think of this through the example of geometry, a Greek invention almost as significant for Husserl (and Valéry in fact) as philosophy itself. Before a science of pure ideal forms comes on the scene, there would have been expressions of human interest in shapes and surfaces. Carpenters, for example, would have concepts of "flatter" surfaces, "squarer corners" and so on, as well as numerous shape concepts. But in what Husserl regards, like philosophy, as a completely new development, geometry brings into play *ideal* concepts – perfectly flat surfaces, perfectly square corners, pure triangularity, and so on. Geometers thus form a community of purely ideal interests which are purely theoretical, and whose tasks are properly infinite tasks, "building theoretical knowledge upon theoretical knowledge *in infinitum*" (CES, p. 286). Husserl would often call the kind of idea involved in such pure inquiry with an infinite task an idea "in the Kantian sense" (*Ideas 1*, p. 342). It is given, that is to say, only as a (interminably) regulative ideal (a norm) and not the attained grasp of a final sense or truth: the teleology of inquiry reaches forward without end towards an "ideal pole". Philosophy would be the ideal science of all science with infinite tasks, and its "function", its "particular infinite task", to engage in "free and universal theoretical reflection, which encompasses all ideals and the total ideal, i.e., the universe of all norms" (CES, p. 289), an inquiry which "brings with it a universally transformed praxis" affecting all "traditional norms, those of right, of beauty, of usefulness, dominant personal values", etc. (CES, p. 287).

The "decapitation" of philosophy as a universal science by positivism is, as we saw in the last chapter, fundamental to Husserl's sense of Europe's life-crisis, and it is clear what, in his view, must be revived, and what that revival entails. Once again: the philosopher specialises in the sense of the universal. For Husserl, the first community of philosophers created "a human posture" which "intervened in the whole remainder of practical life", "first within the home nation" and "then in neighbouring nations", giving rise to "a supranationality of a completely new sort" that is "spiritual Europe". On this view, philosophy "exercises its function as one that is archontic for the civilisation as a whole" (CES, p. 289), but one that is in no way limited to geographical Europe and its inhabitants. On the contrary, philosophers, as I have indicated, are understood by Husserl, not as the *functionaries of a singular civilisation* but the "*functionaries of mankind*" (CES, p. 17). This is "the West's mission for humanity" in general: Europe's promise "as the pledge of a great and distant future for Man" (CES, p. 299).

Husserl accepts that the universal attitude of the "functionary" of "a civilization living in the natural sphere" (what he calls "the mythic-religious attitude" or "mythic-practical attitude" of the "priest caste"), can and does "give rise to much knowledge of the factual world…that can later be used scientifically" (CES, p. 284), and their "mythic interpretations" of their "mythical-natural world" really can, in virtue of their "morphologically general features", resemble "philosophy" (CES, p. 284). Indeed, Europeans "raised in the scientific ways of thinking created in Greece" have understood them as such – but they do so, says Husserl, by interpreting them from out of their own world, and hence "in a European way" (CES, p. 285).

For Husserl, then, understandable though it may be to make such interpretations, it is simply "a mistake": "this universal but mythical-practical attitude" should be "sharply distinguished" from the "theoretical attitude" of philosophy (CES, p. 285), even if "mythic" elements can sometimes reappear in the latter (CES, p. 199). Husserl thus rejects the idea that Greco-European philosophy is just one among other historical forms "under one and the same idea of culture" (CES, p. 279): "European philosophy" is for Husserl, just as it is for Heidegger in fact, "a tautology" (WIP, p. 31).

VI

One is not obliged to take Husserl's word as the last word on this issue. Indeed, there is a movement of thought in Husserl's own work that we have already caught sight of, and which I will segue here back onto our earlier discussion of the right to philosophy, which can take us in a very different direction concerning other ways for philosophy to be. The argument here is that precisely because (what the Greeks called) "philosophy" is already not "tradition-bound", not tied to any particular cultural tradition, precisely because it is not "bound to the soil" of any given human community, precisely because it de-localises in a spirit of endless critique as self-critique, so that the resolve of the philosopher is precisely "not to accept unquestionably any pregiven opinion" (CES, p. 286) – because of all of this we should recognise that (what the Greeks called) "philosophy" is, in its concept, constitutively open to styles, traditions and models other than those which have dominated its history. While forever tied to something particularistic, "the 'idiomaticity' of languages", and is never simply "abstractly universal", (what the Greeks called) "philosophy" is nevertheless, and constitutively, not tied to "a unique language or to the place of a sole people" (UNESCO, p. 8). In short, and *pace* Husserl's official line of thinking, philosophy – and that means philosophy as that is understood "under its Greek name and in its European memory" (UNESCO, p. 8) – "has always been the other way" (UNESCO, p. 8).

"European philosophy" – and within that its national and linguistic variations or models, as well as "the opposition between the so-called continental tradition of philosophy and the so-called analytic or anglo-saxon philosophy", which is neither simply national nor wholly linguistic (UNESCO, p. 9) – may be a sort of tautology, but in *keeping to this subject* we can and should also speak of "Indian philosophy" or "Chinese philosophy" or "African philosophy", and so on. Philosophy under its Greek name and European memory nowhere defines philosophy as a Greek or European thing. Moreover, what philosophy is, and how to go about it, is itself given in that heritage as a philosophical question, a question for philosophy. What philosophy is, is given, as it were, as not given, and *a fortiori* not given as something that has one only way of being properly or "genuinely" done or legitimately inherited. (This competition between styles, traditions and models is evident even in the localised history of geographically European philosophy, as we have just recalled.)

The subject Europeans call "philosophy" hasn't got one "legitimate heir" only (see BB, p. 28 and p. 62), and is not and never has been tied to any people or place either. What Europeans of the nineteenth century called "Indian philosophy", "Chinese philosophy", and indeed "African philosophy", were not unproblematic identifications, and more often than not were run through with "mythological conceptions" and "ethnophilosophical" presuppositions of the non-European "other" of a distinctively orientalist type (APMR, p. 66). But that does not mean that literatures deserving the title "philosophy" are simply absent in non-European places. Husserl speaks blithely of the "new stage of humanity" presupposing a "genuine" philosophy, and builds a racist air-castle to distinguish this from what really are "morphologically" related traditions outside ("spiritual") Europe. But it is not "knowledge of the factual world" or even a specialist interest in the whole of life ("round here") that draws those traditions into relation to what the Greeks called "philosophy". Philosophy concerns an interest, for sure, in "what we really know and find interesting", as Wittgenstein puts it (RFGB, p. 6), and this will doubtless always give it a "round here" or "somewhere where we are" character. But – and here I take a stand – philosophy is characterised by an interest in what is *most* familiar, existence itself, and nothing warrants excluding that interest from non-Europeans. Wherever and whenever the living of life in the world itself becomes an issue or an interest, thinking concerning what is, in this way, right before our eyes deserves the title "philosophy", as Wittgenstein for one did not hesitate to affirm, and also in the 1930s (RFGB, p. 6; see also PI §129). Indeed, for Wittgenstein, such thinking will have belonged to the lives of human beings from its historically earliest times, since the times of "*den erwachenden Menschengeist*", since the first awakening human spirit (RFGB, p. 6).

Heidegger strikes a related note – and one that perhaps provides the most radical justification for Derrida's claim that he may not be the one who throws the "non-Aryan" outside Europe. Heidegger says that Dasein's "familiarity" with "existence", is "*constitutive* for Dasein", adding that this familiarity "goes to make up Dasein's understanding of Being", the question concerning which Heidegger identifies as the most basic for philosophy (BT, p. 119). Coming to terms with the *most* familiar: that is philosophy.

Heidegger's "method" is to "make a study" of "average everydayness", as the preliminary "horizon" for investigations of "the kind of Being which lies *closest* to Dasein" (BT, p. 94). But this preliminary study is already philosophy underway, and understanding the most familiar in terms of an "understanding of Being" means that Heidegger is moving in a space where (inherited) "decisions" concerning "the living in life itself" are already in play (see BS, p. 176). Anticipating everything, Heidegger begins *Being and Time* with the claim that a pre-philosophical "vague average understanding of Being" is, for us, "a Fact" [*Faktum*] (BT, p. 25). Derrida is surely right to think that "nothing is less pre-assured than such a *Faktum*" (FK, p. 3). What we are being asked to take Heidegger's word on at the start of his investigation, right from the start, is not simply the "fact" that, for example, we use the little words "is" or "be" (or equivalents), but that we "already live in an understanding of Being" (BT, p. 23). Philosophy is up and running, and to read Heidegger at all demands a certain "acquiescence" to a "zone" where nothing can be taken as read, understood or known (FK, p. 62). His starting *Faktum* is not an empirical fact. Derrida says that this requirement of acquiescence to a zone where nothing is pre-assured is "not alien" to "faith" (FK, p. 62). Wittgenstein might have said that Heidegger's work of words (like the words of his own *Tractatus*) is not alien to "a kind of magic" either: what else could free our words for "something higher" ("meta-physics") than effectively banishing their familiar, everyday character (RFGB, p. vi)? Nevertheless, the attempt to find the liberating words that can effectively zone in to the most familiar, the effort at taking an interest in what is "closest and well known" (BT, p. 59), the effort at taking an interest in "what we really know and find interesting" (RFGB, p. 6), is the first moment of philosophy – in each case its beginning words taking a stand on what will afford us the best recollection of what is most familiar, in each case competitively arrogating itself to the position of the exemplary witness of what lies closest. And *no one* is "thrown out" of that competition.

Produced in and from the different languages, histories, and idiomaticities internal to the "somewhere where we are" of (what Husserl called) the "home-world" [*Heimwelt*] or "homeland" [*Heimat*] of human lives, thinking of this distinctive type, thinking that is concerned with what is most familiar, *wherever it takes place*, attests to an interest that the Greeks called "philosophy". Under the cover of "mythic" Eurocentric prejudices about "genuine" philosophy, this philosophical *Faktum* has been powerfully repressed by the onto-theological, humanist tradition of European philosophy.

VII

In a situation where one or other of the "two models" of European philosophy ("the so-called continental tradition…and the so-called analytic or anglo-saxon philosophy") have become virtually hegemonic across the world, Derrida takes up the question of the cosmopolitan right to philosophy in our time, and calls for "the deconstruction of these hegemonies", and for developments that would cultivate "the appropriation of but also the surpassing of languages which…are called foundational for philosophy, i.e. the Greek, Latin, German or Arab languages. Philosophy should be practiced, according to paths that are not simply anamnesic, in languages that are without filiational relation with these roots" (UNESCO, p. 10). Engaging in a space, then, where European philosophy and its foundational languages dominate, Derrida seeks a response that neither simply reaffirms one or the other of its two contemporary models nor simply rejects them, a response that would enable us to "go beyond the old, tiresome, worn-out and wearisome opposition between Eurocentrism and anti-Eurocentrism" (UNESCO, p. 8):

> What we have lived and what we are more and more aiming for are modes of appropriation and transformation of the philosophical in non-European languages and cultures. Such modes of appropriation and transformation amount neither to the classical mode of appropriation that consists in making one's own what belongs to the other (here, in interiorizing the Western memory of philosophy and in assimilating it in one's own language) nor to the invention of new modes of thought which, as alien to all appropriation, would no longer have any relation to what one believes one recognizes under the name of philosophy. (UNESCO, p. 8)

The call for a universal right to philosophy is not over; the will to make a contribution to the universal community is not over. The future of that right cannot and should not be confined to its European heritage, but it cannot and should not altogether do without its European memory either – and we should defend ("at any price") the maintenance of the ancient canons against anti-Eurocentric recoils that want simply to reject them. Moreover, philosophy needs that European memory, and not only because it provides a guide to what, beyond it, might still be recognised under that Greek name, and hence be translated by that name. Today, in addition, an affirmation of the right to philosophy for all cannot and should not be made or thought without reference to the specifically political idea that belongs so centrally to philosophy's European history: it cannot and should not do without "the European, and uniquely European, heritage of an idea of democracy" (OH, p. 78). Considerations concerning the right to philosophy from a cosmopolitan point of view in our time are, Derrida suggests, simply inseparable from efforts at an "effective democratization" that would challenge "what, in every cultural, linguistic, national and religious area" would want to limit making philosophy accessible to all, accessible regardless of "class, age or gender" (UNESCO, p. 11).

As I indicated in the discussion of Lenin, the idea of democracy in play here is thought by Derrida as itself essentially historical, and hence, like philosophy itself, its "ideal" content cannot be reduced to anything "simply given" from its heritage, European or not, not even as an infinite task or "regulative idea in the Kantian sense" (OH, p. 78). The content of the concept of democracy – the commitment to ongoing public deliberations over matters of public concern – must be applied to itself as part of its own ideal concept, and hence this concept, again like the concept of philosophy itself, always retains within itself (as part of its "ideal" identity) the promise of self-critique, and hence the possibility of another inheritance, another heading, from another shore. Both democracy and philosophy thus stand, in every here and now, as "something that remains to be thought and to come" (OH, p. 78). This is a concrete commitment to critique as self-critique which never ends, and which wants never to end, and hence for which, *pace* Lenin on genuine democracy, and *pace* Husserl on genuine philosophy, there is no last word. It is a promise. In both we will find what I have come to see as Europe's still unexhausted promise. In the second volume of this philosophical history of Europe, I will track this promise into our time, and send it on.

12

THE GRAND TOUR

Looking back and looking forward

This book has attempted an exploration of a self-understanding: the self-understanding of those who call themselves, and have called themselves to be, "We, the Europeans". This exploration of a distinctively European self-understanding has been guided by an effort to identify its fundamental "sources", its *archē*. At issue here is the basic formatting of the understanding of the world and the significance of our (human) lives that most profoundly marks a European, and especially "modern" European subjectivity, most radically imprinting itself "somewhere where we are". The basic claim has been that the modern European self-understanding is fundamentally rooted in a Greco-Biblical anthropology; a quite particular understanding of the meaning of "Man". Following Derrida, I have tried to show that this anthropology, this *archeo-teleo-eschatological* conception of Man, is at the root of all European discourse about Europe. This has taken us into a detailed investigation of European texts on Man thus understood, works of philosophical history, as the privileged site for tracking the ongoing development of Europe's self-understanding. We have followed an historical sequence of writings in philosophical history in which we see this self-understanding unfold from eighteenth and nineteenth century optimism, and unravel into twentieth century despair; a sequence in which an Enlightenment promise of peace, freedom and well-being for all humanity falls apart. Emmanuel Levinas, who gave us our first summary introduction to the European *archē* in his formula "Europe is the Bible and the Greeks", also provides us with a fitting summary conclusion:

> That history of peace, freedom and well-being promised on the basis of a light that a universal knowledge projected onto the world – even unto the religious messages that sought justification for themselves in the truths of knowledge – that history is not recognizable in its millennia of fratricidal struggles, political or bloody, of imperialism, scorn and exploitation of the

human being, down to our century of world wars, the genocides of the Holocaust and terrorism; unemployment and continual desperate poverty of the Third World; ruthless doctrines and cruelty of fascism and national socialism, right down to the supreme paradox of the defence of Man and his rights being perverted into Stalinism. Hence the challenge to the centrality of Europe and its culture. A worn-out Europe! (AT, p. 132)

Like Marxism, its inseparable adversary, Nazism did not fall from the sky into a European world from elsewhere. We have already noted the role of Gobineau's work in the formation of Nazi raciology, and interested readers should consult Robert Bernasconi's ground-breaking studies of eighteenth and especially nineteenth century race thinking to see how both Kant and Hegel, in different ways and in some of their writings, affirmed and even defined race categories in Europe (see, for example, Bernasconi, 1998, 2000, and 2010). Further, there is no doubt that the "horizontal" Eurocentric philosophical histories of the self-realisation of Man were always amenable to a racial translation and "vertical" transposition of exactly the kind we find in the passage on the golden thread by Hitler.

On the other hand, neither Kant nor Hegel actually refers to or deploys immutable racial categories in their own texts on philosophical history, and Kant, in particular, seems clearly to regard the movement of world history as genuinely universal. His view of what "naturally" (i.e. providentially) divides human beings are "*linguistic* and *religious* differences" (Kant, pp. 112–3). These are not (as far as the eye can see) going to be overcome, and we know too that they "may certainly occasion mutual hatred" (Kant, p. 114). Nevertheless, it belongs to a cosmopolitan hope that such differences can be lived in ways that are likely to cultivate respect and "mutual understanding" rather than antagonistic conflict and war (Kant, p. 114).

Marx conceived the disappearance of national and religious differences as well within the purview of foresight, and his supposedly "philosophical and scientific" discourse of a world history of class struggles seemed to promise (naively, I think we can now see) a far more radically undifferentiated future for a peacefully united humanity. Hitler, recoiling from Marxist internationalism, brought an interminable (and still providential) racial and national struggle onto the stage, with "peace", achieved only by racial subjugation. Not even Kantian hopes of making war less likely between nations and peoples could be countenanced by Hitler, who affirmed that it is "exclusively by the tie of blood that the members of a race are bound together" (MK, p. 258). Husserl's philosophical history, which, as we have seen, is not free of seriously troubling gestures, is certainly much closer to the spirit of Kantian cosmopolitanism than Hitler's racial history. It is not a "community of race which unites [Europeans]" (MK, p. 348), but a "community of spirit" bound together by its *telos* towards self-responsibility, which is the *entelechy* "essential" to universal rational humanity (CES, p. 15). And this opens out, first of all, as it does too in Kant, onto "the practical ideal of Europe": of "the harmonious unity of the life of nations with its sources in the rational spirit" (cited, CES "Introduction", p. xxvii). We will return to that "practical ideal" of Europe in the next volume when we explore the historical emergence and structure of the European Union.

Paying (some) attention to both Lenin and Hitler in this book, I have been willing to follow two particularly murderous turns of European thinking about Man and his history. They form a perfectly vile dialectical pair. On the one hand, the international socialist "scientist" of human equality, and, on the other hand, the national socialist "scientist" of race inequality. The first of these "nature doctors" might seem slightly less objectionable because more in tune with the progressive spirit of democracy ("democracy is the fore-runner of Marxism", says Hitler, probably correctly (MK, p. 71)). But, actually, with all the decency one can muster, one has to reject both. We have made a start puncturing Lenin's claim to have the final word on democracy, and I will regularly return to that theme in the second volume.

"Speaking according to [his] best lights" (CES, p. 18), Husserl attempted to provide a universal history of spirit that could wrest Europe from the racist biologism that was making its way there in his time. But that attempt only magnifies the complicity of philosophical history with the worst. Perhaps the time of the old discourse of Europe's modernity, and hence also the time of a compelling non-novel-like philosophical (hi)story of the world, and the European culture of "Man as the rational animal" that it belonged to, was, in Husserl's time, already nearing its end. Today it is, I think, as Levinas puts it, "worn-out", exhausted. But it does not end there. The next volume will return to Europe in the aftermath of the Second World War, with its division between the capitalist and liberal-democratic West and the planned economies of the communist and Stalinist East – and of Europe's subsequent unfolding in the new geopolitical realities of a Cold War between two new quasi-European global superpowers. We will follow it further through the fall of the Berlin Wall and the emerging "enlarged" European Union with its contemporary challenges, including Brexit. The European Union is a fundamentally "modern" European formation, and carries the Enlightenment cosmopolitan hope into our time. The project of integration has been beset by crises – of political legitimacy and economic stability. Yet, as Wolfram Keiser notes, the idea of a pacific union in Europe continues its remarkable, if uneven and unspectacular, progress:

> Despite such recurring crises, which now frequently also affect democratic institutions and political parties in many member-states, the EU has proved – surprisingly for some – a durable legal-institutional supranational framework for the peaceful regulation of conflicts and decision-making on common policies. That its history should not attract the same attention as Hitler and Stalin owes much to the fact that it has not left the same deep tracks of blood across twentieth-century Europe. (Keiser, p. 11)

With the ambition to achieve a durable peace through "ever closer union among the peoples of Europe", the European Union is an institution with a cosmopolitan and teleological sense inscribed in its treaties. What that implies in terms of a final formation is notoriously contested, and a cause of ongoing political unclarity, economic instability, and probably Brexit too. However, while the modern tradition we have been exploring in this volume provides its ineluctable memory, the idea of Europe that it inherits has also proved open to developments beyond this modern tradition. I will try to articulate and promote those developments in the next volume. I am not optimistic about the European Union as a still-modern institution, but I am not unhopeful that what Kant called (to be) a "great political body without precedence in the past" on our continent also has a future.

To begin again on this grand tour of Europe's philosophical history, I will start the next volume with a preliminary step back, and take in the first great thinker of the modern European self-understanding as caught up not in a "crisis" but in a "worn-out" condition, a condition of "exhaustion": Friedrich Nietzsche, and his thought of a distinctively European exhaustion event of unparalleled significance, the death of God. In Nietzsche's wake, we will track further the unravelling of the old discourse of Europe's modernity, an unravelling taking place right inside a European movement of democratisation. That movement carries a threat of the "levelling" of Europeans into "herd animals" fleeing from self-responsibility. However, as we shall see, it also carries a still-cosmopolitan hope that heralds a newly promising future for a democratic Europe to come.

BIBLIOGRAPHY

Benedict Anderson, *Imagined Communities*, London: Verso (2006)
Deland Anderson, "The Death of God and Hegel's System of Philosophy", *Sophia* 35: 1 (1996)
Aristotle, *History of Animals*, Cambridge, Mass: Harvard University Press (1965)
Aristotle, *Politics*, London: Penguin (2000)
Samuel Beckett, "The Capital of the Ruins", in *The Complete Short Prose: 1929–1989*, New York: Grove Press (1995)
Geoffrey Bennington, "Demo", in *The Politics of Deconstruction*, ed. Martin McQuillan, London: Pluto Press (2007)
Geoffrey Bennington, *Scatter I*, New York: Fordham University Press (2016)
Jeremy Bentham, *An Introduction to the Principles of Morals and Legislation*, Mineola, New York: Dover Publications (2009)
Isaiah Berlin, "Two Concepts of Liberty", in *Four Essays on Liberty*, Oxford: OUP (1969)
Isaiah Berlin, "Message to the 21st Century", accepted speech on the occasion of receiving an honorary degree of Doctor of Laws at the University of Toronto. Unpaginated online text, archived at https://www.nybooks.com/articles/2014/10/23/message-21st-century/ (1994)
Robert Bernasconi, "Hegel at the Court of the Ashanti", in *Hegel After Derrida*, ed. Stuart Barnett, London: Routledge (1998)
Robert Bernasconi, "With What Must the Philosophy of World History Begin? On the Racial Basis of Hegel's Eurocentrism", *Nineteenth Century Contexts*, Vol. 22 (2000)
Robert Bernasconi, "The Philosophy of Race in the Nineteenth Century", in *The Routledge Companion to Nineteenth Century Philosophy*, ed. Dean Moyar, Abingdon: Routledge (2010)
Robert Blanch and Julian Wasserman, *From Pearl to Gawain*, Gainesville: University Press of Florida (1995)
Allan Bloom, "Editor's Introduction", Alexandre Kojève, *Introduction to the Reading of Hegel: Lectures on the "Phenomenology of Spirit"*, Ithaca: Cornell University Press (1980)
Allan Bloom, *The Closing of the American Mind*, London: Simon & Schuster (1988)

Bibliography 197

Pim den Boer, "Europe to 1914: the making of an idea", in *The History of the Idea of Europe*, eds. Kevin Wilson and Jan van der Dussen, London: Routledge (1995)

Andrew Buchwalter, *Dialectics, Politics, and the Contemporary Value of Hegel's Practical Philosophy*, Abingdon: Routledge (2015)

Judith Butler, "Uncritical Exuberance?", unpaginated online text, archived at https://angrywhitekid.blogs.com/weblog/2008/11/uncritical-exuberance-judith-butlers-take-on-obama.html

Stanley Cavell, *The Claim of Reason: Wittgenstein, Skepticism, Morality and Tragedy*, Oxford: Oxford University Press, 1979

Stanley Cavell, *Conditions Handsome and Unhandsome: The Constitution of Emersonian Perfectionism*, Chicago: Chicago University Press, 1990.

Stanley Cavell, *Philosophy the Day After Tomorrow*, Cambridge, Mass: Belknap Press of Harvard University Press (2005)

Gabriel Citron (ed.), "Wittgenstein's Philosophical Conversations with Rush Rhees (1939–50)", *Mind*, 124: 493 (January 2015)

I. Bernard Cohen, *Revolution in Science*, Cambridge, Mass: Harvard University Press (1987)

Mitchell Cohen, "Rooted Cosmopolitanism", *Dissent* 39 (Autumn 1992)

Rebecca Comay, "Hegel's Last Words", in *The Ends of History: Questioning the Stakes of Historical Reason*, eds. Amy Swiffen and Joshua Nichols, Abingdon: Routledge (2013)

Simon Critchley, "What's Left After Obama?" unpaginated online text, archived at http://16beavergroup.org/articles/2008/12/08/adbusters-simon-critchley-whats-left-after-obama/ (2008)

Simon Critchley, "The Problem with Levinas", unpaginated online interview with *Four by Three Magazine*, archived at http://www.fourbythreemagazine.com/issue/deception/simon-critchley-and-alexis-dianda-interview (2015)

Norman Davies, *Europe: A History*, London: Bodley Head (2014)

Jacques Derrida, *Of Grammatology*, Baltimore: Johns Hopkins University Press (1976)

Jacques Derrida, "Violence and Metaphysics", in *Writing and Difference*, London: Routledge (1978)

Jacques Derrida, *Glas*, Lincoln: University of Nebraska Press (1986)

Jacques Derrida, *The Ear of the Other*, ed. Christie McDonald, Lincoln: University of Nebraska Press (1988)

Jacques Derrida, *Of Spirit*, Chicago: Chicago University Press (1989)

Jacques Derrida, *Edmund Husserl's 'Origin of Geometry': An Introduction*, Lincoln: University of Nebraska Press (1989)

Jacques Derrida, *The Problem of Genesis in Husserl's Philosophy*, Chicago: Chicago University Press (1990)

Jacques Derrida, "The Ends of Man", in *Margins of Philosophy*, trans. Alan Bass, Birmingham: Harvester Wheatsheaf (1991)

Jacques Derrida, *The Other Heading: Reflections on Today's Europe*, Bloomington: Indiana University Press (1992)

Jacques Derrida, "Back from Moscow, in the USSR", *Daimon: Revista Internacional de Filosofía*, Issue 5, (1992)

Jacques Derrida, *Specters of Marx*, Abingdon: Routledge (1993)

Jacques Derrida, *Politics of Friendship*, London: Verso Books (1994)

Jacques Derrida, *Deconstruction in a Nutshell*, New York: Fordham University Press (1996)

Jacques Derrida, "Faith and Knowledge", in Religion, eds. Jacques Derrida and Gianni Vattimo, Stanford: Stanford University Press (1998)

Jacques Derrida, "Of the Humanities and the Philosophical Discipline: The Right to Philosophy from the Cosmopolitical Point of View (the Example of an International Institution)", Studies in Practical Philosophy, Volume 2, Issue 1, (2000). This text is also available online, with free access, in *Surfaces* 4: 310 Folio 1: https://www.pum.umontreal.ca/revues/surfaces/vol4/derridaa.html

Jacques Derrida, *Of Hospitality: Anne Dufourmantelle Invites Jacques Derrida to Respond*, Stanford: Stanford University Press (2000)

Jacques Derrida, *On Cosmopolitanism and Forgiveness*, Abingdon: Routledge (2001)

Jacques Derrida, *Acts of Religion*, ed. Gil Anidjar, Abingdon: Routledge (2002)

Jacques Derrida, "The University Without Condition", in *Without Alibi*, ed. Peggy Kamuf, Stanford: Stanford University Press (2002)

Jacques Derrida, "What I would have said…", in *Negotiations: Interventions and Interviews, 1971–2001*, Stanford: Stanford University Press (2002)

Jacques Derrida, "Economies of the Crisis", in *Negotiations: Interventions and Interviews, 1971–2001*, Stanford: Stanford University Press (2002)

Jacques Derrida, "Globalization, Peace, and Cosmopolitanism", in *Negotiations: Interventions and Interviews, 1971–2001*, Stanford: Stanford University Press (2002)

Jacques Derrida, "The Aforementioned So-Called Human Genome", in *Negotiations: Interventions and Interviews, 1971–2001*, Stanford: Stanford University Press (2002)

Jacques Derrida, "Politics and Friendship", in *Negotiations: Interventions and Interviews, 1971–2001*, Stanford: Stanford University Press (2002)

Jacques Derrida, *Philosophy in a Time of Terror: Dialogues with Jürgen Habermas and Jacques Derrida*, ed. Giovanna Borradori, Chicago: Chicago University Press (2003)

Jacques Derrida, *Rogues: Two Essays on Reason*, Stanford: Stanford University Press (2005)

Jacques Derrida, *Learning to Live Finally, Derrida's Last Interview, with Jean Birnbaum*, New Jersey: Melville House Publishing (2007)

Jacques Derrida, *The Beast and the Sovereign*, Volume 1, Chicago: Chicago University Press (2009)

Cora Diamond, "Eating Meat and Eating People", in *The Realistic Spirit*, Cambridge, Mass: MIT Press (1991)

Myrto Dragona-Monachou, *Stoic Arguments for the Existence and Providence of the Gods*, Athens: National and Capodistrian University of Athens (1976).

T.S. Eliot, *Notes Towards the Definition of Culture*, London: Faber and Faber (1948)

Simone Emms, *The Modern Journeyman*, thesis submitted for a Master in Education, Auckland University of Technology (2005)

H.A.L. Fisher, *History of Europe*, Volume III, London: Eyre and Spottiswoode (1935)

Sigmund Freud, "Civilization and its Discontents", in *The Standard Edition of the Complete Psychological Works of Sigmund Freud*, Volume 21, Oxford: Macmillan (1964)

Peter Frick, *Divine Providence in Philo of Alexandria*, Tübingen: Mohr Siebeck (1999)

Francis Fukuyama, "The End of History?", *The National Interest*, No. 16 (Summer 1989)

Francis Fukuyama, *The End of History and the Last Man*, London: Hamish Hamilton (1992)

Rodolphe Gasché, *Europe, or the Infinite Task: A Study of a Philosophical Concept*, Stanford: Stanford University Press (2008)

Simon Glendinning, *In the Name of Phenomenology*, Abingdon: Routledge (2008)

Simon Glendinning, "Derrida and the Problem of Consciousness", in *Consciousness and the Great Philosophers*, eds. S. Leach and J. Tartaglia, Abingdon: Routledge (2017)

John Gray, *Isaiah Berlin: An Interpretation of His Thought*, Princeton: Princeton University Press (2013)

Denis Guénoun, *About Europe: Philosophical Hypotheses*, Stanford: Stanford University Press (2013)
Jürgen Habermas, *Between Naturalism and Religion*, Cambridge: Polity Press (2008)
Jürgen Habermas, *The Lure of Technocracy*, Cambridge: Polity Press (2015)
G.W.F. Hegel, *The Philosophy of History*, trans. J. Sibree. London: Bell (1894)
G.W.F. Hegel, *Faith and Knowledge*, New York: SUNY Press (1977)
G.W.F. Hegel, *Introduction to the Philosophy of History*, trans. Leo Rauch, Indianapolis: Hackett Publishing Co. (1988)
G.W.F. Hegel, *Philosophy of Right*, Kitchener: Batoche Books (2001)
Martin Heidegger, *What is Philosophy?*, Lanham, Maryland: Rowman and Littlefield Publishers (1956)
Martin Heidegger, *Being and Time*, Oxford: Blackwell (1962)
Martin Heidegger, "Memorial Address", in *Discourse on Thinking*, New York: Harper and Row (1966)
Martin Heidegger, "Nietzsche's Word: God is Dead", in *The Question of Technology and Other Essays*, New York: Garland Publishing (1977)
Martin Heidegger, "Letter on Humanism", in *Basic Writings*, ed. David Farrell Krell, London: Routledge (1993)
Martin Heidegger, *Introduction to Metaphysics*, New Haven: Yale University Press (2000)
Martin Heidegger, "Heidegger Speaks: Part 1", online video archived at https://www.youtube.com/watch?v=1ngHZr8sAj0
Adolf Hitler, *Mein Kampf*, trans. James Murphy. All references are to the pagination of the online copy of the text at www.greatwar.nl/books/meinkampf/meinkampf.pdf
Jonathan Hopkin and Caterina Paolucci, "The business firm model of party organisation: Cases from Spain and Italy", *European Journal of Political Research* (1999)
Paulin J. Hountondji, *African Philosophy, Myth and Reality*, Bloomington: Indiana University Press (1983)
Stephen Houlgate, "World History as the Progress of Consciousness", *The Owl of Minerva* 22: 1 (1990)
Edmund Husserl, *The Crisis of European Sciences and Transcendental Phenomenology*, Evanston: Northwestern University Press (1970)
Simon Jenkins, *A Short History of Europe: from Pericles to Putin*, London: Penguin (2019)
Daniel Johnson, "Seven Minutes that Shook the World", Standpoint Magazine, unpaginated online text archived at http://www.standpointmag.co.uk/seven-minutes-that-shook-the-world-features-november-09-daniel-johnson-berlin-wall?page=0%2C0%2C0%2C0%2C0%2C0%2C0%2C0%2C0%2C0%2C3 (2009)
Anjali Joseph, "Us to Them: The pesto is now another aountry", *The Times of India*, unpaginated online text archived at https://timesofindia.indiatimes.com/home/sunday-times/all-that-matters/Us-to-them-The-pesto-is-now-another-country/articleshow/52919052.cms)
Immanuel Kant, *Critique of Pure Reason*, trans. Norman Kemp Smith, London: Macmillan (1973)
Immanuel Kant, *Kant's Political Writings*, Cambridge: Cambridge University Press (1991)
Immanuel Kant, *Opus Postumum*, Cambridge: Cambridge University Press (1995)
Alexandre Kojève, *Introduction to the Reading of Hegel: Lectures on the "Phenomenology of Spirit"*, Ithaca: Cornell University Press (1980)
Wolfram Keiser, "Introduction", in *Christian Democracy and the Origins of European Union*, Cambridge: Cambridge University Press (2007)
Philipe Lacoue-Labarthe, *Heidegger, Art, and Politics*, Chichester: Wiley-Blackwell (1990)

Philipe Lacoue-Labarthe, *Heidegger and the Politics of Poetry*, Urbana and Chicago: University of Illinois Press (2007)

V.I. Lenin, *State and Revolution*, London: Penguin (1992)

Jean-François Lyotard, *The Postmodern Condition*, Manchester: Manchester University Press (1984)

Emmanuel Levinas, *Is it Righteous to Be?* Stanford: Stanford University Press (2001)

Emmanuel Levinas, *Alterity and Transcendence*, New York: Columbia University Press (2001)

Karl Marx, *Critique of Hegel's Philosophy of Right*, Oxford: Oxford University Press (1970). References give the pagination in the online transcription at https://www.marxists.org/archive/marx/works/download/Marx_Critique_of_Hegels_Philosophy_of_Right.pdf

Karl Marx and Friedrich Engels, *The Communist Manifesto*, Oxford: OUP (2008)

J.S. Mill, "On Nationality and Representative Government", in *Three Essays*, London: Penguin (1975)

J.S. Mill, *Utilitarianism and On Liberty*, Oxford: Blackwell (2003)

J.S. Mill, *On Liberty and the Subjection of Women*, London: Penguin Classics (2006)

Dermot Moran, "'Even the Papuan is a Man and not a Beast': Husserl on Universalism and the Relativity of Cultures", *Journal of the History of Philosophy* 49 (4):463–494 (2011)

Stephen Mulhall, *Philosophical Myths of the Fall*, Princeton: Princeton University Press (2009)

Stephen Mulhall, *The Self and its Shadows*, Oxford: OUP (2013)

Iris Murdoch, *The Book and the Brotherhood*, London: Penguin (1987)

Kalypso Nicolaïdis, "Braving the Waves? Europe's Constitutional Settlement at Twenty", *Journal of Common Market Studies*, Vol 1, no. 17 (2018)

Kalypso Nicolaïdis, "European Democracy and Its Crisis", *Journal of Common Market Studies*, Vol. 51, no. 2 (2013)

Friedrich Nietzsche, *Human All Too Human, Part II*, trans. Paul V. Cohn, New York: MacMillan (1913)

Friedrich Nietzsche, "The Anti-Christ", in *The Twilight of the Idols and The Anti-Christ*, Harmondsworth: Penguin Books (1969)

Friedrich Nietzsche, *Beyond Good and Evil*, Harmondsworth: Penguin Books (1973)

Friedrich Nietzsche, *The Gay Science*, New York: Vintage (1974)

Friedrich Nietzsche, *The Genealogy of Morals*, London: Penguin Classics (2013)

Friedrich Nietzsche, *The Will to Power*, London: Penguin Classics (2017)

Friedrich Nietzsche, "Twilight of the Idols", in *The Twilight of the Idols and The Anti-Christ*, Harmondsworth: Penguin Books (1969)

Friedrich Nietzsche, *Untimely Mediations*, Cambridge: Cambridge University Press (1997)

Louisa Passerini, *Memory and Utopia: The Primacy of Inter-Subjectivity*, Abingdon: Routledge (2014)

Robert Perkins, "Hegel and the Secularisation of Religion", *International Journal for Philosophy of Religion* 1 (3):130–146 (1970)

Robert Pippin, *Modernism as a Philosophical Problem*, second edition, Oxford: Blackwell (1999)

Karl Popper, *The Open Society and its Enemies*, Fifth Edition, London: Routledge and Keegan Paul (1966). References give the pagination in the online scan *at http://www.naturalthinker.net/trl/texts/Popper,Karl/Popper%20-%20The%20Open%20Society%20and%20its%20Enemies.htm*

Rush Rhees, (Ed.), *Ludwig Wittgenstein, personal recollections*, Oxford: Blackwell (1981)
Richard Rorty, *Contingency, Irony, and Solidarity*, Cambridge: Cambridge University Press (1989)
Pierre Rosanvallon, *Society of Equals*, Cambridge, Mass: Harvard University Press (2013)
Jean-Paul Sartre, *Existentialism and Humanism*, London: Eyre Methuen (1980)
Jean-Paul Sartre, *The Family Idiot* (Vol. 4), Chicago: University of Chicago Press (1990)
Carl Schmitt, *Political Theology*, Chicago: University of Chicago Press (2006)
Hagen Schulze, *Germany: A New History*, Cambridge, Mass: Harvard University Press (1998)
Judith Shklar, "The Liberalism of Fear", in *Liberalism and the Moral Life*, ed. Nancy L. Rosenblum, Cambridge, Mass: Harvard University Press (1989)
Paul Valéry, "La Politque de L'Esprit", *Variété III*, Paris: Gallimard (1936)
Paul Valéry, *The Collected Works of Paul Valéry Vol 10: History and Politics*, New York: Pantheon Books (1962)
John Adams Wettergreen Jr., "Is Snobbery a Formal Value? Considering Life at the End of Modernity", *The Western Political Quarterly*, Vol. 26, No. 1 (1973)
David Wiggins, "Truth, Invention, and The Meaning of Life", in *Needs, Values, Truth: Essays in the Philosophy of Value*, Oxford: OUP (1998)
Bernard Williams, *In the Beginning was the Deed: Realism and Moralism in Political Argument*, Princeton: Princeton University Press (2005)
Bernard Williams, *Shame and Necessity*, Berkeley and Los Angeles: University of California Press (2008)
Rowan Williams, "Rome Lecture: 'Secularism, Faith and Freedom'", unpaginated text archived at http://aoc2013.brix.fatbeehive.com/articles.php/1175/rome-lecture-secularism-faith-and-freedom (2006)
Rowan Williams, *Dostoevsky: Language, Faith and Fiction*, London: Continuum (2008)
Ludwig Wittgenstein, *Tractatus Logico-Philosophicus*, London: Routledge and Keegan Paul (1974)
Ludwig Wittgenstein, *The Blue and Brown Books*, Oxford: Blackwell (1958)
Ludwig Wittgenstein, *Lectures and Conversations on Aesthetics, Psychology and Religious Belief*, Oxford: Blackwell (1966)
Ludwig Wittgenstein, *Remarks on Frazer's Golden Bough*, Doncaster: The Brynmill Press (1979)
Ludwig Wittgenstein, *Culture and Value* (Revised Edition), Oxford: Blackwell (1998)
Ludwig Wittgenstein, *Philosophical Investigations*, Revised Fourth Edition, Chichester: Wiley-Blackwell (2009)
P.G. Wodehouse, *Right Ho, Jeeves*, London: Everyman (2000)

INDEX

abstract internationalism 92; *see also* internationalism
abstract universalism 91–92, 98, 182
Africa 33, 42–43, 82
African philosophy 188
aggression 64, 66
Alexander the Great 52
Ancient Greece 39
Anderson, D. 112
Anderson, P. 60
androcentrism 10, 103
Anglo-Saxon 164, 180, 188, 190
animal rationale 54–55, 60, 101–102, 174
antagonisms: conflict and 110; differentiating 20; history of 70, 129; identity-forming 19; mutual 98; national 27; political 69; pugilistic 137; social or cultural 92; within society 84, 98; towards science 86
anthropology: archeo 21; of Christianity 54; of Claude Lévi-Strauss 7; distinctive 2; evolutionary 42; Greco-Biblical 192; traditional 54–55, 62, 67
anti-ethnocentricism 7, 12
anti-Eurocentric/anti-Eurocentrism 4–8, 9–11, 29, 47, 56, 190
anxiety 82; about complaint against old courses 3; about Nazism 163; of displaced 21; to establish cultural domination 26; historical portrait 84; Kantian 110, 128, 159
archē 54–55, 80; European cultural identity 80; European *Dasein* 42–43, 55; European subjectivity 2; Greek and Biblical/Greco-Biblical 45–46; modern European world 14; in ontological questioning 54
archeo-anthropology 21
archeo-teleo-eschatologism 79, 84
Aristotle 36–37, 80, 111
Arnold, M. 45, 58–59
Asia 18, 33, 35, 42
Association for Convenience & Fuel Retailing (NACS) 77
attained freedom 104–119
Australasia 33, 36, 42
Australia 180

barbarian 55, 58–60, 72, 183
barbarism 57–60, 72–73, 85, 94
Being and Time (Heidegger) 54, 62, 189
Bennington, G. 129
Bentham, J. 101
Berlin, I. 3, 93
Bernasconi, R. 193
Bible 43
Biblical Christianity 81
biopolitics 148
Bishop of Seville 44
Bloom, D. 33–35, 37
Bloom, L. 36
Blooms of Europe 37
Boer, Pim den 44
Bolsheviks 135, 148
British Empire 180
Bush, G. W. 99–100
Butler, J. 100

Canada 180
Carr, D. 157
Catalan nationalists 32
Catholicism 115
Caucasus 33, 35, 52
Cavell, S. 3, 139, 152
Charlemagne 52
Chinese philosophy 188
Christendom 4
Christianity 54, 111
Christians 37; conviction 57; creationism 80; cultural identity 4; discourses 14; eschatology 69; fathers 37; history 43–44; hope 69; life 124; theology 54; transcendence 62
civilisation/civilization 57–58, 63, 71, 73
Civilization and its Discontents (Freud) 63
Clemens, A. P. 142–143
cohabitation 173, 177
Cold War 3, 78, 93, 194
Collected Works (Valéry) 142, 149
commercial materialism 163
communalisation 176, 179
communism 65–66, 136–139
Communist Manifesto (Marx) 125, 133, 135, 137, 157
communitarianism 124
consciousness 121; European cultural 97; of freedom 107, 109–111, 114, 116–117, 119–121; intellectual 115; public 114, 131; Subjective freedom 107
continuous transformation 72
Copernicus 78
cosmopolitanism 82; ambitious 82; androcentric 79; feelings 101; nationalism and 9; optimism of Enlightenment 1
cosmopolitan society 93
cosmopolitical animal 75–88
Critchley, S. 100
Critique of Hegel's Philosophy of Right (Marx) 125, 127
Critique of Pure Reason, The (Kant) 94
cultural antagonisms 92
cultural identity 4, 92; community of nations 4; *Dasein* 22; Europe 2, 19–20, 26, 28–29, 51 *see also* European cultural identity
cultural self-perceptions 31
culture 17–29; belonging to some culture 19; characteristic form 29; conceptions 28; Europe 10, 20, 23–25; history 21; human 19; internal differences 20; progress of disintegration 26; race and 18; reality 20; self-contained 24–25

Culture and Anarchy (Arnold) 45
Cyprus 33

Darwin, C. 61, 78, 146
Dasein 20–23, 27, 42, 44, 52–55
Das Kapital (Marx) 150
Davies, N. 3–4, 9, 38–40
da Vinci, L. 143, 147
Dead White European Males 3, 10–11, 13, 186
deconstructionism 13
de Gobineau, A. 150, 193
democracy 135–153; electoral 109; formal 129; inheritance 28; liberal 109; motif 7; political 102; real universality of 125; safe harbour of 60; true 130
democratic perfectionism 7, 139
democratisation 28, 102–103, 140, 195
Derrida, J. 3, 7, 11, 14, 21, 32, 45, 53, 65, 70, 73, 78, 83, 93, 96, 101–102, 104–105, 108–109, 145, 174, 179, 182; axiom of cultural identity 22; citation of Valéry's text of the European Hamlet 141; contradicting the hypothesis "precisely not perversions" 136; cosmopolitan right to philosophy 190; cosmopolitan tradition 79; democracy 152; *Diplôme* 176–177; effective democratization 191; English Dominions 180; Eurocentrism 9; European cultural ideal 25; geopolitical horizon 66; German spirits omitted from self-citation 142; international institution 92; Kant's cosmopolitan hope 91; Marxist successors 140; on Marx statement "I am not a Marxist" 144; other Europe 12; *Other Heading, The* 19, 97; paradox of the paradox 55; right to philosophy 82; sense of deconstruction 13; someplace else 142; thought of the trace 18; thrownness 17; unacceptable obscenity 27; UNESCO lecture 185
Descartes 115–116
"*Die Freundschaft*" ("Friendship") (Schiller) 122–123
Diplôme (Derrida) 176–177
discourse: disintegration of European culture 25; of Europe's history 53; Europe's modernity 2–3, 53, 75, 88, 102, 105, 141, 150–151, 153, 161, 171, 174, 184, 194; Greek and Christian 14; historical progress of Man 40; historiographical 41; teleo-eschatological 105

disorder 86–87, 144–145, 150–151
dispiriting Europe 173–191
distinctive anthropology 2
Divine Being 113
Divine Providence 113
Durkheim, E. 68
DWEM 6, 10

East Prussia 81
ecclesia 81
Egypt 43
Eichmann, A. 93
electoral democracy 109
Eliot, T. S. 20–24, 26, 36, 51, 63, 65, 67, 92
embourgeoisement 159
Engels, F. 129, 138, 149
England 24, 114, 118–119
English Dominions 180
eschatologism/eschatology 57, 69–70
Essai sur l'inégalité des races humaines (de Gobineau) 150
ethnocentrism 7, 10, 73, 177–178
Eurobarometer 31, 41
Eurocentrism 4, 6–7, 9, 11–13, 29, 56, 73, 103, 175, 178
Europe 42, 46, 64, 74, 84, 106, 125, 129–130, 158; boundary 34–35; community of race 166; crisis 152–153, 157–172; cultural identity 2, 19, 51; culture 160–162, 178; democratisation 140; empirical history 38; exemplary modernity 75; future 22; geopolitical 12; Greek origin of 39; Greek-Roman-Christian-Germanic/Modern civilisation 165; heritage 11; history 1–2, 39–41, 53, 81, 86, 110; humanity 2, 166, 169, 175; identity 34, 38; legitimate heir 188; life-crisis 187; missionary culture 159; modern culture 102; modernity 2–3, 29, 39–40, 76, 78, 81, 102, 105, 115, 141, 146, 150–153, 184–185, 195 *see also* Europe's modernity; modern self-understanding 173; openness to "perpetual self-critique" 12; optimism 1; origin 9; past reality 3; perfectible heritage 12; political and economic union 28; political modernity 134; pre-War 87; race 18; rationalism 175; religion 20; sciences 166, 179; self-citation 145; self-responsibility 35, 37; self-understanding 1, 37, 47–48, 141, 147, 159, 192, 195; supra-nationally 150; unity in uniformity 29
European Blooms 36

European cultural identity 30–48; genealogy 38; non-national-identifying 32; self-identify 32; *see also* cultural identity
European Hamlet 105, 135, 140–142, 145, 147, 149, 151
European idea of Man 61–74
Europeanization 178, 185
European Union 1, 27, 33, 35–36, 53, 83, 106, 194
Europe's modernity 51–60; discourse 53; Greco-Biblical heritage 55; humanity 59
Europoethnocentrism 177
evolutionary anthropology 42
exclusions: and prejudices 4, 6; subject identity 5

Faktum 189–190
feudalism 158
Finisterre 34
First World War 140, 163
formal freedom 107, 111, 119
Foucault, M. 148
France 31, 110, 116, 118–119, 140
freedom: consciousness of 107–108, 110–111, 114, 116–117, 120–121; formal 107, 109–110, 114, 116–117; individual 94, 116; lawless 94; political 106, 109, 117, 151; renunciation of 95; of speech 110; Subjective 107–109, 119, 133; of thought 5–6; universal 91, 107; *see also* attained freedom
French Ministry of Foreign Affairs 26
French Revolution 82, 99, 101, 103, 106, 116–118
Freud, S. 2–3, 60–61, 63–64, 66, 68, 71–73, 78, 109, 146, 184
Fukuyama, F. 3, 57, 105

general culture 164–165; *see also* culture
Genesis 44
geopolitics 65, 136
Germano-French 114
German U-boat 143
Germany 31, 86, 106, 119, 129, 148, 158; anachronistic 133; criticism of religion 126; culture 163; developments in 161; disappearance of 145; nationalism 161; public affair 131; racist National Socialism 177; universal human development 135; universalisation of voting 134
Gide, A. 104
gigantomachia 112
globalisation 46, 70, 98–99, 101, 136

Index **205**

grand tour 192–195
Great Britain 25, 31, 36
Great War 140, 143, 159
Greco-Biblical 46, 55, 58, 61, 70, 78–80, 175, 192
Greece 69, 102
Greek-Roman-Christian 58
Greek-Roman-Christian-Modern 151

Hamlet (Shakespeare) 105
happiness *see* real happiness
Hegel, G. W. F. 2–3, 39, 56–57, 61, 63, 65, 81, 83–85, 88, 98, 103, 105–109, 111–124, 129–130, 150–151, 183, 185, 193; antipathy towards Kantianism 125; citizenship an abstraction 132; denial of political citizenship 131; disappearance of name of Kant in 141; empirical actuality 127; infinite grief 125; philosophical history 128, 157, 159; political philosophy 124; public consciousness 131; subjective freedom 133; view on State 129
Hegelian Subjective 107
Heidegger, M. 2, 11, 20, 38, 54–55, 59, 62, 67, 182, 185; *Being and Time* 189; Dasein's "familiarity" 189; "thrownness" 17
Hellenistic Greeks 39
Herder, J. G. 61, 63
Herodotus 43
History of Animals (Aristotle) 80
Hitler, A. 163–164, 179–180, 183, 193–194
Hitlerian National Socialism 165
Holy Roman Empire 52
Holy Scripture 113
Homo barbarus 59, 72
Homo homini lupus 72
Homo humanus 59
hospitality *see* universal hospitality
Houlgate, S. 119
human culture 19; *see also* culture
human diversity 97
humanism 59
humanization 59
human rational/rationality 61–62
Hume, D. 169–170
Husserl, E. 2–3, 11, 86, 105, 153, 161, 180, 185; English word "prosperity" 163; Eurocentric racist biologism 175; Eurocentrism 178; European humanity 174; Europeanization 178; Europe's life-crisis 187; general lament 165; inherent teleology 171; obvious objection 186; phenomenology 160; philosophical history 174, 178, 193; physiological sense 167; pre-scientific humanity 167; problems of reason 168; "purely natural" human beings 181; race difference 182; racist National Socialism 177; spiritual Europe 173, 179, 181, 187; spiritual shape of Europe 171; universal history of spirit 194; universalism 175, 181; Vienna Lecture 173, 178–179; writing on European humanity 161

ideological illusion 92
India 180
Indian philosophy 188
inner focus 121
intellectual comprehension 57
intellectual consciousness 115; *see also* consciousness
internal schism 55
internationalism: abstract 92; Marxist 65, 193; proletarian 91
Irish Free State 180
Isidore 46

Japheth 44, 46
Jerusalem 93

Kant, I. 2–3, 39, 56, 61, 64–65, 67, 70, 80–84, 86, 88, 91–108, 111–118, 130, 193, 195; anxiety 159; liberal modernity 122; opposition to prescientific and scientific objectivism 170; philosophical history 128; political liberalism 121; political philosophy 124; skull of 146–147, 149
Kant-Hegel-Marx 105, 146–147
Kantian 107, 131, 134
Kantianism 125
katholikos 81
Keiser, W. 194
Kierkegaard, S. 124
Königsberg 81
Ksiazczakova, A. 31
Kurds 35
Kuttner, R. 148

Land's End 34
last judgement 69
Lebey, A. 146
Leibnitz 88
Leibniz, G. W. 28, 143, 147
Le Monde 11

Lenin, V. I. 88, 91, 102, 105, 129, 134–140, 142, 149, 151, 191, 194; discourse on democracy 136; equality 139; political rivals 137
Letters to the Editor 33, 35–36
Levinas, E. 45, 93, 192
Levinasian formula 46, 54–55
Lévi-Strauss, C. 7
Lévy-Bruhl, L. 184
liberal democracy 109
liberalism 109; communitarianism and 124; European 73; evangelical 57; political 106, 117–118, 121, 125
Libya 18, 43
Lionardo 87–88
London Review of Books 60
Luther, M. 5–6, 114, 120
Lyotard, J.-F. 3

Man: archeo-teleo-eschatological conception 192; bee and 80; defined 54; European philosophy about 147, 183; European science about 147; Greco-Biblical conception 175; historical progress 40; humanization 59; progress and de-alienation of 157; rational animality 179; rational being 39, 62; self-realisation of 193; teleology and 140, 151
Manifesto 69
Martinique 33
Marx, K. 2, 8–9, 37, 57, 60–61, 63, 65–66, 68–73, 77–79, 85–86, 88, 102, 104–105, 112, 122, 124–125, 130, 135–136, 150–151, 157, 171; bourgeois-democratic republic 137; Communist promise 134; crisis 157; criticism of Hegel 129; critique of Hegel 125; democracy 139; dialectical movement 127; epochal social order 158; public affairs 131–132; real human beings 128; Scientific Socialism 149; self-determination of the people 133
Marxism 8, 20, 65, 91, 105, 136, 138, 149, 193
Marxist criticism 91
Marxist internationalism 65, 101, 193
materialism 159; commercial 163; shallow 163
material prosperity 164
Matthews, J. 149
Mediterranean 42
Mein Kampf (Hitler) 163, 165

men of universality 70
Merleau-Ponty, M. 160
Mesopotamia 143
metaphysics 11, 79, 147, 160, 169–170
methodological nationalism 65
Middle Ages 77
Middle East 33
Mill, J. S. 9, 73–74
Moran, D. 178–179, 184
Munkler, H. 60

nationalism 57, 119
National Socialism 160, 173
Native Americans 181
Nazi raciology 193
Nazis 162, 179, 181, 183
Nazism 86, 149, 162–163, 165–166, 193
Newfoundland 180
New Zealand 180
Nietzsche, F. 2, 13, 47, 64, 67, 85, 152, 173, 195
Noah 43–44, 46
non-DWEM 8
non-Europeans 6, 8, 18
non-refoulement 95
Northern Hemisphere 53
Norway 36

Obama, B. 99
Observations on the Feeling of the Beautiful and Sublime (Kant) 82
Of Grammatology (Derrida) 7, 18
Of Spirit (Derrida) 179–180
Origin of Species, The (Darwin) 69
Other Heading, The (Derrida) 19, 97

paideia 59
Papuan 182, 184
perfectionism 139, 152
Perkins, R. 124
pernicious institutions 116
perpetual peace 91–103
phenomenological event 40
phenomenology 160
Phenomenology of Spirit (Hegel) 122, 125
philosophy: African 188; Chinese 188; decapitation of 187; European 188, 190; Indian 188; theoretical attitude of 187; universal 169
Philosophy of History (Hegel) 83, 106, 122, 124–125, 131
Philosophy of Right, The (Hegel) 124–125, 131
Pitt Rivers Museum in Oxford 42

Index

Plato 13, 111
political antagonism 69
political liberalism 106, 121
political representation 109
politikon 37
Popper, K. 110
positivism 86, 152, 187
post-War Europe 160
Prague 162
prejudices and exclusions 4, 6
pre-Reformation Christendom 52
pre-War Soviet Union 148–149
proletarian internationalism 91
proletariat act 130
Protestantism 115
public consciousness 114, 131; *see also* consciousness

quasi-national rivalry 55

race: community 165–166; culture and 18; difference 182; human 98–99; inequality 194; theories/theorists 18, 183
racism 73, 100, 161, 165, 173, 178, 182, 186
radical critique 8–9
radically non-relational conception 19
radically relational conception 19
rational animal 60, 62
Rauch, L. 110
real happiness 120–134
Reiter, H. 148
religion,: abolition of 126; antagonistic 67; criticism of 126; culture and 20; ideological illusion 92; nationality and 63; positive 67–68, 75; transcendence 102
religious suffering 126
religious truth 113
Rhodes 33
River Nile 46
Rivers, Pitt 42
Roman-Christian-Modern 110
Romanity 55
Rome 52
Russia 33, 36, 134; politics 150; revolution 140

Sartre, J.-P. 5, 38, 160
scepticism 64, 160, 162, 169
Schiller, F. 107, 122–123
Schmitt, C. 68, 72
scientific racism 148; *see also* racism
scientism 86, 92
Second World War 2–3, 140, 148, 194
secularization thesis 68, 92

self-citation: European Hamlet 141–143; first and second omission 145; paradox 144; singular omission 144; State names 146
self-consciousness: of freedom 121; non-abstract 120; reconciliation 121; self-esteem of man 126
self-critique 8–9, 11, 14, 187
self-understanding: Europe 3, 9–10, 29, 37, 39, 46–48, 55, 73, 141–142, 147, 159, 192, 195; historical 1; teleological 184
Shakespeare, W. 87, 105
shallow materialism 163
Shklar, J. 3
since Marx 66–68, 75–76, 98, 101, 136, 147
social antagonisms 92
social contract 93–94
social violence 94; *see also* violence
sovereignty 95–96, 118, 128
Soviet Union 66, 70, 148
Spain 32
Specters of Marx (Derrida) 8, 105, 136, 141
St. Augustine 13, 37, 43–44
Stanford University 3, 6, 8
State and Revolution (Lenin) 135, 137
State power 94, 137–138
Subjective freedom 107–109, 119, 133; *see also* freedom
subjective will 121, 124
Switzerland 36

Taylor, A.J.P. 38
teleo-eschatological discourse 105
teleologism 57
teleology 48, 69–70, 92, 140, 146, 151–152, 171, 174–177, 179, 186
terrorism 60, 193
Theodicaea (Hegel) 57, 81, 84
theoria 62, 176, 186
totalitarianism 12, 60, 106, 136
traditional anthropology 54–55, 62, 67
transcendence 57, 62, 85, 102, 123
Turkey 33–35, 44

UNESCO 82, 106, 185
Union of South Africa 180
United States 33, 42, 100, 180
universal hospitality 96
universalism 160; abstract 91–92, 98, 182; *katholikos* 81
universal philosophy 169
University of Oxford 42
Urals 52

Valéry, P. 2–3, 9, 11, 22–26, 42–43, 47, 52–53, 86–88, 104–105, 108, 134–135, 140, 142–144, 149, 160, 173, 185; conception of Man in politics 148; "critical phase" 146; European crisis 158; European Hamlet 141; Europe's modernity 152; foreign country 148; great virtues 144; "Politics of Spirit" 151–152; removal of names of States 145; retaining names of cities, regions and landmarks 150; self-citation 141; someplace else 145; text of the European Hamlet 141
violence 37, 73, 94, 96–98, 137

Weber, M. 68
Western Civ (course) 3–5, 9
Wiggins, D. 3, 41, 51, 78–79, 85, 105, 123
Williams, B. 3, 51, 67–68, 92, 101–102, 117, 124
Wittgenstein, L. 188–189

xenophobia 73

Zhou Enlai 118
zōon cosmopolitikon 80
zōon logon echon 37, 54–55, 60, 80, 101
zōon politikon 37, 80

Printed in the United States
by Baker & Taylor Publisher Services